W9-CCO-830

THE COYOTE'S BICYCLE

THE COYOTE'S BICYCLE

The Untold Story of Seven Thousand Bicycles and the Rise of a Borderland Empire

KIMBALL TAYLOR

TIN HOUSE BOOKS / Portland, Oregon & Brooklyn, New York

Published by Tin House Books, Portland, Oregon, and Brooklyn, New York

Distributed by W. W. Norton & Company

Library of Congress Cataloging-in-Publication Data

Names: Taylor, Kimball.
Title: The coyote's bicycle : [the untold story of 7,000 bicycles and the rise of a borderland empire] / by Kimball Taylor.
Description: 1st U.S. edition. | Portland, Oregon : Tin House Books, 2016.
Identifiers: LCCN 2015033873 | ISBN 9781941040201 (alk. paper)
Subjects: LCSH: Human smuggling—Mexican-American Border Region. | Illegalaliens—Mexican-American Border Region. | Bicycles—Mexican-American Border Region. | United States—Emigration and immigration—Government policy. | Mexico—Emigration and immigration—Government policy.
Classification: LCC JV6475 .T39 2016 | DDC 364.1/3709721—dc23
LC record available at http://lccn.loc.gov/2015033873

First US edition 2016
Printed in the USA
Interior design by Jakob Vala

www.tinhouse.com

For Angelene

I want to extend special thanks to José Antonio Castillo Garcia, Dan Watman, and Ben McCue, without whose collaboration and generosity of spirit this book would not have been possible.

A Note to Readers:

Names have been changed and identities have been obscured in order to protect migrants and the smugglers who cross them.

"The bicycle will be found," said the Sergeant, "when I retrieve and restore it to its own owner in due law and possessively. Would you desire to be of assistance in the search?"

—FLANN O'BRIEN, *The Third Policeman*

Prologue:
EVERYBODY LOVES A BIKE

This is the story of several thousand bicycles that made an incredible journey. They were very ordinary, used bicycles. Mountain bikes, with their knobby tires and sturdy frames, made up a large percentage of the total. Some of these sported shocks and disc brakes—accessories you might think necessary for a trip of this distance and nature. But there were also fragile-looking ten-speeds, three-speeds, and fixed-gears. I once glimpsed a pink-and-purple girl's bike with a small white seat and frills at the handle grips. Heavy American beach cruisers rolled on comfortable balloon tires. English roadsters and Dutch *omafiets* suggested sleek market runs down grass-lined lanes. The bikes were made in France, the United Kingdom, the United States, Italy, Japan, Indonesia, Vietnam, Taiwan, and China. They were adorned in all manners, but the consistent theme was an admirable patina of road wear, rust, dings, dents, and scrapes. The seats and handle grips took the shapes of the bodies that touched them. Yet there were bikes with no seats, no brakes. Some bore labels of origin—shop emblems, registration stickers, or evidence of sale at auction by a police department. In a superstitious, totem-like fashion, an unknown cyclist had drawn simple, elegant waves along the black rubber sidewalls of an unremarkable bike's tire—giving it the blessing of oceanic drift. There was another cycle I remember because of its brilliance: a classic lowrider fashioned from a boy's Schwinn, with the "ape-hanger" handlebars, crushed velvet banana seat, gold piping, and gold-colored rims. The bike lay on its side, spokes sparkling in the dirt like a roulette of icicles. Many of the bikes fell into the category of "utility," a style that peaked in the 1960s and conjured the image of a straight-backed professor pedaling between ivy towers. There were a number of rugged BMX racing bikes that evoked sunny suburban lots and dirty socks. A few high-tech-looking road bikes and classic gems turned up, but soon vanished. I never saw a tandem bicycle, but could easily have missed it. A high-wheel would have been impossible. Clown bikes, depending on personal definitions, abounded. Most of the bikes were not worth much. Some of them were missing important parts. All of them had generated thousands of dollars in their life spans. They had been snatched up by criminals, confiscated by police, purchased by human smugglers, dumped in a swamp, sold to a movie studio, contracted to the military, utilized in war training, co-opted in prisoner reform, donated to orphans, sold at swap meets, cycled and recycled again and again.

Not one human being who influenced the course of the bikes understood their full trajectory or end destination. No one knew how far they had traveled in a group. Few who handled or pedaled them were aware of their specific bike's origin, its next step, or even its next owner. The bikes were not invisible, but at important stages, they were unseen.

The journey was not made entirely on their own two wheels.

The bicycles rode in trucks packed tight alongside boxes of AK-47s, grenade launchers, and pyrotechnics. They shipped out to a small, craggy, restricted island off the coast of California called San Clemente. They were crammed into the backs of border-enforcement vehicles.

They flew to the Hawaiian archipelago. They drove north to Canada, east to Texas, Louisiana, North Carolina, and Virginia. The bikes rolled over the Mexican border powered by the feet of illegal immigrants. They rolled under the seats of actors and horse trainers and pumpkin farmers. Convicts rode them in prison. Real soldiers preparing for battle in Afghanistan took time out to pop wheelies on them. Finally, after years of service, the bikes again coasted under the feet of regular citizens, boys and girls. The bikes are out there now, still rolling. You might own one yourself. Most of their riders have no idea how well traveled their well-worn wheels really are.

When I tell the story of the bikes, listeners invariably ask, "How do you know?" or "Who arranged it all?"

To the first question, all I can say is that I happened upon a large pile of ordinary bikes in an unlikely place, under bizarre circumstances. Everybody likes bikes, I'll say, and when I saw this motley collection of tubes and cranks and frames and wheels—the bicycle equivalent of a shipyard after a hurricane—I discovered that I liked these bikes most of all. I am a person attracted to thrift stores and yard sales. The more battered and unloved an item's appearance sparks an equal and opposite sentiment in me. But I wasn't the only one. A small, feverish cadre of people—ranchers and farmers and alley-trawlers—drawn by the mysterious arrival of bicycles in the bushes, in the river, abreast trails, by the roadside and under bridges, bicycles that poured down with a winter rain that seemed never to end, stopped to pick them up without knowing why. Or, maybe, even caring. Lucky finds don't inspire deep inquiry.

I, however, am also attracted to a yarn, to irony, circularity, and meaning. It is a documentary flaw, I know. Phenomenal events take place without portent or meaning every day. And so, despite the mystery of the bicycles in plain sight, it is understandable that not many who wheeled their prizes homeward ever bothered to ask why—*why here?* A front-page article in the city's only major newspaper reported the event but never asked as much—emitting only a "Huh, look, a bunch of bikes."

And yet, varying ideas of value just might help answer the question of "Who arranged it all?" Because, maybe, we all did. A pile of discarded cars is an eyesore called a junkyard. The last time I entered a junkyard, I needed a rear turn-signal assembly for a 1982 Nissan extra-cab. I didn't look around or admire the other clunkers. Bikes, however, belong to that class of essentially elegant innovations of travel—an airship, an airplane's wing, a sailboat's hull, a keel, a kite, the fin of a surfboard, a bicycle in motion. Bicycles execute the willpowers of the people who buy, find, steal, trade, and use them; they mark the memories of the people who love them. I like to think that it was the curious sight of ownerless cycles descended from nowhere that sits at the heart of this tale—because suddenly they became available to the will of whoever came upon them next; suddenly their destinies were without limit. I didn't collect the bicycles myself. I merely wanted to know where they came from and where they were going and how far they could get. I began to understand the nature of their remarkable journey only by seeking out, speaking to, and investigating the people who had handled them one to the next.

At a certain point, as I charted the expanse of the bikes' adventure, I tried to draw rude diagrams and flow charts. I once tried to draw a map of the journey, but this was difficult; I needed to illustrate things as big as the world yet include details as small as a ditch. In truth, I felt as though I'd caught the tail of a comet, all of the glinting and glittering bits shooting past in the darkness and somehow the very trailing end slowing just enough to get me all tangled up in it. The question of the bikes cost me a good few productive work years when I could least afford it. Following worthless bikes, I was warned a number of times, could cost me everything. On a couple of occasions, I was told, "Don't end up with your head in a bucket," and "You might end up off in the desert somewhere." This was due to the fact that on my own, I was unqualified to sniff this story out. My Spanish is questionable. I'm not a criminal. I'm not affiliated with the military. My motives to expose the story ran at odds with the interests of those who knew the story best. There was no way I could ever keep up with either the speed or trajectory of this comet. It was headed for strange places and worlds that wouldn't admit a regular, unassociated citizen like myself.

So on the trail, I made unlikely allies: movie makers, a Border Patrol agent, a Homeland Security investigator, a couple of Navy SEALs, a few ranchers, some environmentalists, human rights activists, human smugglers—people Mexicans generally refer to as "*malandros*" or bad guys—bike freaks, social agitators, artists, architects, academics, and people obsessed in various ways with small aspects of a story I couldn't always explain. Everybody likes bikes, was my simple premise. Everybody likes to talk about bikes. And to get this story right, I had to believe that people like to talk about bikes to the extent that they'll talk about them even while they're stealing them, fencing them, breaking them down into sellable pieces.

The most critical part, however, the questions of where the bikes I was interested in had come from, and how they ended up in ownerless piles, was only answered after I made an alliance that became a friendship, with a fifty-year-old, ex-con deportee who worked at the public bathrooms in Tijuana and lived in a fake ship. Our meeting was not preordained, but it was meaningful in a way that defied logical connections. Because, as it turned out, El Negro was not just a man with entrée but an extraordinary investigator who delved into the border slums. And from his underworld interviews—with the dons of Tijuana smuggling and itinerant cycle mechanics alike—I was able to piece together the story of El Indio, an impoverished child of *campesinos* who walked out of his tiny Oaxacan village, arrived at *la frontera*, and built an empire on the strength of a single foolhardy idea.

Abandoned bicycles hold the unique ability of reflecting the desires of their finders. They are equally junk and prizes. Art and vehicles. They move people and goods and plans along. They become machines in the service of their riders' willpowers and destinies. By following the mass of these bikes that caught my eye even as they rested, I thought I'd discover just where that collective willpower and destiny led.

Everybody likes bikes.

1

We know that the important early bicycle was a milkman's bike, and that it was saddled with a large wire basket designed to hold fifteen-liter milk canisters. It wasn't likely the first bicycle in the village, but it was the only one in living memory. And aside from Don Ricardo's ancient tractor that, even in good times, none of the farming families could afford to rent, the bicycle was the only mechanized vehicle for many miles around.

Pablo, or Pablito as he was known at age twelve, woke every morning at four with the cackle and crow of the village roosters. By then, his mother had already been awake and working for an hour or more. Her quiet shuffling was an integral part of his morning. Like many of the other families, Pablito's lived in a one-room wood-and-thatch house with a dirt floor. There was no sink. There were no cabinets or bureaus. The stove consisted of three stones enclosing a small fire. In cool weather, this was the heater. And still, the home wasn't as cramped as it might have been if his two older brothers and two older sisters hadn't, one by one, as each came of age, walked out of their small Oaxacan pueblo on the thin, rutted road, and headed off into *el Norte*.

For breakfast, Pablito was given a few tortillas left over from those made the previous evening on the *comal*. Clutching the now cold tortillas, he stepped out into the dark morning and made his way across the yard to a spindly ranch gate. It was constructed of tree limbs and wire, and was attached to the gatepost by leather hinges. Pablito had known the cow whose pieces of hide formed those hinges. Every morning Pablito waited there, next to the gatepost, for the arrival of his best friend, Solo.

The fresh air, the smell of dew on the earth, and the rich scents of the surrounding mountain forest all mingled in the predawn. Pablito listened to the noises of his village as each of the families, 150 residents in all, began to wake and prepare for the day. Morning fires flickered here and there in a rolling landscape that held cold, wet vapors like little clouds in the folds and depressions. When Solo arrived in the bluing light, Pablito hardly had to look.

We know that each wore leather huarache sandals with soles made from car tires. Their patched, loose-fitting clothing had been handed down by Pablito's brothers and Solo's one male cousin who was also in *el Norte*. Sometimes it was very cold as the boys hiked an hour or more into the mountains. At that time of day, before the sun broke above the peaks, the shroud of green forest looked black.

In the foothills, they approached the tree line and fanned out to scour the forest floor, gathering pieces of dry wood. Each boy needed enough to last his family's fire the entire day and following morning. As the season wore on, the boys walked deeper and deeper into the trees to gather the necessary amount. They filled slings, simple frames formed from sticks. A cloth headband was attached, and when they slipped it over the crown of their heads, it relieved some of the load from their backs. They bent low and heard the sounds of small life scuttling all about. There were skunks and fox and anteaters and snakes. Leaves shook above, too, as birds and squirrels passed through the branches. Teardrop oriole nests hung from the outer limbs of the great guayacan tree like rattan lanterns marking the way. Now and again Solo fabricated noises, pitching sounds or deep gravelly groans.

Or he claimed to see things, like the swish of a tail or any slight hint at the presence of the *onza*—a large cat related to the jaguar that few in the village had ever seen. In the stories, the toothy creature was sometimes said to be yellow with spots and sometimes black. When people didn't know what they'd seen, they generally called it a *tigre*, the catch-all word for any big feline. And it was this image that Solo relished. He'd played this teasing trick with the noises so often that it wasn't funny anymore so much as tradition.

Of the two boys, Pablito was slightly shorter. The village was known to produce small people, so minute differences in height were noticed. Solo could comfortably carry a full sling of wood. Pablito took pains to match the size of Solo's load, plus a stick or two. He rarely spoke on their descent into the village, perhaps due to the discomfort—the cloth headband put a strain on the neck—but Mixtecs were well known for their reserved demeanor. Those from other provincial states believed Oaxacans to be tough, perceptive, and cunning, but they were also notorious for masking these qualities with a kind of rural quiet city people sometimes took for ignorance.

Not Solo, though—he was a talker. If Pablito didn't care to chat, Solo didn't mind carrying both sides of the conversation. As he left the tree canopy, the words seemed to awaken. The boys squinted into the rising sun. The vapors and mists were gone and the blue land they'd left below in the darkness was now a patchwork of deep greens and browns. Gray trails of trash fires lifted column-like into the air, and Solo's need to talk seemed to rise with the temperature.

"My friend," he said, "I know you're always caressing your dream of one day going to the United States and working alongside your brothers. I will ask God to help satisfy this yearning because I know you are too proud. You believe He thinks this dream a little piece of nothing, but maybe not."

A yellow-bellied flycatcher darted from bush to bush before them. A hawk wheeled in the sky above. This was not a new conversation for the boys, but one that evolved in the telling and the things they'd learn from those who returned or who passed through. Fathers and sons tended to leave one at a time, and once established, they'd send money and, eventually, send for the others. Women composed most of Solo's family, and he hadn't heard from his cousin in a long time. So it was expected that Pablito would go first—at the request of one of his brothers, perhaps. "And someday in appreciation of my assistance," Solo said, "you will help me to get to the United States as well."

This had always been the plan.

Solo stopped to adjust the sling on his back, and then he hurried to catch up to Pablito, who never dallied. When the idea of leaving was talked through, it often seemed too big an undertaking. The village was an entire world where everyone knew and helped each other. Nearly everything outside of it was foreign to the boys. At these times, Solo would apply subtle brakes to his narrative—lest Pablito up and depart before both of them were grown and ready. "Even though you hold on to your dream," Solo pointed out now, breathing more heavily as his full sling weighed on him, "you also love your family. Your grandfather is old but he's strong and he knows a lot of things."

Solo could think of three aspects of Pablito's life in the village that might keep his friend around: the boy's unique connection with his paternal grandfather, the bountiful wildlife and natural beauty that surrounded them, and the best time of their day, when Pablito and Solo set out on the milkman's bicycle. "Those are some things you love," Solo said.

Pablito didn't agree, or even nod. He didn't shake his head or avert his eyes. He was simply quiet in the rhythm of walking the hard-packed path with the sandal soles made of car tires.

They came to a familiar curve in the trail and discovered that a dark bull had taken up a position directly on the track. To the left stood a marshy papaya grove where two pale heifers hovered like ghost cows in the deep greenery. To the right ran a wire fence covered in brambles. The boys were about as tall as the wheels on an oxcart. Even if it were not angry but merely startled, the bull could trample Pablito and Solo. It settled its great bulbous eyes on them and shuffled its hind legs around until its whole mass pointed at them like a compass needle. It became clear that the animal would not move without prodding. The boys whooped and whistled. Solo raised his arms to appear taller. Pablito then bent and grabbed some fallen papayas—he instructed Solo to do the same—and they lobbed the green fruit into the path of the bull until, as if receiving the message after some delay, it shuffled off into the grove and casually joined its mates.

The boys continued on. Eventually, Pablito said, "My brothers sent some good money this time."

"*Verdad?*" Solo asked.

Pablito didn't answer. He'd never lied to Solo.

"It's a good thing," Solo said. "Maybe your father will rent Don Ricardo's tractor and working the fields will be a snap."

But Solo knew that Pablito's father would not rent the tractor, that he would harness the oxen as always. Remittances like these were coveted—to build new rooms onto shacks, for example, sometimes even of cinder block. A family could invest in a gas generator or a horse or a cow. Regrettably, overdue maintenance had a way of diminishing hopes for wholesale improvements. Thatch roofs needed to be replaced every eight years. And at seven pesos for each palm frond, even if friends and neighbors contributed their labor, the costs could add up. As often as not, however, the patriarch of a family would simply drink the money away.

Pablito waved off the idea of renting the tractor.

"So what will your family do with the *plata*?" Solo asked.

"They say, maybe, the school," Pablito answered.

Their grammar school education was coming to an end. This was the limit for the majority of villagers, as families had to pay out of pocket for anything further. Transportation to the school was another challenge. Pablito might have hesitated to mention the possibility because it was no secret that Solo's family, despite the boy's desire to attend, wouldn't be able to pay. Solo and his siblings sometimes sustained themselves on local fruit for days, and occasionally went to sleep with nothing in their bellies. Still, Solo's optimism didn't wilt. "The lucky ones get to go," he said. "We just need to get lucky."

The boys footed it down out of the hills. Open land gave way to fenced sections. They came upon the small outlying ranches where scarecrows commanded the fields. Soon, they separated to drop the firewood at their respective houses. A farmer worked a light green plot of sesame in the distance, but not many of the men remained this time of year. A cadre of women would be down at the little river, standing to their knees in the brackish water, scrubbing laundry. The lady standing farthest out handed a clean article off to the next woman, and then a third set the pieces to dry over bushes, warm cobbles, and branches. Solo, whose walk home passed that way, always noted the conversation. Occasionally he re-created it for Pablito upon rejoining the path to the dairy: "They're talking about washing machines again," he said. "As if it's something new. Everybody knows about washing machines."

Husbands and sons returning for Christmas often rode with workmates in secondhand cars acquired in *el Norte*. They'd drive night and day to get home, sputtering through the badlands of the interior and over the sierra. Big towns and notoriously dangerous regions were avoided. Both bandits and police were a concern, as the workers often packed the autos with goods too expensive or unavailable in Mexico. The women dreamed of conveniences, but neither the cars nor large appliances ever entered the village. The men, likely as not, would hike in, bearing used clothing but first-rate baseball bats for the village team.

"When we are old men, Pablito," Solo would say, "the river talk will still be about washing machines."

The milkman's bicycle was a very sturdy, very old utility bike with solid rubber tires, two parallel top tubes, and wide, level handlebars. The steel basket was mounted astride the front wheel. A metal dipper with a hooked handle hung from the bike frame. When the boys stopped at a home, one called for the proprietor and the other lifted the dipper and measured the correct amount of milk from the canisters. The bike's seat was made of petrified leather and wobbled on worn springs. Fenders, front and back, helped protect the dairy and the riders from mud splatter in the rainy season and loose rocks in the dry. The rear axle bolts held little posts threaded on either side, which the boys called *diablitos*, or little devils. One kid could stand over the rear tire with a foot on each of these *diablitos* and balance while holding on to the bike rider's shoulders. If done right, the sensation was like flying.

Braking, however, was a matter of art. The milkman's bicycle boasted only a front brake, and with the weight of the load over the fore wheel, even a modest squeeze could send the boys over the handlebars. So, whoever was in back had to apply the sole of his huarache to the rear tire. The foot quickly became hot, and the *diablito* rider would switch to the other foot. Usually, this was Solo's position. Pablito would yell, "Brakes," and Solo would lift his skinny leg like a flamingo and place it on the tire.

The dairy farmer was not young, but from his choice of deliverymen, his appreciation for youthful adventure was evident. His cheeks were deeply lined and he wore his graying hair in a short pompadour that shook as he worked and made his proclamations. And he always made proclamations when filling milk canisters and loading them into the basket. In many ways, globalization was coming to rural Mexico. There were trade agreements and monetary reorganizations and food and currency crises like the Tequila Crisis and the Tortilla Crisis, the demand for imports increasing even as corn prices tumbled, all putting pressure on small farms and businesses like the milkman's, and always with the same result: people left the village.

The boys held the bicycle by the handlebars, and listened.

"There you go, men," said the milkman finally, as he lifted the canisters into the basket. "That should be enough. Don't worry about the Garcia house. They left yesterday."

Pablito made a low whistle, slipped a leg over the frame, and mounted the saddle.

When the canisters were full, the bike was heavy. Pablito stood on the cranks and pushed with all he had. It was a matter of will to keep it righted at the slow revolutions he could muster. Solo jogged behind to give the occasional push. In this way, Pablito eventually gained momentum. Solo followed, and when the bike reached the proper speed, he hopped up onto the *diablitos*. The milkman waved them off.

It wasn't a small thing that the bicycle offered the sensation of balance without a foot or the hoof of an animal, without a single living part having to touch the earth in any way. The stability was in the movement, and the movement was like a trick. Nothing else in their experience offered such a sensation. When Pablito and Solo experienced flying, in some very real ways, it was. The falling was real too. The roads of their village weren't much more than ox trails cut by rivulets and irrigation ditches. When they'd started this job, the milkman offered the usual tips of bicycle instruction: maintain your speed, steady your hands, keep your eye on the road. The bike will follow your gaze. Then the milkman simply walked off to tend to his cows. In truth, Pablito and Solo had taught each other to ride, one running alongside the other and spreading his hands as if to catch a fall. This hadn't been easy on the rutted roads and trails. The bike's bent kickstand and brake lever were proof of the challenges. And yet, they were the only two kids in the village who knew how to ride at all.

We know the delivery vehicle also provided something special that, maybe, another bike couldn't—unquestioned entry into the lives of their neighbors. The boys rolled into the yards, barns, up to the homes of any villager. When Pablito or Solo gave a kick to a tire-chasing dog, no one scolded them. Permission was never required to open a gate or to cross a field. They absorbed the news, attitudes, and gripes of the families in wisps and snatches of conversation. They could appraise their neighbors' crops and yields, and thus their futures.

By the time the boys made their stop at Pablito's house, if there was any news to share, his grandfather would be there to listen. The gate was always open and with Solo on the handlebars, Pablito bumped one wheel and then the other into and out of the dirt sluice that lined the property, steered between the gateposts, and rolled into the yard. A rooster and some hens peeled away. The bike came to a crisp stop and Solo popped off the bars, landing on his feet. Pablito attempted to use the kickstand out of habit, even though it was bent beyond repair, but finally laid the bike on its side.

"*Dime*," the old man said—tell me. He rested in a threadbare hammock tied between posts under the thatch porch. He was wide-shouldered, round, and powerful. His bright eyes peered from under a straw hat set askew and his hands were clasped over a bright T-shirt celebrating an American sporting event. This was tucked into dirty trousers.

"They're talking about the May rain and about corn and washing machines and the United States," Pablito answered.

"The Garcia family left for *el Norte*," added Solo. "They are going to Kentucky to twist the necks of chickens in a factory building as big as the village. The hens live in tiny boxes stacked up to a metal ceiling—higher than the trees. The cousin, Yonny, he works there now and he told Garcia there's lots of work. So they left."

"Is that so? And how will they get to Kentucky?"

"They took the bus," said Solo.

"But how will they cross?"

"I don't know."

"In my day, we were invited."

Pablito's *abuelo* tended to brag in the manner of old men, mentioning just a few succinct facts that suggested a not-too-obvious elevation above most others—an attitude he would naturally deny if confronted. In this case, he referenced his involvement in the Bracero Program, a guest worker agreement struck between the United States and Mexico during World War II. That history was lost to the boys, however. They merely looked at the man.

"These days, to cross, the people associate themselves with *malandros*," he said, "and who knows what they'll get for their efforts."

"They say, maybe, ten dollars an hour," said Solo.

The *abuelo* invited them to sit and be educated. In the shade of the porch, they shared a dish of cold beans and salsa. Afterward, they said good-bye to the old man, mounted the bicycle, and pedaled off to the dairy. They parked the bike in the barn and draped a dirty piece of canvas over it. Then the boys walked to the schoolhouse, a pale yellow cinder-block building with square windows, a tin roof, and a mural depicting turtles along the side. Pablito and Solo sat in the schoolhouse, where, along with the dozen or so village primary students, they studied reading and math from two in the afternoon until seven in the evening—school hours for the children of *campesinos*.

We know from Solo's narrative—details he relayed well over a decade later while living thousands of miles from his childhood pueblo—that one day surely stood out from all of the other days on which the boys hiked into the hills to gather firewood and delivered milk on the milkman's bicycle and went to primary school—a moment that cleaved their childhoods into two distinct pieces.

Pablito returned home in the early evening to find his parents in the house, having themselves recently arrived from collecting the money his brothers had wired to a bank office located in the municipal seat. On special occasions like these, Pablito's mother prepared a meal of mole and hot peppers and beef—a rare treat.

Pablito's father would have worn a baseball cap that was a gift from his eldest son, a collared shirt, loose trousers, and huaraches. He looked like a version of Pablito's grandfather, one that could sit neatly inside the original, differing only in the slight mustache, dark hair, and obliging sensibility. His mother always wore a traditional dress with an apron on top that she'd embroidered with jacaranda flowers. A lantern lit the room. After the plates were wiped clean, Pablito's mother and father likely exchanged glances, and his father cleared his throat. When discussing family matters, they tended to become more formal, even with the children. Pablito would have been alert to the change.

His parents then informed Pablito that they'd be using a portion of their windfall to send him to secondary school. "It is a blessing we are very thankful for," his mother said, "a gift we weren't able to provide for your brothers or sisters." But also—it was his father who spoke this time—they told the twelve-year-old that the two of them would be using some of the money to travel into *el Norte*. Pablito's brothers and sisters had arranged their way, and had prepared a home there in a city called San Diego that was so close to *la frontera* that it seemed not so far away from the village, despite the miles. Pablito would be staying behind to attend school and to take care of his grandfather. If his parents were prosperous, after Pablito finished his studies, they would send for him. If not, they would return to the village.

We don't know Pablito's expression on hearing the news or his response if he made one. We don't know what his grandfather might have said, if he offered advice drawn from his extensive experience or anything at all, and we don't know what the body language of Pablito's parents expressed once they'd unburdened themselves of the decision because Solo, who was at home with his own family, wasn't present to witness the event, and Pablito never conveyed more than the essential facts. That was his way.

Only once, soon after the parents departed, when the boys were working in the side field with Pablito's grandfather, was the topic addressed. Solo heard the old man say, seemingly in response to no one: "It's okay. The country is good. Everything over there is very clean. That's what people say, right? It's so clean. The roads are straight and machines come by to sweep them. Can you imagine? But some things are more important: family and the pueblo and peace and nature. These are treasures; better than clean noisy cities where things cost so much you have to work daily just to remain poor."

Later, Solo explained that it wasn't exactly as if Pablito had been deserted; simply left in a shack with a solitary old man. In the village and nearby, Pablito had two aunts and one uncle and several cousins. And a few nights a week one of the families in the village who owned a television and a gas generator would set white plastic chairs out in their yard. They'd place the TV on their windowsill with the screen facing out. All of the village kids and a few of their parents would come together and watch. Some brought nuts and dried mangos with salt and chili powder or fruit juices tied off in clear plastic sandwich bags. These would be passed around. Most of the villagers were related in one way or another, and gatherings were always very family oriented.

Pablito attended secondary school most of the day and his studies required additional time. But throughout the years, he and Solo continued to meet each morning to walk into the hills to gather firewood, and after Pablito came home from school, they delivered milk. Solo noticed that when *Pablo* did speak, which is how Solo began to refer to him, he didn't sound the same anymore. The words he used had changed. And we know through Solo that one day not long after Pablo had finished secondary school, the teenagers met as usual to hike into the forest, and on returning they split to go to their respective houses. When Pablo reached his yard, he felt something amiss. The place was too quiet. The hens were still locked in the hutch. Inside the house, Pablo found his grandfather. "He still looked strong, lying there," Pablo told Solo, "but he had no breath."

The boy's grandfather had simply failed to wake in the little one-room wood house, but we don't know why. It's likely that the family doesn't either. He was old, they said, that's all. Pablo received some inheritance, but he sold livestock to pay for the service. His aunts and uncle helped out too. Pablo's parents had yet to send for him and he didn't know if they would. He didn't know much about them anymore. In the old days, workers had returned for Christmas, but those days were gone. Communication from *el Norte* was patchy.

Around that time Pablo and Solo took work as laborers to help build a *tiendita*, or little corner store. The job started on a Monday. The town bricklayer played shortstop for the village team, and the Sunday before work was to begin, the team played a game in another pueblo. Pablo and Solo didn't attend, as the hosting village was far away, but they saw the players whooping and strutting into town on the heels of their victory. The boys heard the men celebrating that afternoon and well into the night. The entire village could hear them. And everyone woke to a traveling crescendo of barking dogs and laughter as the players made their ways home in the blackness that preceded the roosters' first cries.

"I guess that shortstop isn't going to show up for work today," Solo told Pablo as the sun rose in the sky. "I heard someone brought turtle eggs to the party—steamed—which are supposed to make you strong, right? Not strong enough, I guess. If the boss comes yelling one more time, I'm going to quit."

"You can't quit something you never started," Pablo said.

"Start where? How? We've never set any bricks before."

Pablo stood and picked up the mason's trowel. He grabbed the wooden wheelbarrow and the bucket of water. He lifted a bag of cement, ripped it open, and began to make a mixture for the footing.

"Just wait for the shortstop," Solo advised. "You're going to mess it up."

"Nothing is going to be messed up," Pablo said. "We're going to pull this work off today, before the *dueño* fires us."

The first side wasn't pretty, or even level, but at a quick glance, Pablo passed as a mason. Nothing in the village, made by man anyway, was ever level.

"I bet you're a good shortstop, too," Solo said. "No point in sticking around here with talent, *hombre*."

Building the walls of the *tiendita* was not the most memorable work. And frankly, if Solo reflected on it, it was only to question whether the bricks remained in place beyond a wet season or two. Solo remembered his exact words to Pablo only because they came true faster than he'd thought.

Two days after finishing the *tiendita*, Pablo asked his friend for a favor. "Solo, I want you to do the thing you promised, and pray to God for my travels. I'm going to *el Norte*."

"You're finally joining your parents?" Solo asked. Eight years had come and gone since they'd left, so much time, Solo thought, that it seemed as if the parents might never send for him.

"I don't know," Pablo said. "I'm just going." And he walked out of the village on the thin dirt roads.

We know that he had no arrangements to cross into the United States, and little knowledge of what the process entailed. He didn't know Mexico City, or Tijuana, or anything in between. Pablo walked to a village bigger than his own. He hopped aboard a local *colectivo* and rode it to a small town, and there he caught another to a bigger town. He arrived in Mexico City after dark and boarded a three-day bus that rarely stopped. The drivers took turns sleeping in the motor coach under the cabin. The bus had televisions in the headrests and a bathroom with a plastic toilet and running water. Out the window he saw types of cars that had never wheeled into the village. He saw mountains and deserts. And at the terminus of a string of marvels, Pablo landed in Tijuana with a few thousand pesos—the sum of his grandfather's estate—which was enough to feed him for a few weeks as long as he purchased nothing else and slept in the open. For safekeeping, he placed the coins and dirty bills in a little pocket he'd sewn into his underwear.

The main bus station would have looked like a gleaming international transit hub—Paris or Kuala Lumpur—to the country kid. Its floors shined. It held shops and restaurants. Pablo would have seen other *campesinos* who looked like he did, wearing sandals, patched trousers, and weathered hats. And immediately, in the presence of city dwellers dressed in suits or crisp jeans and leather shoes, he would have known the difference. He would have known, before learning the term, that he was a *pollo*, a chicken, something to be preyed upon. And likely, he would have seen the men who approached *pollos* fresh off the buses from Michoacán and Zacatecas to offer their services. He would have seen the local police who competed with these men to snatch up *pollos* and sell them body and soul to the coyotes.

But like the other newcomers without money to pay the smugglers, and looking so poor the police had no interest, Pablo found his way to the border fence—*la línea*—and walked along its rusted arc and curve to a broad river that was paved with cement, filled with trash, and smelled of sewage. This wasn't a river anybody would wash his family's clothing in. Pablo walked the paved shore until it ended in dirt at the boundary of the United States. He saw the Border Patrol waiting there in white-and-green trucks and observed the gangs of deported men who idled along the river. Some broke the concrete and dug burrows and caves into the banks, where they lived. Others congregated to smoke and snort *chuki*—methamphetamine—and to huff paint or glue or gasoline under the walking bridge from the United States. Men lined up at a public water spout to bathe their blackened bodies in view of tourists passing by.

Pablo would have known that the only difference between himself and these men was time.

It was in January, six months after Pablo walked out of the pueblo, that Solo learned his friend had wired him money, an intimidating sum. The wire arrived with instructions for Solo to meet Pablo in Tijuana. Solo was surprised that his friend hadn't made it to the inside, to San Diego, yet. He worried that something was wrong with Pablo's family, and that this was the reason they hadn't sent for him long ago. The instructions included a personal note: "Thank you for your prayers. There's good work here in Tijuana."

Days later, when Solo stepped off the red, white, and blue bus from Mexico City—wearing trousers, a worn linen shirt, huarache sandals, and a cowboy hat—he was nearly knocked over by the hustle of the bus station. He took in the gleaming floors and bright ticket counters. He saw women in uniforms. He saw the people in fine clothing. And at some point, Solo noticed a short, dark man in square black sunglasses, standing still among all the travelers hurrying to and fro. This figure wore a loose-fitting T-shirt untucked over baggy canvas pants, and spotless black tennis shoes with bold white stripes. The man made a low whistle.

"Pablito," Solo said, "you are a *cholo* now!"

2

It took a flood. My interest in the world's most crossed international border zone—a sprawling complex not thirty minutes' drive from my doorstep—was piqued only after it lay under a blanket of water. When Americans talk about a flood of marijuana or cocaine or methamphetamines or migrants or violence pouring over the boundary with Mexico, it's for rhetorical effect. With the use of the word *flood*, journalists and politicians mean to say "a larger than normal volume" of something. To put this idea into perspective, our southern border is nearly two thousand dusky, desert miles long—two-thirds the length of the United States, half the span of the Great Wall of China, almost a third of the circumference of the moon. Its parched landscape of surging mountains and mesas could absorb all the drugs of Colombia and, for that matter, all of its rain forests too. It is a place one can walk into and keep on walking into.

But on a micro-level, the canyon lands of the Southwest do struggle under bursts of rainfall over short periods of time. So what the metaphor makers have missed is that ours is a region prone not only to drought but to real deluge as well—unexpected walls of water that come quick and serious. The winter flood that caught my attention brought several forty-foot Dumpsters' worth of used tires floating with it. The receding waters of the Tijuana River left tires hanging from branches like kids' tree swings. American-made rubber clogged drainage ditches, got stuck under bridges. Black, steel-belted donuts were strewn throughout a half-dozen American horse ranches. But the odd thing about this situation was: it wasn't all that unusual.

Some estimate the flood cycle at seventeen years. But heavy rains do sometimes fall in consecutive years, even in a string of them. Clogged culverts, riffraff stuck under bridges, sluices and ditches that go unmaintained—all have allowed relatively minor rains to turn into disasters. In worst-case scenarios, reservoirs and dams fail. It doesn't always happen in the same manner or at the same portion of the waterway or, for that matter, in the same country. It always makes for a surreal scene. In 1895, the cast-iron obelisk called Monument 255, a pillar commissioned by Congress to mark the international boundary at San Ysidro, was caught by currents, washed away, and buried. In 1916 and 1927, storm water caused the often dry Tijuana River to swell to a mile wide, the Far West's replica of the Mississippi. The Mexican customs house was destroyed twice. The region's first church was pushed off its foundation. The bridge to San Diego collapsed three times. Tijuana's original horse track, and its famous multistory mountain of manure, were simply washed away—the manure hillock receding whole like an island in the rear view of an ocean liner. In a Mexican neighborhood butted against the boundary, a flash flood caused a landslide that carried several houses down with it. One of them was full of paper money. Neighbors jumped into the brown river to rescue the notes. In the United States, a commune of farmers called the Little Landers was completely wiped out. One hundred families were left homeless in a matter of hours. There were bloating dead horses and cows and snakes. A dairyman complained of having to milk his surviving cows under water. A raft of wooden casks filled with Mexican wine once washed clear into the San Diego Bay. Local boat crews were seen fishing them out of the brackish water. An observer noted, "The casks were well made, so I bet there was plenty of good wine left inside."

In 2008, an assignment to cover yet another incident involving flood and debris brought me to the Tijuana River Valley and the borderline. I was asked to document the recurring nuisance of these mysterious car tires and how it was that they so consistently ended up in the Pacific Ocean. At the heart of the reporting was the fact that, even though the tires came floating into the United States from Mexico, they weren't Mexican tires at all. California's drivers had paid good money to have their used tires properly disposed of—recycled even. These tires had gone through the legal channels. But there they were, scads of animated and willful Dunlops with the directional sense of snow geese.

As the Tijuana River enters the United States from Mexico, its northwesterly run elbows straight west toward the ocean. The valley that holds the river then spreads out like a fan. Saltwater marsh rolls away from the channel flat and green. Recessed in the tidal lands, snaking waterways meander through oxbows and torpid shallows up to the banks of a small town called Imperial Beach. A few farms and ranches occupy the southern shore of the riverbank. Then, across Monument Road, tan, chalky palisades surge three hundred feet from the valley floor and stagger parallel to the river and wetlands. From the ranches below, this escarpment looks like a fortification of sorts—not all, but most of the high ground was ceded to Mexico in 1848.

It was hard to believe, driving along Monument Road, that one of Mexico's fastest-growing cities simmered just on the other side of this rise. The country beyond the windshield looked every bit of rural California: towering green juniper served as windbreaks along property lines, sycamores shaded ranch houses. Beefy trucks towed horse trailers. It was so American there was no need for the frequent flags.

I rode shotgun in environmentalist Ben McCue's SUV. The thirty-year-old looked just about what the last name would suggest: curly blond hair, a sprinkle of freckles, a lean Irishman. McCue liked to be awed by natural or extra-normal events; he liked to be bowled over by volume and numbers and synchronicity. For the oddities produced by this strange valley, his temperament was a perfect fit. Luckily for my story, he also knew a lot about wayward car tires.

"When I bought my last set of new tires," he said as we eased through a curve in the tree-shaded road, "I paid an environmental fee of $1.75 for each one. By state law, that buck seventy-five is supposed to follow that specific tire through its life span and aid in its eventual recycling or disposal. But I also paid the shop a 'disposal fee' of $2.50 for each of the used tires I left with them. I could have taken the worn tires home with me and skipped the shop's disposal fee, but they would have just taken up space and I would have had to throw them out anyhow. I could have driven on that set a few more miles, but for safety, I let them go. There are over thirty million registered motorcycles, cars, and trucks on California's roads, nearly a vehicle for every person in the state. But neither the state nor the shops have the capacity to recycle or dispose of all of those tires."

"So where do they go?" I asked.

"You'll see," he said with smirk. "A lot of them go to Mexico."

McCue and I had met in Spain years before. He was studying at a north coast university. I was covering the European leg of a professional surfing tour for American sports magazines. The pay was so low that I traveled in a class with students, backpackers, and bearded men who slept in parking lots. McCue's roommate, Zach Plopper, happened to be a professional surfer from California, and on account of that connection the three of us formed a rollicking fan club of Spanish food, wine, and waves. We surfed windblown beaches on the North Atlantic. We each carried an empty wine bottle to be refilled by local vintners. I drove a hot-wired silver Peugeot with no registration or known owner. It had just been handed down surfer to surfer, year after year. On departure, I left the Peugeot with an Aussie surfer in France. Instead of keys, I handed over the screwdriver that opened the door. Following that season, McCue and I lost touch. I learned that he'd found work as an environmentalist on the boundary about the time I received a series of magazine assignments concerning pollution and development issues in Mexico. McCue's was an easy call to make.

"What usually happens is that the tires I paid a disposal fee to get rid of are sold to a tire-hauling middleman who takes them across the border. The tires I left with the dealer weren't bad, they just wouldn't have been safe for much longer. But that gap, between safe and impossible, is what Baja California drives on. The middlemen sell their load to tire shops called *llanteras*. Most likely, my tires were put on a car owned by a regular Mexican driver for a fraction of the cost of a new set."

There was actually a guru of this used tire business. According to a 2009 study led by Paul Ganster, director of the Institute for Regional Studies of the Californias at San Diego State University, the state of Baja California accepts about 750,000 used tires as legal imports per year, but a significant volume is also imported "informally." This usually means tires are slipped into Mexico through the noncommercial lanes on flatbeds or in vans and personal trucks. Another eighty thousand tires cross the border attached to vehicles destined for the scrap heap. To add to the mess, tires hauled from Oregon, Nevada, and Arizona that are never unloaded in California never get counted. All of these tires don't carry the drivers of Baja as far as they might, either. Owing to the quality of the roads, tires have to be replaced frequently. The state of Baja has no real way to deal with what are now "waste tires." The stacks that appear in open lots and along waterways like the Tijuana River are called "legacy piles." These often catch on fire and emit acrid black smoke for weeks; water collects in their wells and mosquitoes take up residence. Tires don't like to be buried in the dump, either. Because they don't biochemically degrade, tires almost magically shimmy up as layers of landfill settle around them over time. When it rains, those waste tires float, most often downstream.

"That $2.50 I paid to have my used tires disposed of only covered the gas money to get them to Mexico," McCue said, "but the Tijuana River will bring them back for free. And that $1.75 environmental fee, it was added to a fund that grows by about $40 million a year with nowhere to go."

"This valley is forgotten," hollered Dick Tynan. He'd stepped down from his tractor. The machine coughed one last belch of smoke, sputtered, and died, but Tynan was still yelling above its roar. "We've picked up five hundred tires already. Some spots are this deep in it," he said, pointing to his waist.

From Monument Road, McCue had turned onto a dirt lane and into the Kimzey Ranch, a historic parcel at the foot of Smuggler's Gulch. Adjacent to the hundred-year-old ranch house was a barn with its doors thrown open. This is where we found Dick and his son Terry. As Dick parked the tractor, Terry migrated over from some outbuildings. Together, they looked like facsimiles of the same man at different ages—white T-shirts and blue jeans, ample bellies, slack shoulders, breast pockets taut with packages of Marlboro Lights. Their postures gave the impression that they'd been molded from river clay. Both had burned necks and stubble on their faces; Dick's was white and Terry's salt-and-pepper. Dick wore his hair loose—a white Beatles cut from that period just before the band turned hippie. The bangs framed piercing blue eyes. Terry's were shaded by a stained baseball cap that read INTIMIDATOR. But the nose was the same straight short nose as his father's. They withdrew their Marlboro Lights and tapped the filters on the packages with what looked like a practiced synchronization.

Nearby stood a forty-foot Dumpster that was slowly being filled. McCue pointed out that this was just one of the ranches in the river's path. Once the tires crossed back into the United States, they were immediately designated as toxic waste. Instead of costing $2.50 each to dispose of, the price was now estimated at twenty dollars. This was why Dick and Terry were out collecting the flood tires themselves.

Dick Tynan had married into one of the few remaining horse ranches in the valley. The Kimzey place got its start raising thoroughbreds for the action at Tijuana's Agua Caliente track. This was not a lonely business in the early part of the twentieth century. Until Santa Anita opened near Los Angeles in 1935, the Agua Caliente Handicap had been the premier event in North America. Gambling was the big draw. Even in the trough of the Great Depression first place garnered a purse of $23,000 or, adjusted for inflation, nearly $400,000 today. Dozens of stables and breeding operations occupied the American side. Famous actors and horses passed through on their way to Tijuana's casino and race track. Movie star cowboy Roy Rogers' famous palomino Trigger (originally called Golden Cloud) was acquired from the rodeo grounds right down the street. Actor Jay Silverheels, who played Tonto in *The Lone Ranger* television series from 1949-1957, boarded race horses in the valley. At the eastern end of the floodplain, San Francisco automobile magnate Charles S. Howard built a stable that housed, among other champions, Seabiscuit, arguably the most celebrated thoroughbred in American racing history.

Now, ranches like the Kimzey place got by renting stalls to urban horse owners who liked to take slow rides through the wetlands, down the beach, and up the mesas. Many of the renters, however, were tired of getting flooded out. Horses had even drowned on the Kimzey place. In this way, environmental issues had become a major concern for the mostly conservative ranchers. As a leader in a local river valley association, Dick had worked with Ben McCue on a number of these problems. (Later Dick would tell me, "The original horsemen in the valley thought the surfers [professional environmentalists] were assholes, but we've linked up on the environment deal and it's been all right.") Each flood seemingly brought their interests closer into alignment. So when McCue and I rolled up, there were no greetings, really, just grievances couched as lists and updates. When Dick said this valley was forgotten, I understood that he meant in the eyes of city government. But we all knew it went deeper.

He waved his cigarette like a wand. "This all used to be farmland and cattle through to Chula Vista. The farmers took care of the water channels. Now that the city owns 'em, there's no maintenance at all. They get clogged up, and when it rains even a little, we get flood. I lost renters, had to drop rents. If this doesn't get taken care of, we'll be washed out of here." Dick took a drag and added, pointedly, "And anytime you get flood, you're going to get tires—always, it's that consistent."

We looked at the Dumpster. There was a long silence. The ocean breeze picked up and riffled through the trees.

"And then there's the bikes," Terry said, speaking for the first time. Our attention fell from the trembling green leaves and landed on Terry.

"Bikes?" I asked.

"The Mexicans," said Dick, nodding across Monument Road to Smuggler's Gulch.

"Mexicans?"

"On bicycles!" said Terry, suddenly animated. "They come banzai down the canyons. They drop the bikes on the trails. They run into the estuary. They run into Imperial Beach!" Pointing, he thrust his cigarette to the north. "I've collected a thousand bikes in the last six months."

"A thousand bikes?" McCue said.

"More," said Terry.

"Where are they?" I asked.

"Right on over here." The younger Tynan turned on a heel. We followed. And around the side of the barn, we came upon the collection. Anything professional in our demeanors—McCue's as an environmental advocate, mine as a journalist—evaporated with each step we made into the heap. Bikes for every stage of our lives lay mashed together. A change came over all of us, even Terry. Being confronted with that many used and distinctive bicycles, each one a history, laid in piles and rows, on their sides, upright and upside down, poised on seats and handlebars—it does something to the imagination.

I was immediately transported to a childhood vacation. My parents had wedged us kids into the 1978 Volvo station wagon and pointed it east. Around Rye, Arizona, we came upon a fenced industrial graveyard called All Bikes. Inside were acres of bicycles and motorcycles and three-wheelers. You may know the feeling when, on mountain roads in deep winter, the passing of a snowplow has created a hallway within a snow shed that extends far overhead—you travel between the walls guided only by headlight and depth perception. This was a boy's experience of navigating the footpaths between these piles and piles of bikes, bikes on top of bikes, machinery without end. For a kid who'd caught the bug of going fast and taking chances, there was nothing to compare it with. The place oozed possibility.

Sometime before, my first brand-new bike, a white Huffy BMX with blue gel grips and matching rims, had vanished. As the neighborhood rumor mill had it, the Huffy had been stolen by local toughs who'd lifted a manhole cover on an unnamed street and dropped the small bike into the black hole. In my young mind, in my imagination, the bike had fallen like a stone into a dark abyss and continued on forever—through the sewer with the rain and wastewater as if on a journey to the center of the void. When I saw the bicycle Valhalla of Rye, Arizona, I realized where my personal BMX had ended up. If only I had a compass, I thought, and provisions, and years to search for it.

About as soon as I lost sight of my family members—we'd all cut our own trails—I encountered a man holding an old motorcycle tank. He was trying to flag down the proprietor. "Hello," he called, "hello? Anyone running this place?" A gray-bearded man with a lank ponytail stood up from a pyramid of parts about twenty yards away. He wore coveralls and held a carburetor in his left hand.

"What'll you get for this tank?" asked the customer.

"That'll be five hundred."

"I could get the motorcycle for that," the man said knowingly. "How about fifty?"

"You asked the price, mister, and I told you."

"It's rusty."

"Yes."

"Dented."

"That too."

"You Solomon? Think all this junk is gold?" asked the man. "I'll give you sixty-five."

"Five hundred."

The customer dropped the tank. It clunked between the frames of bikes. He walked off, disappearing into the metal. The proprietor watched.

I decided to try my luck. People had a soft spot, I'd learned, for youths. "What about this bike?" I said, pointing to a burnt-orange Schwinn.

"You don't have enough, kid," he said, and bent to his work in the pile. Whatever the cost, he was right, because I didn't have any. Back in the car, the family exchanged their various encounters with the owner, and we came to the conclusion that All Bikes was not, in fact, a retail operation. It was a hoarder's paradise, the treasures an obsessive-compulsive had laid up for himself on his acre of heaven in Rye. He didn't want any of the other kids to have any of it, not one little piece.

No one deserved to be that lucky, I thought for a long, long time. And decades later, I felt the same way about this Terry Tynan.

"You can have any one of 'em for twenty, that's what I sell 'em for at the swap meet. Long as they work; if not, maybe less."

Terry, God bless him, was not as particular as the proprietor of All Bikes. Someone dropping by the ranch with a twenty-spot was all the better for Terry. He liked bikes, but he liked to sell them from the same piece of dirt where he'd found them even better. "That's a pretty good markup, don't you think?" he asked.

Within ten minutes of sifting through the possibilities, McCue and I had each mentally separated a bike for ourselves. Still, something inside me reserved the option for a change of heart. There were just so many. And despite our awe at the variety, complexity, and sheer number of his bikes, I'd later come to discover that Terry gleaned what he considered the very best and kept them stored away in a shed right next to the pile for safekeeping. But even if I'd known, I couldn't have begrudged him because as soon as we'd marveled at his commitment and compulsion for collecting bikes, the three of us were smashed into the truck so Terry could show McCue and me how he tracked them. "I know where there's three right now," Terry said. "Let's go."

We bumped along. Terry explained how, a year or so earlier, he'd been standing on the family property and his eyes happened to travel up the slope to Spooner's Mesa. There he saw a man descending the trail on a bike. It looked like a flea dragging a dust plume down the hillside. Terry realized that this must be "an illegal."

"A bold break," he thought aloud. It was an educated appraisal. Terry and his family had seen just about everything—on the last flood a man had ridden a Boogie Board into the United States and gotten stuck in a tree. It took all kinds.

One time a young woman crossed the border alone while in labor, lay down in the Kimzey fields, and delivered her own baby—now a US citizen by birthright. The mother mustered enough strength to carry the newborn to the ranch-house door. Sharon Kimzey-Moore, Terry's aunt, answered the knock and was confronted with the young woman, the baby, and the wet umbilical cord that still connected both. In a state of bewilderment, Kimzey-Moore brought a chair and a glass of water. Terry's aunt didn't speak much Spanish but offered to call an ambulance. The woman said, "No ambulance," and signaled that she wanted to use the phone herself. Fifteen minutes after she placed her call, a taxi pulled up to the house. The new mother simply stepped into the cab with her baby and the driver accelerated off to who knows where.

For Terry, however, the first bicycle rider represented something new. Sunlight illuminated the dusty contrail for everyone to see. Wind whipped it into an alarm. The man disappeared behind a bend. Terry ran down the ranch lane to catch a view of the rider as he hit the flats. Once at the road, Terry imagined, the man had a number of options. He could veer onto Hollister. He could ride Monument to Dairy Mart Road and run straight into the freeway. In between, there were a dozen farm roads to blend into. But as soon as the rider reached the valley floor, just a few yards from the ranch gate, a white-and-green Border Patrol jeep swooped in—sirens wailing.

Terry made the scene as the Mexican cyclist was cuffed and escorted into the vehicle. His bike lay in the dirt. The agents stepped into the jeep themselves and slammed the doors. Terry stopped the men to point out the neglected bike. They shrugged. "Take it," one of them said.

"The Border Patrol doesn't mind someone helping 'em out," Terry reasoned.

Not long afterward, Dick was out making his rounds on horseback when he rode down to the river. "I saw about ten bicycles abandoned down there," he said. "And I came back and told Terry."

"That was the start of it," he said.

As we drove along the valley's back roads, Terry described the geography in the framework of this new history. "Got one on the side of that bridge," he said, or "I found a real nice beach cruiser in that ravine," and, "Seen a big group come down Goat Canyon."

The Border Patrol graded the dirt tracks each night by dragging chained tires or logs behind a truck. This way any new marks on the road could give agents an idea of where an illegal crossing might have taken place, how many crossers there were, and a reasonable block of time in which this traffic passed. In the eastern deserts, the technique also allowed BP to track migrants who came in on foot or on horseback. But the wetlands in the Tijuana River Valley halted any northbound sign, as did the pavement at Monument and Hollister. "Cutting sign" didn't aid enforcement here as much as it did in the wilderness.

The road grading seemed to benefit Terry a great deal, however. He'd developed a habit of leaving the ranch in the early morning. And he followed any writhing tire tracks he found, often into the bush. After fifty years of steady migration through the valley, the footpaths off the road were obvious. Terry would walk them as far as they went, about to the water's edge, and that's where he'd find the bikes.

"Ten here, fifteen there—day after day after day. It seemed like each group had a scout with 'em. Sometimes I'd just watch 'em hightail it down the road. Then I'd go find the bikes."

Once, while driving the ranch four-wheeler, Terry came upon a man he'd never seen before. The man was pushing a bicycle and he waved. Terry stopped. "The *bici*, it has a bad wheel," the man complained in broken English. He pointed at the rear tire. It was as flat as a run-down snake.

"Give me a ride on back?" the man asked, indicating the quad.

"No way, José," Terry said.

Despairing, the migrant dropped the bike and walked off into the trees. "So I grabbed it," Terry said, nodding.

Knowing his affinity for the bicycles, BP officers he'd become acquainted with might stop by the ranch or flag Terry on the road to tell him the location of a new stash. Once, he drove up on an agent who was waiting on foot with a detainee. Terry said he stopped his truck and waved, and the agent "actually grabbed the bike and put it in the back of my truck *for* me."

"Pull over here," Terry said. McCue parked in a random spot on a ranch road. To our left rose the border highlands; unseen but straight ahead lay the Pacific. Hidden somewhere beyond the greenery to our right was the river. We got out and hiked over a berm.

"There were some points in time where some really nice bikes were being left," Terry said fondly, as he led us across a clearing and toward what looked like a wall of brambles. Only up close was it possible to see a thin footpath like a crevice in a cliff face. On this path, Terry said, he once stumbled upon three young women and four men, their bikes lying in the dirt and against trees. They'd been forced to break off from their group and were now without a guide. Terry found them huddled as if making a new plan. One of the men spoke some English. On seeing Terry, he asked, "What way do we go?"

The rancher gave them directions to Imperial Beach as best he could. "Then I went back and called Border Patrol," he said as we walked. "Well, maybe I didn't that time, but I have in the past."

Terry didn't care about the illegal crossing. It was obvious what interested him lay right there on the ground.

We entered onto the path between the trees and just a few yards in, Terry stopped and swept a leafy branch to the side. There was one beach cruiser and one mountain bike—only two bikes, not three as he'd remembered. These days Terry wasn't the only collector in the valley. One of the neighbors must have come along, probably planning to return with a truck for the other two, as we had. Despite the thousand or so piled back at the ranch, you could see the sting of the missing one cross his brow. Terry Tynan had become as transfixed as a beachcomber by the various multicolored and useful items. Other than a passing interest in the small profit they brought at the swap meet, I don't think even he knew why he wanted them so much. But there they were, new and different every day.

3

Within days of Pablo's arrival in Tijuana in late 2005, the Oaxacan developed a habit of wandering along the fence line that climbed and dipped through the mesas and canyons west of the city center. The paths along the border were chalky and hot, and the car-tire soles of his huaraches would have slipped easily on the loose sand. Aside from the low brush and the occasional cactus, the hilltops were barren. The rusty border fence was an eel's fin writhing into the interior. From any of the heights—Russian Hill, Bunker Hill, Spooner's Mesa—one could see the sparkling blue bay and the gleaming towers of downtown San Diego. Compared to Mexico City's low sprawl, this vertical skyline was stark—a dazzling precipice of glass and steel. A number of the southernmost California neighborhoods were also in view. To the west was the arch of the Coronado Bridge, and to the east, the snaking cul-de-sacs of salmon-colored tract homes that spilled out toward the mountains. If Pablo had known the location of the two-bedroom apartment his parents, two grown brothers, and two sisters shared in a south country barrio, he likely could have fixed its vicinity in the cityscape. The dream he'd harbored in the village would have looked different from up here.

Prospects for food or a roof over his head in this part of Tijuana were slim. It was the absolute margin. Even the shantytowns thinned out and gave way before the boundary. One could sleep in a ditch, maybe, or a culvert. The downtown halfway houses that served migrants and deportees could board passers-through for only a few nights, and then the travelers were sent on their respective ways.

Often the next step for the deported was to take up residence along the Tijuana River, the stinking and paved no man's land. Here, the challenges of the disenfranchised were laid bare for the city to see—scrums of men surrounding acrid trash fires, faces sunburnt and blackened from exposure. Clustered plastic and cardboard hovels evoked a sense of establishment. These aboveground structures had cultivated a regional nickname, *ñongos*. But the crude holes that recent arrivals dug for shelter also had a term, *pocitos*, or "wells." Many river dwellers existed virtually without a nation. Identification documents were consistently lost during the deportation process. In the streets of Tijuana, the lack of a voter ID card subjected one to arrest at any time; and gaining legal employment was impossible. Mexican federal law guaranteed the public use of water bodies and their shorelines, which made the river the only place to turn.

New migrants like Pablo who didn't have enough cash for a hotel room or the ability to pay a coyote soon found themselves in the same boat as the deported. Tijuana police kept their eyes peeled for *pollos* to sell, as each one was worth about a hundred bucks or so. Wandering men and women dressed in the clothing of peasants were stopped and questioned—amiably at first, but always with the threat of arrest. If the migrants didn't have the ability to pay smugglers for their services they couldn't be sold by police. In this instance, officers would take whatever they had in their pockets. Sometimes even belts and shoes were seized. To ensure that victimized migrants couldn't make a claim, the police often took their identification, a wound that was sure to hasten stagnation and hunger. *Tijuanenses* called potential crossers *migrantes* and this term carried a measure of respect for people out to do better for themselves. But just a short stint in the river garnered a new status, *indigentes*, the indigent—which suggested a person with fewer prospects than the outright homeless.

To live in a dirt well, scamper from police, abide in a river community ruled by drug users—to slip farther from the lowly rung of *migrante* into the *indigente*—was not an option for Pablo. It was not the dream he nurtured. Yet it seemed that in the period before Solo arrived, Pablo was at risk of losing sight of his goals. The masses of cars and heavy trucks, the roar of jets out of Tijuana International, the multistory buildings that stretched higher than the tree line of his foothill village—they all created a dizzying sense of dislocation. Pablo coped only by keeping on the move, by hiking and walking.

A lone juvenile who stalked the margins, keeping a distinct distance from the camps of strangers, however, would have led a haunted existence: eyeballs and portions of faces peering from tin-roofed shanties in *el Cañón de los Laureles*, the gazes of passing motorists on the International Road. What did they see? A *pollo* or an *indigente*? One could only duck and run at the sight of the municipal police and their flashing blue lights. At some point Pablo's rambling caught the discerning eye of a well-respected coyote, one of the *polleros viejos*. Roberto did some work along this corridor—not as much here as in the old days, but there were still some opportunities. This was old ground and it was his habit to notice every movement in it.

One evening, Roberto assembled his workers and *pollos* in strategic position at the lip of Slaughterhouse Canyon. The sky was riven with gold desert light. But on the western horizon, a great cloudbank surged into the snowy reach of a mountain range. Once the sun dipped into the peaks and ridges of cloud, Roberto knew, all would become gray. He scanned the terrain, including a perch where a white-and-green Border Patrol jeep was parked just on the other side of the boundary. *El coyote*'s survey continued before locking on the form of a young man—this figure squatted on haunches below a stand of mule fat and sagebrush.

"You, *joven*," Roberto said. "Come here." The drifter obliged—but neither too fast nor too slow. When the hunched youth drew near, Roberto asked, "What's your name?"

"Pablo," he answered. The coyote paused; he already knew.

"That's right, Pablito from Oaxaca." Roberto nodded. "You look surprised. I have a memory for such things. Last time, you said you were waiting for something, an idea you had." Roberto quietly stepped to the side and evaluated the migrant in profile. "Are you still waiting for that idea, *amigo*? Or are you ready to cross tonight?"

Pablo stiffened, but followed the coyote with his eyes. Otherwise, he didn't blink or swallow or respond in any way.

"To be reserved is a good quality, especially here." Roberto looked over at his people milling about. "*Oye*," he shouted, "get in the van." Then he turned back. "No need to say more than is required."

The *jefe* folded his arms before Pablo. He assessed the sky. Pablo followed his gaze out to the cloudbank approaching from the west.

"Or is it that you can't trust anybody?" Roberto asked.

"I trust people all right," Pablo answered.

"Look, I have a whole group going over tonight. You can see them there in the van. Those are my expert guides. They will lead this group across and take them to a safe place. *La migra* won't notice *nada*. Same for you. Name your city, Pablito."

Pablo remained quiet and continued to search the sky for the important thing Roberto had seen in it.

"Over there, *joven*, you see those people. That's you too if you want it. Tomorrow, you'll be toasting Budweisers with them."

"I'm not crossing tonight," Pablo said. "I'll let you know when."

"What's the holdup? Is there someone on the inside who can spot you? A brother, a cousin, someone from the village?"

"I have a family right there in San Diego—mother, father, brothers, sisters. But I haven't seen them in a very long time."

"And you are here. They crossed without you, the youngest, asked to stay behind before you understood what that meant. Then something happened. Am I right? I also happen to know what the true holdup is, *amigo*: it's pride. You're too proud to ask for anything."

Roberto possessed the alert but distant quality of someone who negotiated deals while his hands worked at small tasks. He was a ticket taker with an eye on the crowd, the other on the clock, and an ear for the whistle. The light of the sky flickered as tendrils of vapor passed beneath the sun, and then, with a seeming hush, the *pollo* and *pollero* were left in shadow as the quiet of low clouds fell upon them.

"Consider the passage as good as earned," Roberto said. "People owe me favors. I will set you up with a job, and you will pay me back. I've passed many people this way."

"I'm going to cross when the time is right."

"And this moment is not right," he said, nodding with gravity. "But if you're not a customer there's no point in hanging around, *verdad*? This is a place for workers and *la migra*. You can go on your way wandering around Laureles and Cúspide or wherever you visit."

Pablo turned to leave without a good-bye.

"Unless . . . you *are* a worker. And I sense you might be—a hard worker prepared to learn."

Pablo stopped. He faced Roberto again.

"You've probably noticed in your walking, it's been very hot for over a week. They're calling for a sea fog now, and believe me, when God's blanket comes rolling off the ocean that thick, *la migra* goes blind—the agents, their binoculars, night-vision goggles, the heat sensors, those little laser trip wires they have there hidden in the bush, *todo*. Even the floodlights get trapped by the water in the air and become pale little moons. The light doesn't even strike the ground. *La migra* might as well pack it in for the night. Look here." Roberto pointed at the cloudbank. "The fog is coming now."

The cloudbank that had looked like mountains now filled sky.

"The important thing right now is that some of my people are hungry and thirsty. The key to a long career in this business is to put the people's well-being first—everything else comes after." Roberto reached into his jeans pocket and withdrew a roll of money. He leafed some bills off the roll and handed them to the young man. "Okay, Pablito from Oaxaca, hustle down to the Comercial and buy some tacos and water. There are twelve of us, plus you, lucky thirteen. Don't be stingy. Workers like to eat."

Roberto expected Pablo to hurry, but the youth turned and ran. He sprinted down a switchback trail and crossed the trough of the canyon, threading the ragged edge of a shantytown before heading up a goat path on the following side. As he disappeared over the lip of the canyon's far wall, Roberto experienced a trace of familiarity. This *migrante* was a rare one. It was as if the country bumpkin had arrived at the central station intending to meet a connecting train, but in the lay time between trains, he'd become transfixed with the station itself—the architecture, the steam, the whistles, the buzz of the crowd. And he refused the onward passage. It was rare for economic migrants heading for low-wage jobs to see the real earning potential on the boundary. It was rare, but not unheard of, and this young man reminded Roberto of someone.

"Well, I was interested," he said later. "I really liked this kid."

4

From Terry's pile, McCue withdrew a burgundy ladies' ten-speed. It sported decorative lugs at the joints and a lovely little step-through frame. After dusting off a portion of the down tube, we could see that it was called the Free Spirit.

"My fiancée is going to love this," McCue said.

She hadn't yet learned to ride a bike, and McCue aimed to teach her. He pulled a twenty from his wallet and handed it over to Terry. The bill was crisp. McCue's smile was earnest. Terry wore the pursed lips of a trader. A later Internet search valued the bike at fifteen dollars. And Terry sold dozens like it for ten.

"All right," the rancher said, folding the twenty into his jeans pocket. "Deal."

I've always had a thing for ladies' bikes. The act of mounting a man's diamond frame is accompanied by a certain mindset. You throw your leg over, find the seat, grip the pedals, and the subconscious says, "Okay, we're going to ride now." You don't have to have any thought at all sliding onto and off of a ladies' step-through. It's an effortless motion and, once engaged, the bike disappears and you're simply floating on a parallel plane with the earth.

Victorian women of the 1890s championed this version of the newfangled "safety"—bicycles with same-sized wheels. Entitled young men of means, wearing mustaches, small caps, and tight pants, preferred the stylish high-wheel; the safety was but a curiosity. Yet because it was the first machine to give women independent mobility, the ladies' safety soon became an icon of the suffrage movement. They were such potent symbols of women's struggles for equality that opponents of the movement took to calling them broomsticks, as in, "Did you see Ms. Smith ride past on her broomstick?"

The Free Spirit's rear tire had been slashed through to the tube with a box cutter, a disabling tactic employed by Border Patrol. Still, it was a lucky thing the agents hadn't run the Free Spirit over. In recent days, Terry had come upon several frames that had been "taco-ed" under the weight of a jeep or "kilo" truck. To a bike enthusiast, the tactic seemed a bit hard-hearted.

"Why would Border Patrol do that?" I wondered out loud. "Frustration?"

"Maybe," Terry said. "But there's a definite chance bikes are getting picked up here, taken back to TJ, and then rolling across the same way again. The exact bike could be crossing, shit, I don't know how many times. That's if I don't get to 'em first."

McCue and I loaded the Free Spirit into his vehicle. We said our good-byes to Terry and began to make our way off the property. And then, wondering just how a ladies' ten-speed could cross the most militarized portion of a two-thousand-mile border, we decided to head up to the border highlands, because topography, it seemed, had something to do with it.

The same could be said, of course, about the car tires. But even before the Tynans' forty-foot Dumpster brimming with rubber receded to a green speck in the side mirror, I'd completely forgotten all about the car tires. Now I only cared about bicycles, and how they crossed this prohibitive, fortified, and rugged terrain. And where they went from there, and how many times one bike could cross and cycle back through, and who rode them, and, I guess, where the bikes originated from in the first place. And who, exactly, arranged it all.

"Can you imagine," I asked McCue, "a migrant bombing down into the American dream, from one of these hills, on a bike called the Free Spirit?"

I could see a young woman's face, wind in her hair, a backdrop of roiling dust, and only the light of a radiant future ahead.

At the time, I didn't know that Free Spirit was a brand that Sears department stores had sold for decades. They'd been built in every country that made bikes—some to exacting standards, some not—and around the time this little burgundy gem was produced in Taiwan, the brand represented a good percentage of all bikes rolling through America's suburban streets. The idea that an undocumented migrant crossing via bicycle would ride high in the saddle of a Free Spirit was not ironic. It was the odds-on favorite.

The normally dry hillsides of the Tijuana River Valley were dusted in new shoots of green. In a month or two, wildflowers would flash across the earth. The distance between this desert tableland and the people designing its fate in Washington couldn't have been farther. But McCue could see influence-peddling and well-honed statecraft behind rocks and boulders. He parked on the edge of a bluff—a thin strip of the highlands that belonged to the United States. As we stepped out of the truck, an osprey caught an updraft into the sky. Small mammals scurried into the scrub. You could point a finger at the general source of the Tijuana River in the Laguna Mountains and another where the water spilled into the sea. Everything was visible and still this was an opaque and strange place to be. Despite the rambling hills of cholla cactus and chaparral, the ocean vista and the soaring quiet, I experienced a sensation of being both remote and surveilled. For good reason—McCue and I were, in fact, being watched. Border Patrol agents crisscrossed the state and county parks that constituted this public space. They drove trucks, jeeps, and quads. They put the glass to everything that moved. On the way up, an agent in a white-and-green truck flagged us down. McCue produced a business card and exchanged small talk. He flashed an advocate's smile. The agent drove a small distance away, but continued to observe.

I assumed this had to do with the national terror alert level. It was set at yellow, *elevated*, as it had been for the past five years. And as on most days, nobody really knew why. No indication in the environment seemed to separate the yellow threat from a blue, *guarded*, or even a green, *low*—the two designations that were never applied. Yellow carried implications, however. Citizens were to be "alert for suspicious activity," more so than they might have been at blue. Authorities were charged with a "closer" monitoring of international borders. The ranks of Border Patrol agents doubled during the George W. Bush administration, and Customs and Border Protection grew to be the largest law-enforcement agency in the nation—so there was an extreme amount of monitoring capability. Which explains how it was that, as McCue and I were alert to the suspicious activity of the lizards and hawks in the county park, an agent watched us through binoculars. It explains *how* the agent had the time and resources to observe regular citizens in a park, but not *why*. And this, because CBP was also one of the least open or transparent agencies in the government, was something we'd never know.

That lack of information—regarding the cause, source, location, or duration of the threat, combined with the obfuscating stance of the authorities—created a gap filled by speculation as easily as a footprint in the wetlands filled with water. In his 2009 memoir, former secretary of Homeland Security Tom Ridge confirmed that political pressures were applied to the terror alert level. The department's own website stated that alerts had psychological consequences. But many believed the heightened alerts also gave rise to border-enforcement excess. And the circularity there was troubling: politics instigated heightened threat levels, which spurred overreaching enforcement, which led to abuses and drew media attention, sparking civil outrage, causing increased threat levels. Yellow, orange, red. The same mercurial process was transforming the landscape McCue and I encountered on the hilltop. In Washington, immigration policy had been conflated with the War on Terror, resulting in the construction of a new, higher border fence that was slowly progressing west. We could see its shiny steel—a bright and writhing tapeworm on the back of a camel.

Back in 1980, a collective of grassroots environmentalists and scientists secured a historic victory in keeping the American side of the Tijuana River open and the valley free from major development. There had been plans for a marina, an amusement park, track homes, and even a nuclear power plant. The environmental achievement allowed for the establishment of state and county parks, as well as open space designations such as the Tijuana Sloughs National Wildlife Refuge. And so the Tijuana River Valley remained one of the last unbroken wetland systems in the state of California, and it was key in keeping featherweight species like the clapper rail from extinction.

But in 2002, Representative Duncan Hunter added a rider to the Homeland Security Bill that called for the construction of a "triple fence" along the San Diego corridor—an edifice that required filling in canyons to build a paved road across them. This promised to cause a number of environmental problems for both the wetland below and the native species that lived there. Wildcoast, Ben McCue's employer, allied itself with a coalition of local and national organizations, including the Sierra Club, in opposition to the massive fence. They brought a lawsuit. The California Coastal Commission sided with conservationists and denied permits for the construction. But in 2005, a piece of legislation was slipped into the Real ID Act, a bill intended to bring uniformity to driver's licenses, which allowed Homeland Security to waive any law that stood in the way of the fence. It was a legislative Trojan horse. Among others, laws ambushed by the Real ID Act included the Endangered Species Act, the Clean Air Act, the Migratory Bird Treaty Act, the National Historic Preservation Act, the Coastal Zone Management Act, and the National Environmental Policy Act.

On April 1, 2008, DHS secretary Michael Chertoff invoked the waiver, and construction began. McCue and I could see contractors filling Smuggler's Gulch with 1.7 million cubic yards of dirt. McCue's cause, it appeared, had been lost without any identifiable link between this land and real incidents of international terrorism.

This wasn't, however, the only sight. In the span from downtown Tijuana to the ocean, seven narrow canyons divide the palisades into buttes and mesas. The various incarnations of the border wall—the old rusty brown one and tall shiny new one—rise and fall with every incline and descent. This creates a visual effect that has led many to compare the border wall to a roller coaster careening away toward the inland mountains. Every little nook and hill under its track has a story.

It was on the tops of these bluffs that survey teams from both Mexico and the United States met in 1850 to execute the terms of the Treaty of Guadalupe Hidalgo and draw the boundary line. But the treaty, which ended the Mexican-American War, did not specify exact coordinates. Some language indicated the line should be set at the original division between Alta California and Baja California, in a rich valley fourteen miles south of Tijuana. But the Mexican representatives wanted to retain some portion of San Diego Bay for commerce. The Guadalupe Hidalgo Treaty transferred more than half of Mexico's territory to the United States—a landmass that includes the states of California, Arizona, and New Mexico, as well as parts of Texas, Nevada, Colorado, and Utah. In comparison, the bay seemed a trifle. The American camp refused, however, arguing that San Diego Bay had always been a part of Alta California, which was now theirs.

The parties haggled. Finally, they settled on alternative treaty directions that designated a seventy-year-old map, made by Spanish pilot Juan Pantoja y Arriaga, as the initial point of reference. The treaty then gave directions to mark the border one marine league south of the southernmost tip of San Diego Bay, as indicated by the Pantoja map. Two problems arose immediately. The old map didn't match the topography the surveyors encountered. The bottom portion of San Diego Bay was a shape-shifting wetland that changed through the seasons and sometimes connected to the Tijuana River. Then the parties couldn't agree on the actual distance of a marine league. In the spirit of expediency, they split the difference between the conflicting lengths—a happenstance negotiation that put the uniformed commissioners, topographers, and surveyors on the elevated bluff that would become Monument Mesa. Buffeted by a sea breeze, with full views of the bay and the river, the men designated the initial point. It was October 10, 1850. A journalist from a London newspaper sent to cover the western demarcation of the epic border survey noted that the Mexican delegation displayed a "remarkable degree of gravity"—some described them as weepy—as they gazed north into the 525,000 square miles of country lost to Mexico at the close of a war that lasted one year, nine months, one week, and one day. The Americans on the other hand were drunk with victory.

My favorite image of the border is a lithographic plate based on an illustration made by Boundary Commissioner John Russell Bartlett in 1852. Having missed the founding phase of the survey, Bartlett traveled back to the inaugural point at the Pacific. He encountered the eight-ton white marble obelisk Congress commissioned from a stonemason in New York. It had been shipped by sail around Patagonia's Tierra del Fuego, up the Humboldt Current to San Francisco, and down to San Diego, then dragged across the sloughs and erected on the mesa by captain Edmund L. F. Hardcastle. Until then, the boundary was celebrated only with a pile of stones. Bartlett discovered the new monument framed by a grove of Shaw's agave in bloom. This particular species shoots a panicle, a spear that looks something like a giant asparagus, six feet up. The tip then flowers in yellow and pink. Beyond the monument and the agave spears, Bartlett illustrated a placid ocean and the hummocks of the Coronado Islands. In his diary, he wrote that the white obelisk "is seen from a great distance on land as well as by vessels at sea."

Bartlett has been described as bookish. Many in the commission found him an absentminded and foolhardy dawdler. This could be due to the fact that he used the appointment to fart around the American West like Don Quixote—once stalling survey work for forty-four days so he could return a maiden, who'd been captured by Apaches and traded off, to her small Mexican pueblo. His dedication to the art of illustration, however, was not a priggish hobby but an official element of the commission's charter. Scientific information concerning the almost unexplored territory was to be recorded and collected, and sketches of native people and species were to be made as the surveyors carved out the line. The compilation of illustrated birds, reptiles, and plants that emerged from the field is a chronicle both elegant and otherworldly. One plate depicts white-robed Tohono O'odham people harvesting bulging red cactus fruit from giant nopal limbs by the use of long, forked sticks. Alien, stylized landscapes at the precipice of change: I found the endeavor to hand-draw the wilderness a thoughtful and forward-looking gesture on the part of what was otherwise an infighting gang of scapegrace rascals. The marking of the two-thousand-mile border was an achievement every bit as profound as the dredging of the Panama Canal or the spanning of the Golden Gate. But the men attached to the Boundary Commission went on to become the direct inspiration for Western cinema's most notorious thieves, rapists, and murderers. Some became Confederates. Some rose in the ranks of the Union. Some were hanged, some scalped—most deserved it. Things went afoul from the outset.

Nearly all of this history is invisible—buried, paved over, or fenced off.

Grizzly bear still roamed Southern California when the Arguello Adobe, the Mexican-California ranch house that anchored the original Rancho Tijuana, was erected on a small rise overlooking the bay. Assembled of handmade bricks, whitewashed, and laced with bougainvillea, the compound was the only structure between the Spanish presidio at San Diego and the frontier city that would rise to the south. It was once attacked by Indians—saved only with a concession of beef—and served the Arguello descendants from the Mission Period through the gold rush and California statehood. During World War II American soldiers commandeered it for a lookout. But then, in 1951, a year after the last Arguello descendant died, the historic casa was bulldozed during construction of the I-5 freeway. The native Kumeyaay village marked at the south end of San Diego Bay by Don Juan Pantoja's 1782 map is now the province of third-rate strip malls cornered by discount gas stations. Charles Howard's sprawling thoroughbred ranch, where Seabiscuit trained, is now freeway-adjacent and obscured by subdivisions of asphalt-roofed track homes. Even the eight-ton marble obelisk—inscribed in both Spanish and English and, as Bartlett noted, visible by land and sea—has been permanently gated into Mexico by Homeland Security's eighteen-foot-tall steel fence. In the early 1900s, the monument drew as many as one hundred thousand visitors a year. Now, you can touch the American monument only by traveling to Mexico.

In crime writer Joseph Wambaugh's narrative nonfiction account, *Lines and Shadows*, the border canyons are given menacing characters. The book profiled a real team of San Diego police officers who dressed as poor *campesinos* and cased the boundary for criminals. Their aim was to capture a gang of bandits that preyed on migrants when they were at their most vulnerable, just as they crossed. The true tale highlights a unique period in border enforcement. In the early 1980s, the Border Patrol was a fraction of its current size. Undocumented migration was yet to become a partisan political issue, and the boundary was porous. This maverick SDPD squad may have been the last of a breed as well. Some of them were Vietnam vets, many of them Latinos. They filled in for a Border Patrol agency prohibited from working the boundary at night. Much of the action took place in a basin Wambaugh called Deadman's Canyon. In one scene, the undercover officers are beset by a covey of bandits. The wily *campesinos* pull their guns. "Suddenly [another] group of thugs poured out of the shacks on the hillside, heaving rocks." It dawns on the cops that they are outnumbered. Then, in this canyon that serves as a natural amphitheater, something odd happens. The regular people of the Mexican neighborhood adjacent to the fence come out of their own shanties in droves. They howl at the rock throwers. They begin to march toward the thugs, who quickly melt back into the barrio night. As the officers cuff their criminals on the American side, the regular people of the shanties cheer the officers. They applaud. "There were lots of weird things happening in these canyons," Wambaugh writes, "but this was one of the weirdest."

Wambaugh's Deadman's Canyon is sometimes referred to with the equally ominous name Death Canyon. Both are just lazy misinterpretations of the Spanish, Arroyo del Matadero, or Slaughterhouse Canyon. This wasn't the setting of a Quentin Tarantino movie either, just the site of an everyday butchery on the fringe of the city. As Matadero enters the United States, its name changes to Smuggler's Gulch, and this moniker holds up to history. Cattle rustlers, goat herders, gunrunners, Mexican revolutionaries, bootleggers, traders of highly taxed lace undergarments—they all made use of the canyon. The problem started in the 1880s, when the United States initiated customs duties and prohibitions a couple of miles away, at the port of entry in San Ysidro. In a wide-open country, this tax thing just would not fly among locals and traders accustomed to crossing freely. Mostly ranchers used the canyon. Then smugglers came along, and maybe, at first, the ranchers and smugglers were the same people.

The drug trade, Iaon Grillo pointed out in his book *El Narco: Inside Mexico's Criminal Insurgency*, was kick-started by a Chinese community suspended in Tijuana by the United States Chinese Exclusion Act of 1882. For nearly three decades Chinese laborers had been immigrating to North America to work in mines and build railroads. They brought opium poppies and introduced the plant to the Sierra Madre. As California's gold rush and railroad building came to an end, US legislators shut the door on Chinese immigrants. By then trade routes from the Sierra Madre through Ensenada and Tijuana to the opium dens of Los Angeles and San Francisco were already well greased. The narcotics passed through Smuggler's Gulch with the goats and cows. During Prohibition, smugglers traced the same routes with beer, whiskey, and tequila.

Nearby is Russian Hill. It is true that eighteenth-century Russian trappers made it down this far about the time they'd colonized parts of Northern California (San Francisco's Russian Hill is named after a cemetery established by early traders). But this hill earned its handle through a type of labyrinthine mythology peculiar to border towns. The highland belonged to a ranch owned by a Señor Soler. At one point Soler was a regional player in the Mexican Communist Party. The ideology was popular with Mexican thinkers and artists, and arguably, didn't carry the same stigma that communism did in the US. Soler was ambitious in his ideals. At one point he built a bullring and a theater on his hill in order to attract people to a neighborhood he intended to base on socialist principles. Much later, at some point in the 1980s, a blocky, multistory building was erected on the edge of Soler's growing barrio. Residents set up so many large antennas and satellite dishes on the roof that its position lording over the American valley became noticed. Over time, *Tijuanenses* associated Señor Soler with communism, communists with Cold War Russia, and the USSR with spies. Clearly, the building topped with CB antennas and satellite dishes at the precipice of the United States just had to be teeming with communist spies, and thus its name: Russian Hill.

The naming of Bunker Hill actually was a consequence of geopolitics. Cement bunkers, something like the string of batteries along the coast of France, were dug into the mesa during World War II. They're still there. Somewhere offshore rests a sunken submarine. Residents like to think it's a Japanese sub wounded by the guns of Bunker Hill. There's a kind of dark glee in the idea that the enemy had been so close. But more likely, the sub is an obsolete American vessel junked and sunk by our own navy out of boring expediency.

The submarine is invisible, but scars of war preparation lie all over the dirt. The desert has reclaimed an important landing strip, evidenced only by a stretch of relatively level ground. Historian Charles W. Hughes wrote that early unmanned aircraft, or "drones," were tested in the valley and used this strip. In fact, during World War I, a boy stepped out of his ranch door on the way to milk his heifers just as an out-of-control drone dropped from the sky and decimated the barn.

There's a small basin clogged with bamboo thickets that is popular with illegal crossers. It was named after Tijuana's first health food restaurant, Yogurt Canyon. The namesake eatery is still open just on the Mexican side, where the canyon is called *Sauces*, or Willows. A small, flat-topped mesa next to it is striated in a white residue. The thick layer of chalk looks like a stark geologic phenomenon, but it was actually created from nine thousand years of the Kumeyaay people's clam harvests. They scooped and ate the clam meat, and dropped the shells at their feet. Imagine eating the same thing in the same place for nine thousand years. I imagined consuming nine thousand years' worth of hot dogs—the mound of wrappers rising underfoot year after year, into a mountain. I could look down and see my great-great-great grandfather's wrappers. I could see that he preferred ketchup and pickle relish. There's a story in the waste. But this mound of our ancestors' wrappings, the layers from which we could glean information, was imminently due to be paved over by Homeland Security's new road.

McCue pointed out that the National Guard had also been deployed to the boundary. Their first mission here was called Operation Jump Start. The high ground was key to success, and Guard troops took command of various hillocks, erecting what looked like party tents. The high ground was crucial because they weren't permitted to engage in immigration matters, only to observe and report what they saw. Each soldier was either coming from or going to Afghanistan or Iraq—one could imagine this landscape as just another exotic desert oddity.

"There was one group of soldiers who took a position on Spooner's Mesa and sat in the blowing wind day in and day out," McCue said. The smell of street food wafted across the border wall. "*Perros calientes*," street vendors called. "*Carne asada!*" Banda music was caught in the desert drafts. "They took in a dog that had wandered over from Tijuana—as if it had been a meek stray, and not an opportunist," McCue added. "Those guys had no idea where in the world they were."

The migrant woman I imagined—the one astride the Free Spirit—I mentally placed her at various locations in the terrain. This was the kind of place a competitive mountain biker might take on for sport. I thought of the elegant ten-speed. It was a tough image to jibe. The 1974 model had been advertised in a folksy TV commercial; the background song went: "Hear the wind blowing, see the grass growing. Hear the sounds of love and laughter through the day, now you're on your way. When you have a Free Spirit . . . you'll always have somewhere to go."

Confronted with the border industrial complex—the fences, the roads, the towers mounted with cameras, the jeeps and trucks and the constant buzz of agents patrolling on quad motorcycles—I just couldn't imagine my migrant going anywhere at all on the Free Spirit.

5

Roberto came from a small ranch in the state of Sinaloa, a mountainous and arid region that runs up against the azure Sea of Cortez. In 1979, Sinaloa wasn't the powerhouse of narcotics trafficking that it is today. The Sierra were a badlands so lost in time that the last Apache raiders hid out among its forests and heights even as Charles Lindbergh crossed the Atlantic by plane, the Jazz Age swept America, and Gandhi led his Salt March for independence. Roberto's family's ranch was an isolated spread two hours by donkey from the closest school. But he grew up knowing there was another life out there. One of his father's brothers, he understood through stories, was a worldly man of some esteem who had lived in Tijuana for many years. And the moment Roberto, the eldest of six siblings, had outgrown his dusty little rancho, he found himself walking the streets of a central neighborhood called Cinco y Diez until he found his uncle's ramshackle house. It was not the urban palace he'd imagined, but Roberto didn't care. He hadn't hitchhiked and bused to Tijuana to reunite with the uncle. "I wanted to cross to *el otro lado*," Roberto said. "Well, that was my plan."

The uncle was an old bachelor who lived with several yappy little dogs. He worked as a bartender in one of the seediest bars in a city built on them. His bald head, bulbous eyes, and small features caused many people to mark the similarity between the uncle and his *perritos*. He often said it was a lucky thing the resemblance didn't earn him a nickname. In Tijuana nicknames were inspired by physical traits, defects, and flaws. A guy called Chango (Monkey) likely boasted a protruding jaw and big ears; El Calaca (the Skeleton) would be bony; El Sombra (the Shadow) might be a mute. There was Feo (Ugly), and Moco (Booger). There was even a kid born with his right leg slightly shorter than his left; the discrepancy forced a side-to-side hobble, and inspired the nickname El Pingüino (the Penguin). Roberto's uncle was called, for reasons lost to memory, El Barbero (the Barber).

As a barkeeper in the red-light district of the Zona Norte, the Barber had a lot of contacts. His establishment was frequented by prostitutes, pimps, a sprinkling of sailors, slumming politicians, musicians, artists, jai alai players, bullfighters, jockeys, and a new kind of creature that had come into being right there in the borderlands—*el coyote*.

Although celebrated in the street *corridos* as a wily and mythic character, part whiskey runner and part Robin Hood, *el coyote* had a fairly specific and recent birth date that dipped, at that point, just a generation deep. After the binational Bracero Program—a guest worker agreement struck between the United States and Mexico to fill agricultural vacancies caused by World War II—was ended in 1964, thousands of Mexican workers were repatriated to Mexico on railways, and spilled out onto the streets of windblown border towns like Tijuana, Mexicali, and Juarez.

Within a growing season, a small-time hustle in the guiding of these workers back into the United States was initiated—some say right there in Tijuana. This was a mom-and-pop business, and client recommendations were key. The men and women who filled these positions often had family on both sides and were culturally bilingual. A savvy borderlands operator might sell untaxed cartons of cigarettes from the trunk of a car parked in a Pomona berry field one day, and cross the people who worked in that field the next. Importantly, this first generation of entrepreneurs saw themselves as compassionate hosts. God delivered the migrants to their care and it was their duty to protect them. Over time, their business was compared to that of travel agents, as there were options and classes of tickets to consider. And eventually these transnational travel agents were hung with an umbrella moniker: *el coyote*.

By the time Roberto sat for his first beer in the uncle's bar, the business of crossing Mexicans without documentation into the United States had grown into an industry with agreed-upon codes of conduct and a hierarchy of diverse yet compartmentalized job descriptions. *El coyote* was no longer a lone operator but had become the big cheese, a businessperson who managed a workforce, handled the books, and rarely put him or herself in danger by personally setting foot in the United States. At the base of the coyote's pyramid were any number of freelance recruiters, sometimes called *enganchadores*, who scoured the central bus station, the airport, the slums, the beach, and the borderline itself for potential clients. The customers were called *pollos*, chickens, and all of the people who worked for *el coyote* were generally referred to as *polleros*, chicken herders.

On the ground was the head *pollero*. This was a manager who called the shots and explained the rules of the game to the *pollos*. The first being that once on the inside, the chickens were never to admit even a whiff of *el coyote*. In America there were no *pollos* and *polleros*; they were all job seekers, nothing more.

In a high-ground position crouched *el checador*, a surveillance man who kept track of Border Patrol movements through binoculars or whatever else he deemed necessary. This person was intimate with the agents' shift changes and lunch breaks, with the nuances of each agent's work habits. *El checador* memorized drive times from hilltop to bottomland. He logged response times in every type of weather. And when conditions were right, *el checador* flipped the whole machine into action with a wave.

Primarily, he was signaling a figure who idled in an obvious and open position near the fence line. This figure carried no bundle or provisions. He might wear red or a bright soccer jersey. He might be big, he might be loud, for it was *el gancho*'s duty to make himself known to Border Patrol. Imagine old-timey rodeo clowns—jokers who entered into the ring to protect fallen riders by distracting the agitated and surly Brahma bulls. Whatever means they saw fit to accomplish both was fair game: a challenge, a tease, a sprint. Likewise, the *gancho* might make a show of himself right out of the gate—leading agents away from the migrants' route. Or he might wait as needed—if it looked like the *pollos* could be in danger, the *gancho* might act the clown, a crazy person running in circles, a security danger that required attention. His eyes rolled, he foamed at the mouth. Then he might get caught in a pickle, a pickle among *jalapeños*—which, owing to their green uniforms and hot tempers, was a slang term for Border Patrol.

When the *ganchos* looked to be successful, then the *guías*, or guides, would lead their migrants into the landscape. There were canyons and valleys and ocean and beaches and marsh. There were trails, and no trails. There were culverts and ditches, farms and factories. And at the precise moment, *el comunicador* placed a call to *el levantón*, the getaway driver who waited on the US side to meet the *guías* and the *pollos* and load up and slip off into *el Norte*.

In 1979, Roberto's uncle paid a bar patron, a known coyote, $1,800 cash—a first-class ticket—to pass his hick nephew into the United States.

"I was crossed at Otay," Roberto recalled. "There, you just jumped the fence, ran a little, and you were at the factories where the ride was waiting."

Months passed and Roberto was washing dishes in Los Angeles. He started to wonder how many times he'd washed the same dish. In his stained apron, amid the vapors and steam of the machines and the force of the industrial spray nozzle, he began to rehearse his obstacle run, the jump, the climb, the fall, the sprint, and the skip into the United States. He saw a *camarada*'s face every time, another migrant waiting in the pickup car who'd slapped his leg and said, "Man, that shit is like drugs. I get a high every time."

After a year in Los Angeles Roberto was back in Tijuana, knocking on his uncle's door.

"What are you doing here, *mijo*? Are you okay? Did you get deported?"

"No, uncle," Roberto said, "I'm fine. Everything is good. It's just that I was in Los Angeles and I was washing all of those spoons and forks in a kitchen that was like a hot, white dream and I kept thinking back to the last time I felt good. I mean really good. And the only moment I could find was here on the border—when I was crossed by *el coyote* into Otay."

"What are you saying, son?"

"Well, I want to do that work."

"With the migrants?"

"Yes."

"Dumb kid! I hand over my savings to put you into a new life, and you want to be *el coyote*?"

"Let me tell you," Roberto said, "I had a really hard time finding people who would help do the work. You could almost count all the *polleros* on your fingers. And it was a difficult time. We had to watch out for the police here more than anything. During the shifts of certain cops, you couldn't even walk near the edge of the border. You'd end up in the '70-76' under investigation, which was not pleasant. It'd start with a bag over your head, electric shocks to your testicles—all to see what they could get out of you."

Roberto's critical first associate was a young woman he called La Señora Diana. She was a beautiful, straight-backed Mexican American girl just a few years out of high school, with high cheekbones and feathered hair. Her gender, looks, and citizenship status were all serious bona fides in her role as *levantón*. As with most pickup drivers, La Señora had family and contacts on both sides. She was culturally bilingual, and understood that minutiae like a blown headlight or taillight just screamed for a pull-over. And if she were stopped and couldn't flirt her way out of further inquiries, she could always claim Mexican citizenship, offer an assumed name, get deported with the *pollos*, and, later, saunter right back into the United States.

"Soon, I got ahold of Carlos and Juan, who helped recruit *pollos*. And with me as guide, from 1980 to '83, we crossed about twenty a week in the usual ways, at Otay and San Ysidro. La Señora was always there and waiting. I couldn't complain. Things were going well for me. But then, from about 1984 to '87, my luck changed. To be honest, I don't know how, but people from Central and South America started to come to me in droves—very good, very grateful people."

The coyote from Sinaloa's change of luck was actually a consequence of disastrous geopolitics. Simultaneous civil wars in Nicaragua, Guatemala, and El Salvador—instigated and supported by Cold War powers—had reached a zenith. Death squads and militias plagued Honduras and Colombia. Some countries like Ecuador and Peru were just flat-out destitute. And by the early 1980s, people began streaming north in methods reminiscent of the Underground Railroad.

"Nicaraguans were some of the first," Roberto said, "and later I crossed people from El Salvador, Honduras, Costa Rica, Panama, Chile, Peru, Ecuador, and Colombia. Without a doubt, they made a difference in my work. In my family, we were always taught to help our fellow man. And I was much more careful with these migrants. They would come to my house and I wouldn't take them out until everything was in order."

The custom was that a migrant's contact in the United States paid the fare. So if a crossing failed, *el coyote* was obligated to offer second and third chances. The arrangement required *el coyote* to be contactable by both migrants and their families.

"I gave my phone number to the people I took across," Roberto said. "Later, the uncle would call me, the sister, the niece, the daughter, the godfather, the godmother—you know, I put whole families over there on the inside."

In a short time, Roberto built a substantial organization of *guías*, *ganchos*, *comunicadores*, *checadores*, and *levantones*. His tentacles ran as far south as Mexico City, where international migrants were often met at the airport by drivers, taken to a local safe house, and then whisked north. With an organization reaching into the United States, he could guarantee arrival in any American city—from New York to LA.

The original coyotes played a dangerous game of cat-and-mouse with Tijuana's city police. Roberto was jailed a number of times. A conviction carried a stiff prison sentence, but trafficking was a tough charge to prove unless a *pollero* was caught in the act, by which time, he'd be on the inside. And migrants, who relied on their *pollero* for second and third attempts, should their crossing be thwarted, had no interest in squealing on the operation. Among the discomforts of jail, Roberto explained, was an enhanced interrogation technique called a *tehuacan*, something like waterboarding. The victim was gagged and inverted, and a well-shaken Coca-Cola was forced up his nose—a fizzy, painful, drowning experience that Roberto recalled as "not at all pleasant."

The worst part for the smugglers doing jail time was the loss of business and relevance in the fast-changing field. On top of Central America's problems, a 1982 debt crisis in Mexico led to a period of economic collapse some describe as the "lost decade." Things looked bright for a short time in the early 1990s, but just months after NAFTA was signed in 1994, Mexico was forced to devalue the peso by half, sending the country into another deep recession. Factory work drew thousands to the border towns, but the poor wages and conditions promised a shortened life span. While Tijuana factories made 80 percent of the TVs sold in the United States, few of their builders could afford to buy one. From the hilltop shanties along the boundary, the decision to cross was an obvious one. Globalization had presented *el coyote* with a motivated clientele.

"We got together, the *polleros* of the area. We all needed to do something about the police—simply in order to work," Roberto said. There was a council of eleven veteran *polleros* who sometimes made joint decisions. In this case, those who had a cop in their pocket were asked to share their contact and widen the net. "It was necessary to explain [to the police] that this business would continue with or without their help. Financially speaking, some of the police had already demonstrated the way in which we might be able to work together. And I can say, proudly, that we in Tijuana were the first to convince the police of that fact."

Afterward, Roberto said, the beat cops would "happily" come get their commissions. And the *polleros* started working with less stress. "Of course," he admitted, "we'd never tell the cops the truth about the number we were crossing, and we definitely never told them the exact amount we were charging."

In 1995, Roberto crossed another Central American and put him on to a gardening job in Los Angeles—a contact he'd used a number of times. The business, as it turned out, had been sold to some people from the Philippines. In time, the new employers mentioned to Roberto's migrant that they wanted to bring their siblings over as well, but that they couldn't find the *pollero* who'd crossed them. "So my guy told the Filipinos about me. How he was able to convince them—because those people are extremely untrusting and good hagglers—I don't know. They called by phone. I had a hard time understanding. Can you believe that as soon as I had their siblings at my house they asked how much I wanted for my cat? 'What do you want it for?' I asked. 'Well . . . to eat,' they told me. 'Leave my cat alone,' I said. 'I'll bring you another.'

"So I walked a few houses down where there's a lady with a load of cats and I took three. Then I went to the store with their grocery list and I bought everything they needed in order to cook their cats. And, believe me, they made a delicious meal. Seriously, I thought, 'I have to take the Filipinos over right away or they're going to finish off my neighbors' cats—and mine too.' But listen, because of the gracious way I handled them, I still have work with the Filipinos to this day. I've also crossed Koreans—humble, friendly; Chinese—they're kind of fussy and obtrusive; and Cambodians—good people but they don't speak Spanish at all. I have to pay a translator in order to communicate with them."

In short, Roberto became one of the *polleros viejos*, the old guard, who rose above the fray with their connections and mutual cooperation. Over the years, Roberto crossed a Disney's small world of clients over the fence, through tunnels, past customs stalls, and into airports with, albeit false, documentation. "You can't imagine how much I've enjoyed this," he said. "It is work I love doing—the satisfaction I've given to thousands of families in the United States."

Rooms were added to his house to accommodate international migrants in transit, and as his home literally grew, he brought family members from Sinaloa to stay with him in Tijuana. When the ranch was no longer as viable as it once had been, even Roberto's mother and father moved north. And eventually the youngest and most treasured sibling, his twenty-two-year-old sister Marta, joined the household. On the ranch, she'd been bookish, but in the city she took to wearing miniskirts and short blouses and quickly developed a reputation as a woman afraid of nothing. Roberto noted traces of the La Señora Diana. From the first day Marta arrived, he and his sister were inseparable. She went with *el coyote* everywhere—to the canyons, the slums, the bars. And in doing so, Marta learned the trade.

Roberto had the best recruiters and his work was bustling. “There were nights when I couldn’t get through it all and she started to help out—organizing the people, transporting *pollos*, making crucial calls to *el levantón*, et cetera,” he said. “Marta had a knack for calming the nervous. And people paid very close attention when she gave instructions. The girl was tough.”

6

"I never saw a beat that was more interesting," said reporter Janine Zúñiga.

On January 30, 2009, I came across a photo on the cover of the city daily that showed a man pushing two bikes down a dirt road. Another pictured a man inspecting a pile of them. From the sage and cobbles on the path, the terrain couldn't have been more distinct. My gaze flashed on two words in the subhead—"dumped bikes"—and I experienced a combustible, buzzing sensation brought on by both an instinctive rivalry with this newspaper writer and a grudging companionship in the pursuit: *there was another seeker in the valley.* And indeed, when I'd located Zúñiga through a mutual reporter friend, the river valley loomed in our conversation like a silent monument. Not only did I want to know what secrets she had coaxed from the valley, I wanted to know why she'd been looking at all.

An intrepid journalist, she'd worked for the Associated Press news agency in Los Angeles, New York, and Dallas. But over the most significant decade of her career, Zúñiga covered South San Diego for the city's largest newspaper, the *Union-Tribune.* If not the focus of the metropolitan paper, the south county did offer considerable variety. It was by turns coastal, rural, international, and big city. Mountains crumbled into foothills. Desert wasteland gave way to swamp. It included both the massive border complex at the intersection of two freeways and the tiny hamlet of San Ysidro caught in its shadows. There were a handful of small municipal governments to contend with. And then there was that great rambling valley, that little-known world rife with the remnants of the past.

In July, Zúñiga reported on the annual sandcastle contest—the US Open. She dutifully sat in on city council meetings and redevelopment schemes. She never slouched from menial civic matters but the predictable stories were often punctuated by curious events—the case of the strange tar balls that washed up on the Strand, for example, or the toddlers found wandering the streets of Chula Vista. One of her favorite reporting discoveries was a clutch of rare green turtles found basking in the warm water discharged by a South Bay power plant. There was petty larceny, like the robbery of a pizza deliveryman and, later, a gas station clerk. But when the drug wars began to heat up just across the border, Zúñiga's lens broadened. She cowrote a lengthy series about a fourteen-year-old cartel hit man who'd become infamous for beheading his victims. He was called El Ponchis, or Pudgy. He helped slay a cook, a gas station attendant, a student, and a small-businessman. And then the teen, Edgar Jimenez Lugo, was arrested as he attempted to flee Mexico and reunite with his mother in San Diego. What did this US-born kid's career reveal about Mexico, Zúñiga asked, or America? How many other boys and girls were caught between these two worlds?

In January of 2009, Zúñiga decided to drop by the Gomez place off Monument Road. She wanted to follow up on the flooding story she'd recently covered, and wondered how the cleanup was going. Plus, Zúñiga believed it was just good practice to keep in touch with her contacts. This visit served both purposes.

"People in the valley are quite reserved and skeptical at first," she said on the telephone. "I would go visit on occasion so that I could reach them immediately if there was an emergency."

That emergency potential was rich. The Pacific Ocean offered any number of unexpected stories, be it disabled vessels, smugglers, or natural phenomena—like giant waves, creatures, or sea rise. Amazing things washed up and, often, familiar things washed away. But then there were the immigration patterns, the specter of terrorists crossing from Mexico, and, in recent years, the largest buildup of border security in the history of the United States. Driving past horse ranches, community plots, organic farms, and wild wetlands, one expects the weather stories; the international intrigue seemed, well, so foreign.

A thin strip of bleached country asphalt divides the Gomez property. Thirty acres of flat agricultural land extend north in a patchwork of fields that halts at a wall of dark thickets on the riverbank. The remaining eight acres rise with the border highlands to the south of Monument Road. Zúñiga passed the Kimzey place and then the Martíns' farm, a parcel that had once belonged to a Japanese family that was said to have been interned during World War II. As she rounded the bend in the road at Smuggler's Gulch, Zúñiga caught the old Monterey cypress and pine trees that framed the Gomezes' stucco farmhouse. A barn, with its tin roof caving in, slumped like an auto wreck on the western edge of the farm. Zúñiga passed a small plot of dark brown earth that was sometimes topped with bright orange pumpkins, sometimes with deep red strawberries. Here, she turned off onto a dirt lane and parked next to a little plywood shack that served as the farm stall when the berries arrived. Stepping out into the ocean air, Zúñiga noticed something that she hadn't caught during her last visit. Was it a rummage sale? No. But maybe it was something close. "There were bicycles all over the property," she said. "Upright and in rows, everywhere."

Zúñiga found the farmer, Jesse Gomez, a man in his fifties. He wore knee-high rubber waders, jeans, and a canvas camouflage jacket.

"Hey Jesse, are you starting a bike collection?" she asked.

The taciturn man paused; his sleepy brown eyes were so light they appeared almost a dark yellow. He looked up at the highlands across the street. Then, in his slow drawl, he told her what he knew—which wasn't much more than what she could see for herself: bicycles, just about everywhere.

"The first few bikes, that was exciting," he said when I later caught up with him. "But then it's like, 'Oh, we gotta go pick 'em up.'"

A cobbled track cuts the green hill, covered in manzanita and wild sage, all belonging to the farm. Gomez kept the gate open to give recreational horse riders and Border Patrol access to the mesa above. Sometime around 2007, however, as Gomez lay in bed, he began to hear what sounded "sometimes like cascading water, and sometimes almost like horses trotting." The sound seemed to be roiling down the hill, his house in its path. Soon enough, he realized what it was.

"There'd be fifteen riders at a time—two, three times a night."

Gomez's son, David, wandered over. He said the traffic set a family routine. "We'd get up for work in the morning, and we'd see shiny spots on the hill. I'd go up and collect at least twenty bikes a day."

The family heard motor vehicles in the night too, and they figured that some of the cyclists were getting picked up. They'd just ditch their bikes on the property and hop into a van. But in the daytime, Jesse and David would also see people who "just looked illegal" pedaling bikes. Once, Jesse watched a familiar cycling club ride Monument Road to the beach, a passing whir of color. On their way back out of the valley, he spotted a lone rider in work clothes turn from a dirt lane out of one of the canyons, and then merge into the pack as they sprinted off toward the I-5 freeway. Some of the migrants might have been picked up by people on horseback, as had happened in the past with foot crossers. But there were obviously migrants who rode out to the river as well, leaving bikes on the banks before wading through the wetlands and into the north.

"It was like an explosion," Gomez said.

Jesse and David didn't hunt bikes off of their own property and they didn't sell the ones they found. The wheels just presented themselves, to a point of annoyance. A bearded Border Field State Park ranger once stopped by in a pickup and off-loaded bikes he'd found, as if their place were the depot. Then again, Jesse Gomez did come upon his neighbor, Terry Tynan, who looked to be scavenging on the Gomez hillside. "Matter of fact, I had to kick him off the property," Gomez said.

The phenomenon did not dissolve the rules of the neighborhood. Picking things up wasn't new. There had always been backpacks and excess clothing tossed aside by passers-through. Plastic shopping bags fluttering on the road's shoulder contained hairbrushes, razors, soap, deodorant, makeup—everyday toiletries essential for long trips. These packages likely belonged to migrants who'd been intercepted. Abandoned items read as clear and simple descriptions of the neighborhood's nighttime traffic. But this latest trend brought something else in its wake: looky-loos, people covetous of anything free, people crazy about bikes.

By the time Zúñiga discovered the bicycles on the Gomez place, the family had already donated a big batch to Father Joe's, a homeless services provider in downtown San Diego. Extended family members had been outfitted with the appropriate bikes. Jesse Gomez's immediate family all liked the beach cruisers. Which was not a problem; they'd been descending into the valley for nearly two years. But the best bicycles—GTs and Treks—had been donated to the Church of Jesus Christ of Latter-day Saints. These bikes had been specifically selected for the young Mormon missionaries who rode them house to house spreading the gospel. Gomez was proud of the fact that he could outfit them, because he believed he had benefited from the missionaries' teachings himself. It was an image I particularly liked, too. Clean-cut young men in white shirts and dark ties coasting along on bikes that had violated the sovereignty of the United States—wheels that had served one pilgrimage now serving another.

Zúñiga's piece was titled "A Vehicle for Quick Crossing." At the heart of her reporting was this sentence: "No one is sure exactly when the border-bike phenomenon began or why." These were probably the two most important questions to be found in the front-page story. But they went unanswered. And even the nascent search for clues seemed to become muted and lost amid all the shiny new artifacts in the valley—simple queries drowned in the hubbub emitted by people attracted to the bikes themselves.

"After that newspaper story came out," Gomez said, "we just got flooded with people looking for bikes, looking for parts, just looking, looking."

Tall and thin with her gray hair pulled into a tight knot at the nape of her neck, Maria Teresa Fernandez presented a quiet, almost reverential disposition. Her elegantly accented English and way of choosing artistic metaphors extended the impression—it was an aura that served her work as much as it contrasted with the hardscrabble landscape she delved into. After years of watching the boundary between the United States and Mexico with fascination, the heart surgeon's wife found an unlikely calling in documenting life along the gritty frontier through photographs. The terrain of her milieu included the mountainous Otay section, the dense urban center at San Ysidro, and finally the coastal bluffs, and the beach. There was a lot of driving, walking, and hiking involved. Just to get to the border-adjacent state park she visited every weekend required a mile-and-a-half trek through scrub and sand. When the Department of Homeland Security began construction of the new sea fence extending into the Pacific, access to the public American beach was closed. So every day Fernandez drove into Tijuana, and through town to Playas de Tijuana, where she could walk up and lay a hand on the very same construction.

By the time I met Fernandez, she'd been photographing various aspects of the boundary for a dozen years. She said, "Anything that touches the wall, I want to document." There was everyday graffiti as well as professional artwork: sculptures made of coffins and white crosses representing the numbers of fallen migrants. The Playas portion was a favored canvas. One artist had simply painted the metal pylons of the fence the same blue as the San Diego sky. Viewed at a distance from the Mexican side, there appeared to be no fence at all.

For the purposes of Fernandez's work, however, the detritus of the clandestine traffic—and the increasing fortifications to prevent it—were even more potent symbols.

"I've been able to see a lot of things, watching this living, growing entity. And I have this need to keep in touch with [the wall] all of the time," Fernandez explained. "It's as with any relationship—there is a certain point when you think you understand all there is to know about that person. But that point is just the beginning. The relationship continues. And that's how it is with me and the wall, because the wall just grows and grows."

Certainly, it was true that Fernandez caught the border complex at what she called "a special moment." In her career, the steel and concrete that constituted the fortifications changed textures and sometimes crumbled. There were barnacles and mussels attached to it at the ocean. She'd found a hole in a thin and rusting steel section and pulled crumbling pieces away so she could stick her camera through and make a photo. But mostly, through the efforts of government contractors with their heavy equipment, the wall only became taller and wider and thicker.

Recently, she'd passed through two checkpoints to get to the formerly open area at Friendship Park, dedicated by Pat Nixon in 1971 in a gesture of national kinship. The park is centered around the border monument set in place in 1851. This area was where Fernandez had made some of her most successful images—including photos of Mexican Americans picnicking at the beach fence with their Mexican relatives, or lovers, sitting on the other side. One of them depicts a man seated under a colored umbrella laughing so hard he's brought his hands to his ears to stop the words he's hearing. On the opposite side of the steel pylons, a woman's head is upraised and howling too. Whatever was said struck the family as so hilarious, the pylons of the wall virtually disappeared. Yet in 2012, as Fernandez was ushered through a new eighteen-foot-tall steel gate that had been erected around Pat Nixon's park, a Mexican looking through the fence said to her, "Hey, who do you think is more free? You in America, or me over here? You are being guarded by men with guns. I just walked over from the taco cart."

As a kind of resident artist of the boundary, Fernandez has hosted a number of delegations from other parts of the United States and abroad. A group of German filmmakers came to document the border wall, and Fernandez offered them a tour. They viewed local neighborhoods, artworks by renowned artists, and sites of infamous incidents. Fernandez told stories about her encounters with the crossers and the things they left behind. Once, on the Mexican side, she came upon a migrant camp that looked recently vacated. Searching for images to take, she spotted a bag with a young woman's things tumbling out: lipstick, eyeliner, candies. Inside, she found a girlish diary, and turning to the last page, Fernandez read the line: "As soon as I get to America, I'm going to start losing weight." On the American side, Fernandez encountered a man in his forties with his young son at his side. They'd come because the man's father, a Mexican citizen now in his eighties, had traveled by bus for two days to stand alone on Tijuana soil and attempt a reunification through the fence. It was the father and son's first meeting in thirty years. The grandson was introduced.

"Do you see what you did for me?" the younger man said to his father. "You taught me to work hard, and look, here is my son—named after you. He goes to school and he speaks English, too."

For her German guests, Fernandez also explained her idea of the wall as a living thing, adding, finally, "But like any living, breathing animal, I want the wall to die as well."

The Germans considered this idea. One of them said, "You know, we didn't think the Berlin Wall would ever come down until it came down all at once. The death of a boundary is possible."

"I hope it happens here, too. In my career," she said.

It struck me that Fernandez could have done anything with her time. She was a woman of class and means, and the border was neither a pleasant or safe place to be. Not only was Fernandez's fascination with the wall odd, so was her relationship with it. She had dedicated her life to noting and archiving its various nuances. There was a heat and a passion to her work. And yet she wanted the wall to cease to exist as well. It was if she'd been inordinately enthralled by the growth and mutation of a tumor, had devoted her life to chronicling it, but desperately hoped for a cure at the same time. What would she do if this thing were gone? Twelve years of stalking a beast is time enough to fall for it.

In the interim, Fernandez spent her days bent low, clicking the shutter on items like baseball caps in the dirt—likely lost in a sprint. Shoes were stuck in mud, or hung from the wall itself. Rope ladders were tossed aside. Handmade things that fit the bodies who wore them sat like empty shells. Her face to the camera, the lens to the wall, she always looked close.

Maybe this is why the first few times she became aware of cyclists along trails in the distance, this chronicler of small detail didn't stop to let the sight sink in. People on bikes, it's an everyday occurrence. Maybe these riders were dressed like *campesinos*, Fernandez recalled, but . . . She did catch the curious sight of an adult pedaling feverishly down a track on a child's bike; the revolutions made by the grown-up knees and ankles on the tiny pedals and cranks came to her like an unexpected joke. But it wasn't until Fernandez arrived at Border Field State Park—and found herself on the edge of a significant pile of bicycles accumulated in the dirt parking area—that one of the park's staff ambled up to explain where they'd come from in the same measured, scientific way he might elucidate the sudden appearance of a whale carcass. Her latent memory of crossers on bikes came back to her then. This transnational cycling in plain view, so smooth and forgettable in its arrival, caused her to wonder if the activity was organized or spontaneous to the point of performance. Did its consistency signal something else, something bigger? Migrants, Maria Teresa Fernandez knew through experience, tended to do what worked.

A *Los Angeles Times* review once claimed that Fernandez's photographs "form a knot of narratives." But like the everyday mysteries in her photos, the mystery of the bikes couldn't be untangled by snap observations alone because, as with the hats and shoes, the people who put them there in the dirt had vanished. Phenomena of the border sprang forth and evolved so fast, few of their riddles were ever solved. The bikes were mysterious. But so was everything else. Fernandez could only return to her central premise—the one thing she knew she could accomplish. Anything that touched the boundary needed to be photographed, documented, cataloged. So Fernandez stepped into the bush and shot the bikes that were set there, "hidden between branches, or in hollows," as she said, or simply "thrown away."

I found Greg Abbott on a clear winter morning, walking the sand dunes of Border Field State Park with a tank of herbicide strapped to his back and a spray nozzle in his hand. This was a ritual the state parks ecologist performed during the coldest week of the year, spraying the invasive "highway" ice plant that bloomed and shape-shifted across the dunes like a slow-moving storm.

In his overworked khakis adorned with the patch of the brown bear on a faded field of green, Abbott looked both rugged and intellectual, as if Papa Hemingway had retired from books to take a civil service post in the southernmost corner of the West Coast. He wore a scruffy gray beard, but you could still see the beach boy blond in it. The saucer-like bullring and brightly colored neighborhood of Playas de Tijuana dominated our southern view. We stood a stone's throw from the mouth of the Tijuana River, where it emptied into the Pacific. Offshore, the Coronado Islands broke the ocean's blue plain. Behind us, the green, tawny, yellow, and rust colors of the valley ascended from scrub to tablelands rising into Otay Mountain, a crescendo of the last unbroken fresh-to-saltwater system in Southern California.

As we talked, a black-tailed jackrabbit the size of a small beagle leapt from a low bush and made a wide, loping arc around our position. Abbott sighted the rabbit's evasion technique and suggested we modify our direction in order to keep the animal from bolting into the streets of Mexico. Nodding at the open land around us, he said, "It looks pristine, but it's not." I could clearly see the bunkers in Bunker Hill. Somewhere in the vicinity, bovine skeletons eroded from the earth where American soldiers once shot forty head of trespassing Mexican cattle—the first cross-border incident of the twentieth century. Migrant trails snaked the entire reserve. And of course, there were remnant car tires.

"This is an island—an island surrounded by three million people," Abbott said. "And islands have problems you wouldn't believe."

Greg Abbott had been a pioneering surfer and a legendary lifeguard—occupations that fit together only in the beginning. His surfing and world travel kept him from ever wanting to commit to a career-track lifeguard gig. As he came of age, state lifeguards were suddenly classified as "peace officers" and required to carry side-arms. They filled out paperwork and climbed the bureaucracy to soft pensions. That wasn't Abbott. And yet his heroics saving lives at the beach had earned him injuries that ensured he couldn't be a "seasonal" forever—that was a kid's job.

Remembering when he fit that description, Abbott pointed to the spot where he and some other seasonals had once built a shack and a barbecue pit. It was hidden from their superiors by the large sand dunes. The sight of the empty space made him reminiscent. The driftwood shack was so close to the border, Abbott and his cohorts would often dash into Mexico to make saves off Playas de Tijuana. One September, in fact, brought both sweltering heat and a powerful swell that had originated south of New Zealand. The inland heat prodded a record number of Tijuana's citizens to the beach, an egress timed perfectly for a mass encounter with the treacherous waves. There was no lifeguard service in Mexico. At some stage, while scanning with his binoculars, Abbott spotted a swimmer caught in a rip current on the Mexican side. He grabbed his "can"—a red flotation device—and dashed across the border to make the save. Once he got the swimmer to the sand, a mob of beachgoers cheered. But then Abbott spotted another swimmer in trouble farther south, and after, another. "There were so many people at the beach," he said, "it was like running through a crowded bar." He kept following dangers until he "couldn't see America anymore."

Then the first sea fence was built, an iron gate extending into the Pacific that split one beach between two nations. Lifeguards called it "the strainer" because ocean currents often trapped swimmers against its pylons, holding them underwater.

As enhanced border fortifications went up in the 1990s, crossings became more dangerous and the lifeguards soon found themselves making increasingly desperate saves. Abbott once watched a group of migrants attempt to negotiate the Tijuana River mouth where it meets the ocean. They were already on US soil but their aim was to get to the town of Imperial Beach on the other side. Depending on tide and season, the river mouth will push or pull a tremendous volume of water while appearing placid. "They looked fine at first," Abbott said, "but just as soon as I turned my head, all five were in trouble." He bolted down the dunes and into the swirling water. He gathered the group of fully clothed men and women, most still clutching their few possessions. And then he began to swim them to the farther, northern side of the river—a distant crescent of dry sand. This valley comes with a separate set of rules. Abbott knew that if he did the much easier thing and pulled the "illegals" back to the southern shore where they'd entered, the group would only attempt to cross again. "You don't want to have to save them twice," he said.

In 1998, a North Pacific storm brought the kind of surf the Strand sees maybe once a decade. Some waves approached two stories high. Thirty-knot winds out of the southwest carried rainsqualls, drenching the coast and whipping the waves into a fury. The ocean temperature plunged. In all this heaving gray tone of texture and energy, Abbott spotted a *panga* fishing boat foundering off Coronado Beach. Coming over in *pangas*, open wood boats propelled by outboard engines, had become a popular yet reckless immigration technique. The problem was that *pangas*, while great fishing boats, were poorly designed for long-distance travel. Few migrants swam well enough to justify the risks. Abbott observed a huddle of bodies in the front of this one. His fear was that the person in charge would force the passengers overboard in an attempt to lighten the load. The *panga* pilot approached the surf line but fled out to sea when waves rose up. Then Abbott, as he feared, saw people slipping over the rails. The boat turned and headed back south. Those men weren't going to make it, Abbott knew.

"I called in backup from everybody in the world before I jumped in there," he said. He'd ordered a Jet Ski. He looked at his watch. Slim chance the ski would arrive in time. So he grabbed his gear and started swimming out toward a raft of men drifting into the surf's impact zone.

Drowning victims don't often cry for help. That action requires energy and breath, two resources victims conserve in order to survive. Once out there, Abbott met seven Mexican men in their twenties, all clinging to a couple of life vests and a surfboard. Their expressions were those of men at a wake. Abbott understood the challenge was to get the living out of the surf zone as a group. But he couldn't touch any of them. He knew that one or more, in silent panic, would attempt to claw themselves on top of their savior, simply to fill the lungs one more time. So Abbott tossed a lifeguard strap, tethering himself to about a thousand pounds of drowning people. In Spanish, he warned them to keep their distance. If Abbott led the party straight toward the shore, he was certain to lose a few in the pounding waves. It was procedure to swim them farther out to sea. But as he did this, a rare set of extremely large waves jacked up in front of the group. The timing couldn't have been worse. The first wave landed squarely on top of the men. Abbott felt and heard bone grinding in his neck. He struggled to hold the line. His body was tossed and rolled. The cold felt like a tight belt constricting his chest; the vastness of the sea drained energy and body heat. As he attempted to breathe, his lungs made short, violent convulsions. Nearing the point of blackout, Abbott finally felt a cold wind shear on his face. He'd surfaced. And as the waves passed, men popped back up. All of them. Abbott looked for the beach. But a rescue vehicle wasn't coming, and he knew it.

So the old lifeguard made one stroke and followed it with the next. Steadfast ocean sense helped him negotiate lulls in the swell, locate the currents and rips, and coach the men shoreward. By the time they landed—faces blue and lips purple—the entire parking lot at Coronado's public beach was a theater of flashing lights and bleating sirens. Some of the victims stumbled and fell, a symptom of hypothermia. A migrant wearing a soaked dress shirt threw up blood. All were rushed to the hospital.

The single-handed rescue of seven men in dangerous conditions garnered newsprint and an award. But Abbott thought, "Maybe being a fifty-five-year-old seasonal isn't all it's cracked up to be." Not long after, the ecologist post opened up at Border Field State Park. The beat was the same, but this time the job entailed saving small life. "Yep," he said, "I went from being a respected hero to a bird guard."

It may be due to Abbott's longevity in such an odd and volatile landscape that people seek him out. In conducting research for the novel *Tijuana Straits*, noir author Kem Nunn walked the estuary with Abbott, who enumerated the nine species of endangered birds that nested in the sand dunes, as well as the cats and dogs that crawled out of Tijuana to feed on them. Partly because of their acquaintance, many locals assume that Nunn based his character Sam "the Gull" Fahey on Abbott. As proof, they point to a singular line: "He'd accepted as his charge the protection of certain migratory birds, most notably the western snowy plover and light-footed clapper rail."

I sought out Abbott for less subtle reasons. As my search through the valley narrowed, I'd surmised that Abbott might be one of a select few who knew where the bicycle plague had come from. And maybe even why. It was Abbott who'd piled the bikes in the Border Field parking area where Maria Teresa Fernandez had found them. When Jesse Gomez mentioned a state parks "ranger" who'd left a load of bikes on his farm, that was Abbott too. Most often, when I questioned people in the valley about bicycles, they pointed in Abbott's direction.

In fact, between the time I met Terry Tynan and sought out Greg Abbott, a filmmaker named Greg Rainoff set up his camera to interview Abbott at a location overlooking the valley. The topic of the interview had to do with the Department of Homeland Security's decision to override environmental protections in constructing the new "triple fence." As Abbott spoke before the scenic backdrop, a silky peloton came whistling out of Goat Canyon. The cranks whirred, the wheels rolled. The riders hustled down the dirt track as easy as anything. The sight of them might have seemed unremarkable until one contemplated the only place where they could have originated. The cluster of cyclists became so distracting to Rainoff, his camera wheeled off Abbott to follow its trajectory. Footage of illegal crossers scaling a fence or hoofing through the desert is rare, but this—it was as if a cameraman had set up to interview a zoo official but caught dinosaurs in the background. Rainoff's clip is the only moving image ever captured of the bicycle migrants.

That scene, however, was not new to Abbott. The first time he'd noticed the bikes, he'd been hunched over digging up endemic species of sage from an area of the park soon to be annexed by Homeland Security. Abbott figured that if he collected the plants sure to be destroyed by the new construction, he stood a chance of repopulating these areas later. Bent at his task, he heard a piercing whistle, a signal of some kind. A fluttering of wings then caught his eye. Flushed birds can telegraph any number of events but when Abbott saw a northern harrier shoot from the bush, he knew this was a human disturbance. Then came a sound like a waterfall. Around a bend, a group of riders flanked by a guide of some sort rolled into view, wheels heavy on the road. Abbott watched the lead rider herd the pack and direct it toward the river. The cyclists seemed determined but they weren't sprinting. "The river is one mile from the border," Abbott said. "An all-out foot run would take nine minutes, at least. But on a bike, it's four."

As bicycles accumulated in the valley over the following months, the park's staff began to separate and pile them in the same manner they used to clear waste tires, cobblestones, and trash that washed out of the canyons. The sight churned something in Abbott. His early travels straddled the age of the ship and that of the jet—he once circumnavigated the entire globe with two flights separated by months on deck. Still, he knew his life as a traveler really began on a bike. Those piles of spokes, rims, wheels, sprockets, and metal tubing, Abbott knew, were rockets to unknown worlds. And, well, he couldn't stand waste. So on a number of occasions Abbott loaded bikes into his state parks truck and hauled them to donation centers. But in greeting the AMVETS thrift store staff, and pulling the bikes out of the truck bed, he experienced another feeling that tugged at his better judgment. It was the ecologist in him, he told me, who thought: "I wanted to tag those bikes the way we would a jackrabbit. Just to see how fast they slipped into Mexico, and came right back again. I probably donated the same bike several times."

The Tijuana corridor was the one stretch that the Department of Homeland Security pointed to as secure; this was the example the other 1,942 miles of border might hone to. Abbott remembered the cyclists as just cruising, not racing. At a glance, some could barely ride. And this gave him pause.

"So why?" I asked. "Why are the bicycles successful?"

"The sensors," Abbott said. "The Border Patrol has had seismic sensors placed all over these canyons. Seismic, as in earthquakes. They sense thumping, pounding, jarring, running, walking things—earthshaking things. They don't detect rolling things. Migrants traditionally run and walk. The Border Patrol rolls. These bikes reverse the trend."

7

Before stepping into the fog, the strangely intuitive *pollero viejo* whom Pablo encountered on the rim of Slaughterhouse Canyon made an offer. "Find me some *pollos*," Roberto said. "I will buy them from you."

Pablo produced no response at that time, not a yes or a no. And with a final wave, Roberto disappeared into the clouds.

But a few days later, Pablo sought out Roberto in the canyons—the only place they'd crossed paths. It was hot and arid again. The many rises and drops in the road could confuse any memory of the landscape. Pablo found it necessary to ask his driver to stop at the summit of the last precipice before the ocean. There was a small and infamous turnout there. Before then, a bus would have been a luxury for Pablo. The decision to hire a private taxi had to do with the people in the car with him, a man and a woman from Chiapas whom he'd recruited at the main bus station east of downtown. And the turnout offered the couple a view of their desired destination, the United States.

We don't know what he told these people or why they might trust this *joven* enough to follow him into a roller coaster of wasteland and slums—surely the most exotic sight they'd ever seen. Stories of false recruiters, kidnappers, and murderers were too common to dismiss. Many said that to choose a recruiter was to make a decision with one's life. The couple must have understood that their destiny was, to some extent, bound to this one transaction. Yet they chose a young man whose demeanor revealed nothing. And so it would have been a relief to all when, after a few hours of looking, Pablo spotted Roberto and his gang of *polleros* at work near Playas. The familiar van was there. Pablo was beginning to recognize the guides as well; there was a program and efficiency to their operation.

Roberto acknowledged his aloof young acquaintance with a curt professional nod. When addressing the migrant man and woman, however, a physical change came over his being. Roberto's chest lifted with authority even as his head made the slightest tilt in understanding. The ringmaster of a traveling show, he used his expressive hands to suggest both terrible wonders at his command as well as a fellowship with his guests. This performance was merely an affected version of a transaction that Pablo would soon learn. It was called the "checkout."

"*Señor y Señora de Chiapas*, this is how the deal will be done," Roberto said—ringing in these nonnegotiable terms as a gentle proposal. "You don't pay here in Mexico. You give me the name and phone number of a contact in the United States who will pay for your passage in American dollars. I call your contact to confirm the agreement and fee. Once you are on the inside, and at the home of my associate, we will place a second call to your contact. You will remain with my associate until your contact comes through. A day, a week, a year—it doesn't matter. You will be comfortable, and you will remain with my associate until payment is made. Now, on occasion, I have returned good people like yourselves all the way to El Salvador, at my expense, only to make the point that payment is required. But I'm sure that won't be necessary in this instance."

The warmth of his smile was unassailable.

The migrants looked at each other. They would have known this point—what could only be called detainment—was standard procedure. But the man said, "I don't want to ride in the trunk of a car."

"So you have a contact? Please, give me the name and the number," answered *el coyote.*

"It is my sister's husband. He says we don't have to cross any way we don't want to."

"Do you swim?" Roberto asked.

"No, I don't swim. What kind of question is that? Whatever happens, I'm not riding in the trunk of a car and I'm not going into the ocean."

Roberto turned to Pablo with a handshake. "Thank you, my friend. I will take good care of these two." As he withdrew his fist, Pablo discovered a fold of green bills. It was $300.

El coyote put his arms around the shoulders of the couple and walked them toward others still waiting. It was in that fleeting moment that the youth joined what was called, among his new colleagues, "this work that we do." He was an *enganchador,* a recruiter.

Not much is known about the second bicycle. It was most likely an Asian import that had cycled a portion of its life in the western United States before moving across the line aboard a scavenger's pickup truck—in the same manner that old mattresses, reclaimed construction materials, and used car tires made their way to Tijuana. We can be almost certain it was a mountain bike, or a hybrid of some sort based on that popular design. An overwhelming rack of similar bicycles with names like the Power X, Titan, and Ground Assault were found abandoned in the river valley. These sported imitative relishes, like shocks that didn't really absorb. The bicycle would have gone for about forty bucks on the streets of Tijuana. And though it wasn't in Pablo's character to steal, it's likely that this bicycle had been stolen once, or many times, and that its parts were so mismatched it fell into a category called "Franken-bike."

Pablo purchased his new wheels shortly after his career began. A natural save-all known to forgo meals, he'd nevertheless been industriously acquiring items critical to a life other than a middling position in the hierarchy of the riverbed slums. There was a hole in the dirt there with his name on it, and the thought of its open maw kept him busy.

Colleagues in Pablo's position have said that he was lucky—in ways that could be named and ways that couldn't. For example, he came into the work while America was experiencing an incredible economic surge. And despite the fact that he offered little of his interior life in return, his clear expression and earnest demeanor drew strangers to him. He understood the archaic, impoverished lands from which they'd emerged. He knew the border. And, importantly, Pablo now knew Roberto. Not all recruiters had connections like this.

Pablo took a room in a claustrophobic alley off of La Zona Norte. He'd never lain down in a dwelling with a floor other than packed earth. He'd never slept under a roof alone. But Pablo didn't think of the rental arrangement as a home. Barbers needed mirrors, a chair, some combs and scissors. Bricklayers needed a trowel and a wheelbarrow. *Enganchadores* required a space in which to house their people while preparations were made. The quality of the room depended on the class of the migrants. Pablo's weren't expecting much.

This room belonged to a row of such spaces—a dorm-like situation for drug users and people down on their luck. All shared a community shower and toilet. Pablo's room was sealed off by a plywood door with a flimsy latch. Inside were dirty yellow walls. Pirated electricity lit a single bulb that hung from the ceiling. There was no running water. The quarters rented for fifty dollars a month.

In September of 2005, standing before the bus station's prominent, gold-gilded shrine to a colorful and radiant Virgin of Guadalupe, Pablo was introduced to a handful of his new colleagues. There was Juan, Javier, Rudy, Poncho, and Luis. Word seemed to have gotten around about who was buying Pablo's *pollos*. And being that it was sometimes difficult for freelancing recruiters to find a consistent coyote, privateers like Pablo's new friends often curried favor with those who held a steady connection. Strategies in crossing changed daily, so a part of the game was networking. Competitors quickly became associates.

Juan was Pablo's age and had also come from the south. He'd heard others call the new guy "untrusting," but Juan understood that people from their part of the country were simply inclined toward a solitary bearing. Juan approached Pablo in the same casual manner he might a possible client from that region.

"*Hola*," he said, leaning against the white wall, next to Pablo. Across from them were the ticket counters where employees—young urban women with tight, shiny ponytails, crimson lips, starched collars, and tight jackets—offered efficient and comfortable transport to anywhere in Latin America. Their broad, competitive smiles contrasted with the expressions of the men on the other side of the polished floor, those who promised illicit transport north.

"*Buenas*," Pablo said.

"Nice day, eh?"

"Yeah."

"I've noticed that nice days are good for the work. You?"

"Hopefully."

"You're a strong recruiter, *amigo*," Juan said. "I can tell. The people really seem to trust you."

"Maybe," said Pablo; compliments weren't often handed around in the village. "I'm no different than they are. I got off the same bus with the same idea, and even less money in my pocket."

"You said it, *amigo*. I'm from Michoacán. And you?"

"*De Oaxaca*."

"Ha. Should have known. Everybody's from there—that's why people call us all 'Oaxacas.'" Juan laughed. "Where in Oaxaca, if I might ask?"

"It doesn't matter."

"No, I guess not. I wouldn't know it even if you told me. What's your name?"

"Pablo."

"Pablo," Juan repeated the common name. It was Paul in English, a biblical name. "I've heard the others call you something else: El Indio. That your nickname?"

"Yeah, I guess."

The tag, meaning "the Indian," was often hung on people with indigenous looks or dark skin. There was a Mexican phrase: *no seas Indio*. Most took it to mean "don't be gullible," or "don't be stupid." As with a handful of epithets like it, a hint of mirth in the utterance of "Indio" could be taken as an insult. Mexico's class divisions were sometimes mixed interchangeably with race.

Not long before, in a chance encounter in the canyons, Roberto had overheard another bus station recruiter calling Pablo "El Indio." Roberto instantly reprimanded this rookie—in a manner he reserved for the lowliest of river-dwelling fools. But Pablo stepped in; he told his *patron* that he didn't mind. Roberto couldn't understand Pablo's dismissal of the slight. He thought it poor form to let the recruiter's overreach go unpunished.

The nickname, of course, could also be taken in other ways: a reference to the noble native who employed cunning and skill in defense of his people, for example, or the lone wanderer of the plains. Or maybe Pablo didn't take offense simply because it wasn't a name from the village. Maybe he didn't mind because the nickname built up his borderlands identity.

"I'm Juan, like the song," Pablo's new friend said, making a little shimmy. Pablo offered no response, letting the gesture fall to the tile underfoot. Recruiters didn't take silence for an answer, and it wasn't Juan's nature anyway. "You always get your *pollos* right away, I notice," he said. "But you don't work as much as some of us. Or maybe just not here, eh? What are you doing with your time?"

"I don't know. We can't be *enganchadores* forever."

"A bus station recruiter who studies? Wow, I've seen it all now."

"Me and Indio got to be good friends," Juan said much later, "and we started talking about different ideas and ways of making more money. We both would ask, 'Why not cross *pollos* ourselves?'"

The initial question was how. The trade was highly specialized. Each position required experience, and each technique expertise. The world of those who passed migrants over with rope ladders was separate from that of the *panga* boat operators, or the tunnel diggers. Increased enforcement at border cities pushed the poorest crossers into the wilderness, where guides attempted to elude trackers while also keeping their clients alive. The unseen coyotes who passed their customers through the terminals in *la línea* seemed to exist on an untouchable plateau.

"Then a whole month went by where we barely saw each other," said Juan. "Word on the street was that he was seen around the borderline checking out different spots. There were even some who thought he was on drugs because all he did was hang out, walking back and forth along the edge of the border. And he would spend a lot of time just sitting in certain spots. To me, this wasn't that weird since he usually didn't do anything with others. He was an isolated person."

In early December, Juan and El Indio happened upon each other at the bus station again. It would be for the last time that year. The business was about to shutter for the holidays. Migrants, hoping to spend Christmas with friends and family, didn't want to take the risk of a long detainment should they be snared by Border Patrol. So they migrated early, or waited until after the first of January. *Coyotes*, *levantones*, *guías*, and *ganchos* took a month-long break as well.

"Neither of us had family in Tijuana," Juan remembered, "so we said we'd hang out for Christmas."

The young men spent the day of the Nativity at a famous strip club and hostess bar called Adelita. And during the week between Christmas and New Year's Eve, Juan and Indio lounged at local bars, treated themselves to meals, and talked shop. When conversation turned to business, Juan sensed that El Indio always kept something back. But maybe not, maybe there just wasn't that much to him. Either way, it was great to indulge. There hadn't been a week in either of their childhoods that offered the possibility of meat every day, not to mention the variety. And that was not all. On New Year's Eve the boys found themselves in a bar called La Estrella, The Star, and a few of the girls they'd met at Adelita arrived in a glittering storm of laughter.

"Where have you been all week?" one asked, having noticed the boys slouched over their drinks. She insinuated herself between them and the others gathered. "We all had so much fun on Christmas, I thought for sure you'd come back."

"Well," said El Indio, looking pleased, "now it looks like we're going to ring in the New Year together." The guys invited the ladies out to dinner, but the women said no, they wanted to take out the boys. Tips had been good. They all agreed on a Chinese restaurant called El Dragon in the Cinco y Diez. The group spun out of La Estrella and flagged a taxi. In New York they might have been young artists and actors reveling in the big city far from family. They burned with the same passions, these smugglers and strippers—optimistic young people looking to make a mark and hungry for something better. After dinner, the party careened on to the ladies' late-night shift at Adelita. The group celebrated the arrival of 2006, which floated down upon them in a shower of confetti, colored lights, and dance music. El Indio raised a bottle of *Bucanas*—Buchanan's scotch, a calling card among *polleros*. In the village it would have cost a week's wages. "Happy New Year, Juanito!" he cheered his friend.

Juan, however, wasn't going to let the spirited moment slip by. As the bleating horns and embraces subsided, Juan put a steady hand on his shoulder. "*Amigo*, how are *we* going to start working in 2006? It's time *we* became coyotes, *hombre*."

"I found a way," Indio said—bleary, content, and unusually open.

"All right!" said Juan. "You ever take anybody to the inside?"

"Me? No, never," Indio said. Juan had only assumed. Now his friend seemed somehow younger. Had Juan misread his quiet character for experience, confidence even? Indio put the neck of his bottle against his *camarada*'s chest. "But this is the year, *amigo*."

"And how?" Juan asked with a flick of his chin.

"You want to find out, *mi Juanito*? Meet me at the cathedral tomorrow at 8:00 PM."

Still a bit hung over at seven thirty the next evening—the phrase Juan would have used was *Estoy crudo*, I'm raw—he prowled around the open square underneath the spires of the downtown cathedral. The Catholic edifice stood kitty-corner to several popular markets and shops. It was the last night they'd be lit and decorated for the holidays. People milled about, enjoying the early winter evening. Indio arrived exactly at eight. He looked fit and healthy. The boys bought a couple of tacos at a nearby cart and then caught the bus, in this instance a minivan *colectivo*, and headed west. Stepping off near the Comercial Mexicana in Playas de Tijuana, they crossed to the other side of the International Road where empty lots of desert scrub rolled up to the iron border fence. Before them to the north, the deep dark of the Tijuana River Valley lay like a vast pool—wind-rippled and quiet, it spilled onto a distant shore where lamps illuminated the city streets of Imperial Beach. They made their way along the base of Bunker Hill. Indio led Juan toward a shallow depression not worthy of the name canyon. A portion of it had eroded under the fence, leaving a hole big enough for a man to slide through. This was where Indio had stashed his bicycle. The men found the spot, crouched, and listened.

"Okay, so what's the plan?"

"This is where we're going to enter with the people," El Indio said.

"Through the hole? And then what? That's a long way to the road." Juan made an obvious show of looking west toward a tower that the Border Patrol had erected opposite the lighthouse. Then he turned east and nodded at a kilo truck parked on Bunker Hill. The silhouette of an agent was visible inside.

"We're going to ride in on bicycles," Indio said.

"What? Taking time off had some effect on you!"

"No, *mi Juanito*, the time helped me to see it," Indio said. "This is the way—riding across on bicycles."

"Seriously? Explain."

"Better to show you."

"Okay, and when will this happen?"

"Right now."

"You're joking. Come on. *La migra* right in front of you, cameras over there, sensors in the ground all over the inside."

"I know all of that already. If you don't want in, no problem. I'll do it myself."

"Don't be crazy."

El Indio pushed his mountain bike through the crevice and squeezed in after it. Juan saw the bike lifted out and then Indio's legs climbing out of the pit. Then Juan could not see his friend at all. The solid steel wall blocked any view. He ran up Bunker Hill a ways to get a vantage. And there he caught the silhouette of a man astride a bicycle—a phantom navigating a deep blue slope down to the Border Patrol's very own road. He watched the dark figure fleeting through shadow and light, the tires raising just a quiet puff of dust.

Juan turned to view the Border Patrol agent waiting in the truck. Local smugglers believed that a blue light mounted above the Border Patrol's Imperial Beach station, within view of the valley, flashed when ground sensors detected a disturbance. Juan waited for it. He wondered if the distance created a lag time before the sensors set off the light. But the light did not blink. And by then El Indio had already vanished into the night.

8

On satellite images of the globe at night, the Baja peninsula is one of the last regions of the world—in a league with the Amazon, Central Africa, and Siberia—that recedes into a blackness as deep and thick as the oceans. The two main exceptions on this thousand-mile strip of mountains and deserts are the light clusters of the Tijuana-to-Ensenada corridor on the north end, and the state capital La Paz and resort towns of Cabo San Lucas on the southern tip. In contrast to the Age of Discovery, however, nowadays the lightless, roadless places of the map are not the lands where monsters lurk.

By 2007, the monsters lurked in the cities.

In the 1990s, when Colombia's great Cali and Medellin cartels began to crumble as the main distributors of illegal drugs to the United States, a cadre of Mexican trafficking organizations took control and vertically integrated the business. They were no longer the middlemen. Over the next decade the wealth and influence of the Mexican cartels grew to such an extent that many believed their power threatened the sovereign authority of the Mexican republic itself. Disputes among cartel affiliates concerning the right to traffic through certain corridors increasingly led to public firefights and executions. The showy and gruesome displays revealed a disregard for official authority that put the nation on edge.

In December of 2006, the newly elected president of Mexico, Felipe Calderón, ordered 6,500 troops into the state of Michoacán to tamp violence between two of these organized groups, and to assert federal control. The result, however, was a flash point that broke into an open war between the government and the cartels that would last the remainder of Calderón's term and cost as many as forty thousand lives. Each time government troops arrested or killed leadership in any one organization, the power balance among the mafias fell out of whack, territory came up for grabs, and the assassinations and murders increased. The war revealed veins of corruption within branches of the government itself. And of the many fronts to this conflict, the most disruptive was the one that opened between corrupt local police forces and government troops. Shooting between police and soldiers occurred in public. But as police departments were forced to purge their ranks of tainted officers, many of the newly unemployed took positions within the cartels. The margin between the tactics of civil authority and those of armed gangs only blurred. By 2010, Calderón was accusing Mexico's network of traffickers of attempting to "replace the government" and "impose their own laws." In the United States, pundits began to use the term *failed state* in reference to the nation's closest neighbor and second-largest trading partner.

As two cities on either side of a dry river, San Diego and Tijuana suffered a dramatic split. The younger of the two was quickly becoming too chaotic and violent for the other to comprehend. San Diegans, and most Californians, averted their gaze, simply choosing not to see. Then the housing bubble burst, and in the ensuing economic crisis even those tourists who had been brave enough to visit Tijuana ceased to go. The city built on good times lost its founding industry, seemingly overnight.

During the economic peak that preceded the recession, a magazine editor sent me to cover a heated Baja land grab. Development schemes had been hatched along the coast from Cabo to Tijuana. Gringo speculators were fencing off sections of desert with no access to roads or anything else. Equity-rich Americans, looking to catch the next boom, bought unfinished $300,000 apartments overlooking the gray and polluted beaches of northern Baja. Just a matter of months after I wrote that piece, I was tasked with covering the collapse of those inexpensive retirement dreams—and all of the half-built, ramshackle developments left to Mexico in its wake.

But also, due to the addiction-like drive of the surf bug, I continued to comb the black stretches of the Baja map—tidal flats, basins, headlands, and dusty little fishing hamlets that looked like sets for slasher films. I became more familiar with Baja's windblown coasts and cactus fields than I was with the city closest to my own. During those years, Tijuana sat like a lion at the gates of Baja's wilds. The feat of driving through Tijuana while avoiding Tijuana was something tourists like myself put a lot of thought into.

One of the first events that brought the incipient drug war into my consciousness occurred in September of 2007 on the International Road, a route to the coast I frequently used. A group of American surfers traveling in two trucks looked into their rearview mirrors to catch flashing blue lights—Tijuana's municipal police were behind them. The tourists pulled over to discover that there was not one police car behind them but a short convoy. Once the vehicles had stopped at the side of the road, heavily armed men exited them in combat fashion. The waiting tourists quickly realized this was not normal procedure—they were yanked from their trucks and instructed to get on their knees at the road's dusty shoulder. Guns were trained on their heads. Their pockets were emptied of wallets and keys; then associates of the gunmen stepped into the surfers' vehicles and sped away. In this instance, the robbers let them all live. Back in the States, the victims feared reprisals to the extent that they wouldn't give their names to the media. Mexican authorities said they would recover the two trucks only when the vehicles turned up at another crime scene, which, with the way things were headed, would be very soon.

This incident, and a few others like it, suggested something broader afoot. As had happened in the past, pressure put on the traffickers' traditional sources of income and smuggling routes had provoked them to diversify into robbery, extortion, and kidnapping. The use of police and military tactics and equipment in these events, however, suggested a blurring of the lines between criminal and governmental authority—a signal that the situation was soon to be totally out of control.

Each border reporter could pinpoint the moment when he or she sensed trouble coming. While, as a surfer and a traveler, I might have related more closely to the surfer robbery than to others, it was probably the mellowest of tremors in an incrementally intensifying series that went on to rattle the entire region. Regular citizens were robbed and raped. Police officers disappeared. Human remains were found melted in barrels of lye, or piled in empty lots. Decapitations became routine. Bodies were hung from bridges, including from a familiar bridge in Playas—an incident famous only because the hangman's rope snapped and the body fell into traffic.

A coworker of mine and his friend were intercepted by men wielding assault rifles who suddenly blocked their route with a dark SUV. The two victims were pulled from their economy car and forced into the assailants' Chevy Tahoe. While the vehicle sped through a turn on the way to who-knows-where, one of the abductors began to choke my colleague from behind the headrest. Seated behind the driver, his friend intervened, drawing the choker's wrath. Just then, my colleague cracked his door and jumped out. In that speedy, distracted instant, his friend managed to do the same, but caught a bullet in the thigh as he fell from the vehicle. A few days later, my colleague arrived to work in San Diego with scabs covering half his face—it was the body part that had made first contact with the dirt embankment.

A friend's gardener, a man who sometimes works at my own house, found a gagged corpse on the pavement outside his Tijuana home at 9:00 PM on a Tuesday. He hadn't heard a sound preceding the discovery. The body came with a handwritten note that said, "We told you so." In conference following the discovery, no one in the neighborhood admitted to knowing the dead man, or what he'd been told.

The most vicious year came in 2008 with 843 murders citywide. Then, as now, there was also an unknown number of missing. In 2009, one of the region's warring kingpins was apprehended. By 2010, the homicide rate subsided, prompting a visit by President Calderón. He came to speak at an economic festival called Tijuana Innovadora—Innovative Tijuana. "Crime has dropped dramatically since its peak in 2008," the president said. "Tijuana went from a city seized by terror and focused only on questions of crime to a city motivated by hope."

Within days, however, a new wave of beheadings and executions swept Tijuana. Armed men entered a drug rehab center and assassinated thirteen patients. Shoot-outs erupted on major thoroughfares. Bodies were again hung from bridges. "Obviously, they [narco gangs] don't want it to seem like we are a society of good people. That's why they are doing these things again," a woman attending the Innovadora festival told an Associated Press reporter. Like a last gasp, however, the most torrid violence seemed to end with 2010. Whichever cartel had won the Tijuana smuggling corridor, it had managed to keep it.

During the protracted siege, *Tijuanenses* had simply learned to live for, and entertain, themselves. Rather than dampen the city's culture, the troubles seemed to make it anew. I was aware of these things, but I'd lost touch with Tijuana—it was a place I was happy to drive through. Once I reached the end of the bike trail in the Tijuana River Valley, however, I knew that if I wanted to discover the source of the border bicycles I would have to make Tijuana's acquaintance again, and probably more. I didn't have a clue where to start. So I did what most newcomers to cities around the world do: I took a tour. A weird one.

On an elevated Mexican slope overlooking the border fence—facing north across the wandering and brush-filled river valley to the blue bay pooled at the foundations of San Diego's skyscrapers—sits the oldest cemetery in Ciudad Tijuana. The walled and hoary graveyard is named after an old, secondary border crossing that admitted large freight and lumber into Mexico. This casual crossing once stood just a stone's throw from the cemetery. It was called Puerta Blanca, or the White Gate—an unobstructed dirt route guarded by a single US sentry post. Tijuana residents commonly crossed through to buy fresh fruit and eggs in Monument, the American town just across the line. That town no longer exists, and today, there is no entry point at Puerta Blanca either, only a triple-fenced steel wall. Adjacent to the boundary is the international sewage-treatment plant—built by US taxpayers to treat modern Tijuana's waste—and then the broad saltwater estuary. Since the 1970s the old White Gate's competitor, the official crossing at San Ysidro five miles to the east, has grown. At fifty million crossings per year, the sheer number of cars idling in line, waiting to enter the United States, made the customs complex one of the strongest emitters of greenhouse gases in Southern California.

The Puerta Blanca cemetery is quiet now. Almost nobody remembers the customs gate that lent the graveyard its name. Proximity to the boundary continues to resonate, however, as Puerta Blanca is home to one of Mexico's new and rising people's saints, a deific figure well suited for the vagaries of *la línea*. Like those of the deathly Santa Muerte (usually depicted as the grim reaper) and Jesús Malverde (a mustachioed Robin Hood celebrated by the narco underworld), the legend of Juan Soldado has been canonized not by the Roman Catholic Church but by the disenfranchised citizenry of Mexico. For Juan Soldado is the patron saint of *los inmigrantes*, and the fact that the mountains and deserts of the United States fill the vision of anyone looking north from Soldado's shrine atop the cemetery hill is no coincidence.

On a cool November afternoon following Mexico's Day of the Dead celebrations, I joined a quirky, unsanctioned tour of Puerta Blanca. The small group was made up of former and current Tijuana residents as well as a number of young Americans. The drug warfare had pushed a large percentage of Tijuana's middle class to relocate just across the border to suburban Chula Vista and greater San Diego. On any given Saturday night the waft of Mexican laundry detergent in a number of trendy American bars was palpable enough to suggest what 2010 census takers struggled to document—an exodus. On this tour, some of these natives were reuniting with a dusty but potent little corner of their original hometown.

I might have been lumped in with the group's second half—young urban professionals—but their youth and the vitality of their presence surprised even me. As if in the wake of a storm, an arts resurgence had sprung from the rubble of Tijuana's tourism industry. This in turn drew a cadre of hip, media-savvy Americans south to participate in it. They made music and visual art; they wrote. The city's color, dilapidation, and chaos contrasted sharply with the suburban meditation on the "safe" side of the border. These artists mined that divide. As a result, in print and in conversation, Tijuana had been dubbed "the poor man's Paris," a cheap, liberal, culturally rich city.

Initially, I found the comparison of Paris and Tijuana a strange one. I pictured Hemingway and Fitzgerald sharing a bottle of mescal and a bucket of Tecates in the vinyl booth of a Tijuana bar last updated with pinup posters of the 1970s, discussing a narco soldier nicknamed El Pozolero—the Stew Maker—a body-disposal expert made famous by his technique of dissolving human remains in acid; or maybe how fans and defenders of bullfighting increasingly found themselves put on their heels by animal rights groups, even here in Tijuana. Slowly it dawned on me, however, that Paris had been the poor man's city. For as disparate as Paris of the 1920s and Tijuana of the 2010s might have been in the imagination, the structural elements were there: war ruin, a flexible legality, openness to the arts, lots of space for rent, and a favorable exchange rate. The only element that seemed to have changed in the century between the Gilded and Computer Ages was national culpability for the organized violence and destabilization. I truly wanted to believe my neighboring city was in the process of rebirth. But my on-the-ground sense was that the ceasefire that made this trip to Puerta Blanca seem intriguing and worthwhile existed only in lull, a moment between moments.

White wooden vending carts loaded with flowers, beads, votives, and candles were parked beside the iron bars of the entrance. Inside, a wide cobblestone road progressed up the hill; tombstones ascended with it like stadium seating. The quality of the cobbles was important to note because if devotees of Juan Soldado received the miracle they'd asked for, tradition required that they return to his shrine on their knees—a testament of their faith. This was expected to bloody the knees. Sure enough, we came upon a middle-aged woman assisted by family members who held her at the biceps—an attempt to lighten the weight on her kneecaps. Despite the aid, she grimaced as she set each nub before her. On both sides of this procession, the occasional grand mausoleum or sepulcher rose from the mud in buoyant color. There'd been no obvious plan for filling this hillside, but the fact that the family plots looked regularly visited, added to, and evolving suggested a kind of messy intimate care. Halfway to

Soldado's grave we approached another devotee, this time an attractive, manicured woman with big hair and hoop earrings. She absolutely strode on her knees. Her pilgrimage was slowed only by the two young men who picked up plush car floor mats from behind her, circled, and set them before her again—carpeting the path. This is when I first noticed our tour's hostess amid the crowd, because she began to badger the young woman with a wagging forefinger. "You're cheating, you're cheating," she said to the woman, in Spanish. For the benefit of the English speakers the hostess turned and repeated, "This woman is cheating. She will not receive her miracle."

An amateur Tijuana historian and hometown psychic, our hostess, Martha Henke, wore black velour pants and a black vinyl jacket. She had straight dark hair with a strip of graying roots down the middle. Large-lensed sunglasses obscured a good portion of her face. Though dressed young, she appeared to be in her fifties, and she smacked her lips between thoughts like an *abuela*. After berating the elegant Soldado devotee aboard the floor mats, Henke took the helm of our mob with an upraised finger and led us in a group to the grave.

There, we lined up to enter a small house-like sepulcher. Inside an archway, both a bust and a small statue of Juan Soldado were crowded by candles, wreaths, bouquets, notes, and photos—tight quarters with the paste-up decoration of a child's room. The bust looked like a smooth-faced caricature, a cartoon, something from Disneyland. The saint's eyes were mere black pupils, the nose thin. He wore a green soldier's cap and jacket. I could have easily taken him for a trolley conductor.

The personal notes pasted all about, however, were nothing if not heartfelt. They thanked Juan Soldado for help with immigration papers, the recovery of a loved one, or an unspecified *milagro*. On lined paper, a schoolkid had drawn an image of the saint in crayon with a coffee-colored face and a green bellman's cap. The top of the page read, "Juanito el Soldado"—Little John the Soldier. If the letters came off as sweet, the abundant photos were unsettling. Mostly showing men, most of them young, the collection of images looked to be of the missing. The photo of a teenager cut from his California driver's license was scotch-taped to Soldado's bust, as was a black-and-white mug shot of a serious man in his early twenties, as well as an image of a father figure lost in the North. Engraved tiles thanking the folk saint for miracles plastered both the inside and outside of the little structure—the names of the appreciative family always given but, disappointingly, not the exact circumstances of the miracle. Each item in the mausoleum created an unfinished narrative. Underneath all of this was the supposed body of Juan Castillo Morales, but not his story. For this we traveled farther up the hill between offset graves, to a secondary shrine set against the uppermost cemetery wall marking the place where the twenty-four-year-old army private was executed by military fire in 1938.

"How many of you believe in spirits?" Henke asked the gathered. "How many of you have felt a presence?"

I struggled to remember or imagine some sensory wisp from a night in my past—a hovering light, maybe, or an unexplained chill. I failed to conjure anything. A few timid hands rose. A man standing in a graveyard with his hand in the air came off as an eerie admission, I thought. Most hands quickly lowered. In the back of the small crowd a woman I'd noticed earlier for her looks—strong cheekbones, straight nose, pale green eyes, raven hair, black leather jacket and blue scarf—now caught my eye with the confidence of her stance, her right hand held firmly aloft. Attractive, international, and dressed for a biker's funeral—she evaded assessment. I then looked to Henke for a response to the show of hands. The hostess seemed to take in not the hands but the nature of this crowd, one that quite visually seemed to disappoint her. The sky was overcast, the air chilly, we stood in mud.

She said, "Well, I'll tell you, some of us see things. Some of us feel things, and it is real."

Henke said her mother had actually known the Camachos—a respected Tijuana family raising a string of pretty little girls. The eldest, an eight-year-old, was named Olga. On a Sunday in February, thin light falling on dirt streets the color of cumin, this child was sent to the store for "a cut of meat." The Camachos lived close to the La Corona market so her mother, Feliza, expected a quick return. As the light weakened further on that short winter day, Mrs. Camacho became alarmed at Olga's absence. The mother hurried to the shop as it was closing and spoke to the owner, Señor Mendivil, who confirmed that he'd sold Olga the meat and that she'd skipped off with the package. Outside, Mrs. Camacho saw a soldier leaning against a wall. He'd not seen a little girl. Nonetheless, he said, "Maybe she went that way." He pointed in the opposite direction of the Camacho home. As dark came on, the family's distress caught the hearts of the neighbors. The police, a volunteer force of just five or six officers, enlisted help from the nearby military barracks. They managed to cordon off roads heading north to San Diego, south to Ensenada, and east to Tecate. Still, no sign of the girl appeared until, as Henke told it, the next day, when a couple of boys playing in a field found a bloody sack containing Olga's remains.

The soldier leaning against the wall, Juan Castillo Morales, and another soldier were later detained by police. No one knows why. Some say it was because they stood watch earlier at the garrison, and so may have seen something. Three vagrants were also detained in the sweep. These strangers were quickly released and, eventually, the family of the second soldier provided an alibi. By this time a curious crowd had formed outside the military *comandancia*, a castle-like structure intended to dissuade Americans from encroaching on the empty Baja peninsula. Inside the *comandancia*, at a table within earshot of the growing rabble, Morales vigorously denied any part in the murder of Olga Camacho.

Here, our hostess stopped to tell an interesting and complicating side story. In her childhood barrio it was believed that a corpulent commanding officer of the federal garrison, a man known for making inappropriate advances toward young girls, had seen Morales loitering about in the street earlier that Sunday. He called Morales into his office. He said, "Morales, I've seen you admiring my gold-gilded pistol. I need a favor. I was out hunting rabbits today, and I cleaned them, but now I have this big sack of guts and bones. Take this sack and get rid of it in the desert, quick before it stinks, don't even take the time to look inside. If you're fast about it, when you return, I'll loan you my pistol for the week."

In the 1930s, Tijuana had fewer than twenty thousand residents while San Diego boasted more two hundred thousand. The point that Henke's mother had known Mr. and Mrs. Camacho as neighbors, had from a distance shared in their horror and pain, brought much to the tale. It built a bridge from family history to graveyard legend. But Henke's connection to the Camacho tragedy also brought that odd story of the gold-gilded gun, a Faustian trade with the devil, a nonsensical explanation for the only physical evidence discovered in the case—a blood-stained uniform, an item supposedly found in Morales's home during a search conducted while he sat accused in the *comandancia*. Neighborhood myth has it that the uniform had been stained by rabbit blood during Morales's errand. The corpulent officer, of course, does not exist in the official record. And yet, there Morales was, confronted with the tainted uniform by his prosecutors. A clear confession was sought from the frightened young soldier.

At the time of Henke's tour, I was unaware of a well-researched book exploring the rise of the Soldado myth: *Juan Soldado: Rapist, Murderer, Martyr, Saint.* In a work backed by firsthand interviews, the late San Diego State University history professor Paul J. Vanderwood delivered a more nuanced set of facts and, importantly, he illustrated how it passed that a terrified and outraged town so quickly raised a lynch mob even as Morales and the others were questioned. In their fury, the mob barraged the *comandancia* with stones. Torches and pistols were not far behind. The small Tijuana police force dissolved into the streets. The *comandancia* itself held only a few hundred soldiers. And after business hours the crowd of Tijuana citizens outside grew into the thousands.

Unfortunately, this was not an unexpected response for the period. California's final lynching was still a number of years off. The intent and implications of that angry *comandancia* gathering were understood by everyone. Chants for justice rang up into the interrogation room. Confronted with the uniform and the noise outside, Morales reversed his denials and made a full confession. It might have been a calculated decision to buy time. A trial might have afforded him the opportunity to recant and spare himself a lynching. The mob set the *comandancia* aflame anyway. The authorities weren't waiting around. Within less than three days of Olga's discovery, Soldado was put on trial behind closed doors. He was quickly convicted and sentenced to death—to a rare *ley fuga*, a military execution in which the convict is commanded to run for his life before being gunned down.

The singular piece of evidence—the uniform bloodied either by a messy sack of rabbit skins or by murder—never entered the transcripts of the closed court martial, nor was it saved for posterity, if it ever existed. Further evidence implicating Soldado was never unearthed. Over time, in the minds of the people, that deficit of facts—as well as the speed of the trial, the weak position of the outpost government, the civil unrest, and the strength of the crowd—never fully exonerated Morales, but helped to build a different kind of case for a handsome young man with no one but God in his corner. All of the elements worked toward a confluence of narrative and belief that would have led to conspiracy theory in the United

States but, in Mexico, led to sainthood. As Vanderwood wrote, "Some believed (as many do today) that those who die unjustly sit closest to God. Therefore, they have the ear of the Lord and are especially effective as intercessors."

Henke said she'd returned to Tijuana from New York City in the 1980s—her shot at something bigger had detoured into single motherhood and a situation tipping toward destitution—when she first came to Juan Soldado's grave with a request for a miracle. She needed rent money. And kneeling in his mausoleum she spoke to Soldado, as many do, as though she just couldn't be sure if the heinous charges of rape and murder set against him were true or not, and that if he could see his way clear to granting her miracle, surely she would believe he'd been framed those seventy-odd years ago, framed and shot as he ran, his body then dragged to a shallow grave on that spot. As she kneeled in the sepulcher, Henke said, at the very outer rim of her right earlobe she felt the warm breath and grazing lips of the young soldier—a presence just beyond view. A man's voice said, "I will grant your wish, and then you will believe I am innocent."

As she offered this point, Henke's lips smacked—a period on a statement of fact. We were all free to believe or not. Atop the shrine's steps, behind her the cave-like edifice holding more images of Soldado, Henke conjured a time from her youth when she'd been in dire need, she'd made a petition to the spirit of a disgraced soldier, and then there, days later in the bathroom of a San Diego nightclub, she nearly stumbled over a wad of dollars lying on the floor, the exact sum she'd required.

As we made our way back down through the graveyard, the clouds breaking up and sunlight sputtering through, Henke pointed toward a cleft in a hillock near the rust-brown US border fence. She said that a number of years after Soldado's burial, a group of migrants had huddled there waiting to cross into the United States. On the advice of a local, they hiked up to the gravesite to petition Soldado for success in their crossing, and for a blessing of their travels. Ever since, the intercessor's legend had grown among migrant communities far and wide.

It was often repeated, however, that for one who petitioned by the grave and was granted a miracle but did not make the return pilgrimage to the shrine on his knees, Soldado himself would knock ever so late at night on the petitioner's door—wherever it might be. I imagined that Soldado must make a lot of trips into the United States, himself. Maybe we had crossed paths, at a Waffle House in Alabama possibly, or a Church's Chicken in Kentucky. A member of our party, a man in a red beanie, asked Henke directly: "You received a miracle. Did you return on your knees?"

"No, no," she said with a flip of the wrist. "I will maybe do it sometime."

Her velour pants looked a bit thin in the knees for such a feat. The woman she'd harassed earlier was long gone, luckily, for the sight of her floor mats would have broken the spell of the martyr's tale completely.

Graves set at such random intervals created a Pachinko-like effect as the group funneled down the hill; somehow we were bumping into people we thought we'd just passed. I'd later learn that the existing graves were likewise askew when Soldado was ordered to run for his life before a firing squad composed of, possibly, soldiers he'd worked alongside. Capital punishment didn't exist in this Catholic country—theoretically. The element of running was a go-round. It suggested that the convict was in fact trying to escape the law, and thus stopping him with bullets was justified. There were newspapermen from Los Angeles and San Diego and a crowd in the hundreds. Morales, dressed in a uniform stripped of insignia, understood what was to follow, but he nevertheless bolted when the signal was given. The United States border was within his view, the graves provided cover; an escape looked remotely possible. A witness claimed that as Morales jumped over and around the gravestones, the soldier spotted a small boy paralyzed in his path. The boy had been hiding behind a granite block, having stolen away to watch the pomp of the event. Children were not welcome at the execution, but the festivities proved irresistible. Juan stopped his flight to wave the stunned boy back, out of the line of fire. He then regained some distance through the maze of tombs before the first volley of gunfire sounded. A bullet nicked his skin. He continued to run. Maybe the large sepulchers provided too much cover; maybe his comrades fired into the sky on last impulse. Two more rounds were ordered before Morales finally fell.

Saving the boy was his final act. Although recorded in newspaper accounts, this detail of selfless grace has somehow been edited from the traditional myth. One can only wonder why.

The scattered arrangement of the graves also put me, as we neared the cobblestone road, arm's length from the raven-haired woman with the green eyes. Talking with a girlfriend in Spanish, she paused and turned slightly back and said in English, "We have a lot of ghosts in Tijuana, for a city that is so young."

"What others?" I asked.

"Well, I went to high school at Agua Caliente, the technical school. There was a woman in white called La Faraona. She appeared as a light. Kids saw her all the time, even I saw her," she said.

Agua Caliente sat two miles up the riverbed. It once held a lavish Mexican-colonial-style casino, hotel, and racetrack that attracted Hollywood starlets like Rita Hayworth. La Faraona—the Pharaoh—had supposedly been an entertainer who dressed in white robes. She was murdered somewhere in the resort at the height of its renown. After gambling was outlawed by Mexico's president Lázaro Cárdenas in the late thirties, part of the tourist complex was turned into a school. Much of the rest fell to ruin.

"But I've never been here," she continued with a sweep of the hand. "We lived on the other side of the city. And at that time it was too dangerous to travel about."

The woman and her friend picked up their conversation and continued onto the cobblestone road. I heard her mention that she'd attended a California State University campus, and now lived in San Diego. Here was an elegant, educated woman who no longer lived in Tijuana, but nevertheless adhered to its social codes and superstitions, to mores necessary in the accretion of myths and legends—no matter how dubious.

There were many reasons I began my search for the source of the Tijuana bicycles at the Puerta Blanca cemetery. Among them was the spiritual aspect. The shrine of Juan Soldado had lorded over the history of Mexican migration to the United States—from those invited to work California's fields during World War II to those who crossed just yesterday. Prospective migrants from all over Mexico continued to pay homage to Soldado and their stories were scrawled upon his tomb. I liked to believe there had been migrants who, between 2006 and 2009, trekked up the cobblestones, petitioned the saint, and later mounted a bike and pedaled into new lives and grand futures.

But the geography of the area, to my mind, was also elemental, because the United States lay downhill from Tijuana, and gravity, as both a metaphor and a physical force, defined the entire region. The hemisphere seemed bent along this axis. And everything came tumbling down: flash floods and killer bees and wild parrots and car tires and mountain lions and pollution and people and cultures and languages.

Also just downhill from the cemetery, incidentally, sat one of the closest bike shops to the border. My guess was that even a spiritual journey needed a new set of inner tubes and some brake cables now and again.

9

The Chicago Club lay just off Calle Coahuila, the Zona Norte's main drag, and within view of the red-light district's most popular bars. Inside, past a bouncer and a vacant coat-check stand, a huddle of vinyl booths surrounded a low parquet stage where dancers twirled about brass poles at either end. To the left, a bar extended nearly the length of the room; the wall behind it was mirrored and filled with bottles. The rest of the decor was basic, mostly red and black. Only at the very rear of the room was there a reference to the club's theme. It was a large portrait of the American gangster Al Capone.

Every *pollero* operation chose a local cantina as a de facto base. In the field, communication was often interrupted, and crews were easily divided. So a prearranged spot that provided cover was essential. This one was dark, intimate, and close to the border. It didn't charge a cover. One could see who came and who went. An average patron could easily get to know the bartenders and strippers who worked there. And if a crossing was particularly successful, the ingredients for a celebration were always at hand. That the club El Indio and his *amigos* chose as the base for their cadre of smugglers took its theme from America's bootleg heyday was not a point that garnered mention by any of them.

Early on a Tuesday evening was a slow time at the club. The dancers tended to slouch about like lonely car-wash attendants—women almost unassociated to the elongated and alluring vixens conjured by frequent and healthy tips. Juan was sitting at the bar chatting with a woman in a schoolgirl's plaid skirt when Indio walked in. Juan spotted his *socio*—his partner—but continued the casual conversation. Indio pulled out a seat, said hello to the girl, and exchanged mild pleasantries with Juan. A silence settled. Soon enough, the stripper moved on to some promising tourists seated in a corner.

"You made it," Juan said, excitedly.

"Yeah."

"With the bike?"

"No," he admitted. "I left it."

It was the first vehicle El Indio had ever owned—a dream bike to the kid he'd been in the village. But the *pollero* hadn't wanted *la migra* to spot him riding back on the exact bike he'd just crossed with. Not that the *jalapeños* were bicycle experts, or even aware. He was just nervous, superstitious even.

"Of course," said Juan. "Still, it's too bad . . . that was a cool bike."

"We need more. I'm looking to get, say, thirty. For starters."

"Let me see what I can do. I'll meet up with some friends here in *la Zona*, and I'll put the order in."

"Also, we need someone on the inside who can make the pickup." This was a bigger challenge, one that required strong connections in the United States.

"Yeah, I have some friends," Juan said. "In fact, I called Luis. He should be here soon. He has a green card, never has any problems."

The *polleros* ordered beers. As the night progressed the club began to fill. The PA's volume seemed to rise with the action. Rather than absently circling the brass poles, now the ladies began to kick and lift, to shimmy and spin. The nightly party was unfolding, fresh again, when a big, husky guy stumbled into the club. This man walked along the bar until he found Juan, who greeted him with affection and introduced him to El Indio. The loud music had a way of creating bubbles of privacy. Small groups could talk openly without appearing conspiratorial. Though his small talk was spare, Indio had a way of sizing people up in minute exchanges. Juan's banter eased the situation. Luis was not shy when recounting his feats in the field, and he must have met some requisite borderlands standard. Because at some point, in vague terms, Indio began to convey their scheme to Luis. A particular dancer caught Juan's attention and he turned away to watch. A moment later, he heard Luis erupt in laughter that sheared through the music. When he looked, Luis had his big hand on Indio's shoulder.

"What, Juanito?" Luis said. "You asked me down here to tell jokes? Ha, ha. I hope you're buying drinks, my friend."

Indio was silent, proffering the Oaxacan mask that revealed nothing.

"Listen, *jefe*," Juan intervened on Luis's behalf. "It's a normal reaction, eh? Who would imagine this harebrained idea? He's only surprised."

"Actually, I'm impressed," the big man said before gulping his glass of *Bucanas*. He laughed again. A flush overcame his face and his eyes narrowed as he surveyed the room.

Indio gathered himself before addressing the new associate. "Look, let's say you pick up my people tomorrow night, a trial run only. We've set the place and the hour. You wait there. You pick us up. You drive away with good money. But I have to know it's a sure thing you'll be there."

"As long as the *pollos* are going to be there, so will I," Luis said. He raised a finger. "I don't want to be driving around for nothing." The driver slapped Juan on the chest. "You owe me."

He waved some bills at the bartender, set them on the bar, said his good-byes, and left.

Two *polleros*, Javier and Rudy, waited in the canyon with three young men, migrants El Indio had recruited at *la línea*. Javier was slender with wavy hair, a thin nose, and classic good looks. Rudy was also trim but with a rounder face and a more amiable disposition. They were about the same age as their clients, but the *polleros* had been attempting to strike a pose of experience. The group had spent a good portion of the day driving through Tijuana's slums, drumming up bicycles together. They talked music, soccer, girls. Rudy felt it was a companionable situation; he liked these guys. And resting nearby in a pile was the result of their work: the third, fourth, fifth, sixth, and seventh bicycles.

But now, in sight of *la migra*, the migrants began to look nervous. One of them had a habit of licking his lips. The two others offered weak smiles. Their eyes darted. Against his better judgment, Rudy offered them a conciliatory out. "Still cool with riding across, right?" He nodded at the tangle of rubber and metal. "There are other ways to cross."

"Oh yeah," said the eldest. He was twenty-two and from Sinaloa. "It sounds way better than running, *amigo*."

One of the *pollos* pointed to the lone ten-speed. "This one is strange, no?"

"It's easy," said Javier. He bent his body and bulged his back in an impersonation of a stage-race competitor. He looked over his shoulder and then pretended to overtake the peloton. He straightened. "In the city, we ride these bikes almost exclusively."

"I don't think I want that one," said the eldest.

"No, me neither."

Eyeing Javy, as his associates called him, Rudy chuckled. "I'm just the *gancho, hombre*. It looks like you'll be the city slicker on the road bike."

He shrugged. "It's okay. El Indio says that as long as the tires roll, it will do the job."

Later, Javy admitted that he was plain scared. He'd never been to *el otro lado*. A couple of days before, he and El Indio had gone to the canyon to observe *la migra*, but the agents didn't act in the ways that Indio had said they would. "We checked and double-checked the timing of the shift changes, and the number of minutes it took an agent to reach the bottom of the hill, where we were going to be," Javy said. "That's when I began to get afraid."

Rudy, Javy, and the migrants all heard a rustle in the brush, a scuffing of sandy soil and the scratching of tumbleweeds. El Indio appeared from the darkness. He was short of breath and looked to be in a hurry.

"Okay gentlemen, to confirm, everybody knows how to ride? Everybody is cool with the plan?"

"Yes," answered the young men. "Of course." One rubbed his hands. Another lifted alternating heels, as if already en route.

"Okay. Rudy, you should make your way to the top of the hill. Watch for the fifth bicycle to pass onto the road, and that's your sign to distract *la migra*."

Rudy hustled up a thin path.

As they put the bikes over, light glinted off spokes and the ratchet of gears sounded impossibly loud. Indio guessed *la migra*'s shift change would happen in twenty-five minutes. But nothing happened.

"You see him there on that hill?" he said to the group, pointing at the agent. "He will drive down the backside and we will have ten minutes, more or less, to slip through. I've made arrangements with the *levantón*. He will meet us by a farm. You need to know that the street is called Hollister, just in case. It shouldn't take more than eight or nine minutes to get there."

Meanwhile, Rudy would be on the hill ready to distract the second *migra* if they needed it. "If something else happens and the plan goes wrong," Indio told them, "if *la migra* spots you—don't run back to this place. Jump the fence somewhere else. Don't come back here. Does everybody understand?"

A while later the men saw the Border Patrol truck's headlights flick on. The vehicle reversed from its parking place to the crown of the hill, where it made a three-point turn and then disappeared down the backside.

"Okay, let's go."

Indio led the men under the fence. The migrants emerged from the hole on the other side, the whites of their eyes flittering in the darkness. The *pollero* told them to grab their assigned bicycles. Once the rear guide, Javy, straddled his road bike, the small pod of cyclists negotiated a mild ravine to a graded dirt road. Indio stood on the pedals, a habit from his milk-run days, and each rider in turn rose into a sprint. The men would have been able to hear crashing waves at Border Field State Beach, to smell the rich wetland sages, and to feel the cool, moist night air pooled there in the valley's lowest depression.

The chalky dirt road became old asphalt near some outbuildings. And here the riders experienced the sensation of being observed; every dark construction posed a threat. It was easy to imagine that, inside, faceless people reached for telephones and dialed the police. Around a curve, El Indio made his hand into a fist and pulled into some bushes. The migrants followed, bunching together.

"The *guía*," one of them said. Javy was still on the road, far behind.

Seconds passed.

The sound of an approaching vehicle came from the east. Bold headlights then flashed on the hillside brush, disappearing into a bend. If Javy remained anywhere on the two-lane road, the lights would soon find him. There was nothing the migrants or their *pollero* could do. It was as if Javy traveled along a tightrope: any move by the others would shake the line, and he would certainly fall. If Javy were caught, the others would have to leave him behind.

The vehicle seemed to slow. The lights lit upon the asphalt just ahead of their position. The men squeezed tighter into the bush. A truck—white and green—all but stopped alongside them. An unseen track branched off from the far side of the road. The truck veered onto it. The engine roared as it climbed a hill. Soon enough, the darkened pavement of Monument became the province of raccoon, jackrabbit, and possum again. Like them, the crossers cautiously moved back on to the road.

A voice behind them said, "Wait, wait."

It was Javy on the road bike.

He rejoined the migrants without comment, and from Monument Road, the squad arced onto Hollister. The smell of manure and hay replaced the sages. A long blue road presented itself. The shoulders were clear of foliage and there was little cover. Compared to Tijuana, it was quiet to the point of being surreal. They passed a boarded-up farmhouse that looked like it was slumped in a sinkhole. A street sign read: YIELD TO HORSES. They crossed a low bridge over the river and pedaled a short way before turning off on a dirt side lane. This led to what looked like a shantytown. In plan and shape, it was very much like those in the canyons. But this one was lightless, silent, and foreboding. Only when they stopped could they see that it was constructed of lattices, shacks, and vine racks—a community garden. "Okay," El Indio said, "the pickup isn't here yet. If we crouch, we can't be seen from the road. Lay the bikes down and we'll wait."

A half hour passed, and then an hour. The night cooled and the smells of the river overcame them. The migrants began to ask how long it might take *el levantón*. They asked about *el levantón*'s point of departure, estimations of drive times, and the condition of his vehicle.

Indio finally stood. "The pickup isn't coming," he said. "He didn't think we could do it." As he mounted his bicycle, he told them, "Don't go anywhere."

"Can we have our cell phones back?" one of the men asked.

"They won't work here," the *pollero* said.

"It would be good to have them anyway," another answered. "In case."

El Indio withdrew the devices from his bag and handed them over. He stood on the pedals and moved down Hollister. The *pollos* watched his figure until it passed under the first streetlight and into the night.

A battered Toyota four-door pulled into the dirt lane and slowed to a stop. El Indio stood and walked toward the car. The driver's door opened and a man stepped out. He stared at Indio the way one might at a rare animal: the creature was exotic, too much so to be believed. Indio walked around the door with an open palm. The man merely looked at it. Indio embraced him. They remained that way for what seemed to be a long time. Neither said anything until the man stepped away to have a look, this time with the eyes of a brother. "You look good," he said.

"Thank you, so do you," Indio responded.

Then the driver eyed the men squatting by the garden shacks and said, "We don't have room for the bikes."

"It's okay." Indio turned to Javy and the *pollos*. "Leave them."

The driver opened the rear doors, withdrew white plastic buckets full of masonry tools, and put them in the trunk. Indio waved at the group and told them to get in. He took the front passenger seat himself. The interior was worn and smelled of sweat.

"*Gracias, Martín. Muchas gracias*," he said.

The driver turned the ignition, flipped the lights, and they drove out of the community gardens. The location was surprisingly close to a freeway on-ramp. The overly lit gas stations, the signs and street lamps, and the red-and-white lights of cars passing on the freeway was for the migrants like a grand kaleidoscope.

In time, Martín said, "Kid, you're lucky I was at home when you called." He whistled, his gaze focused on the road ahead. "What were you going to do? Hop on a city bus? I didn't tell your mother where I was going. She would have freaked out. She hasn't seen her baby in, what, ten years."

"I didn't call sooner because I knew that the family was doing good, and I didn't want to make my problems your problems. Tonight there was no other choice; the pickup never came."

"All the way over here I was thinking, *What do I do with Pablito? I can't bring him into the house like this.* Now I realize you forced my hand. If I deny Mother the opportunity to see you before you end up in jail or deported, she will never forgive me."

"Thank you, Martín, for helping me."

"What about the rest?"

El Indio directed his brother to pull into a hotel not far from the family's home. The woman at the front desk spoke Spanish and when Indio paid for the room from a fold of cash, she asked for an extra deposit for the TV's remote control. Handing over the room keys, she started to ask if they needed help with luggage, but observed that they had none and stopped. Indio walked the three young migrants to the room. There was a painting of a ship, a small TV, and two beds. Before leaving, Indio instructed them not to open the door for anyone or step out for any reason. "I will come back soon," he said, "and we'll reach your destination tomorrow."

The family apartment was modest, as Javy remembered it. "The place had two bedrooms and one bathroom. The kitchen was open to the living room. El Indio's parents slept in one room, and the two sisters in the other. The brothers slept in the living room."

While still on the stairwell, Indio heard voices and the sounds of a television. Through a bay window, he could see an entire family milling about a living room and kitchen. Martín entered, and Indio and Javy followed. The youngest son scanned faces lit by fluorescent lights. He hadn't seen any of these people together in the same space since they'd all lived in the one-room shack in the village. This space had windows, countertops, and couches. There were doors and a carpet. Each face looked older, tired—and the men bigger, with bellies. In the village, they were always just skin and bones. Indio's mother wore an apron similar to the one she'd worn at home. There was a little gray in her hair. She stood with a ladle over a pot in the kitchen and peered up only when the room went quiet in their presence.

"Aye, Martín, you have friends," she scolded. "You should have called."

"Mother, I would like to present your son Pablito and his friend Javier. They crossed over from Tijuana just hours ago."

"Pablito?"

El Indio walked into the kitchen and embraced his mother. His father rose from the couch and joined them. One sister stood back, as if hesitant, and the other clasped her hands. The middle brother stood from the couch. Martín and Javy didn't move.

When Indio and his mother broke from their embrace, tears had already reached her round jawline and rolled onto her neck. She wiped at her face with her apron.

"My boy," she said, "it is so good that you were able to come and be with us now. I am so happy. Everything is complete."

Indio surveyed the others. His head lowered a touch. "It is wonderful to see you again, Mother—all of you. But I haven't come to stay. I'm here for just a short time."

"What do you mean?" she asked.

"I have to go on to Los Angeles, for work," he said.

"Work? What are you doing?"

"I'm taking some people to Los Angeles," he said.

"You are a driver?" she asked.

"No. I was hoping Martín would drive us."

"Los Angeles," said Martín. "I have a slab to pour, 6:00 AM."

"Us?" the mother said, indicating Pablo and Javy with a finger.

"There are others," he said. "I brought some men over with me."

"Men? You are a coyote?"

"I am doing some work."

"Were you followed? We don't . . . none of us have the papers, *mijo*."

"No, no. There's no chance."

Speaking for the first time, the father said, "You were expecting rich Americans, son. We're still simple people."

"Everybody has to work," Martín added. "Every day. All of us."

"How much money do you make in a week?" Indio asked.

"About five hundred."

"Take me tonight. I'll pay five hundred. You'll be back in time for the slab."

Martín looked at the other men. The father shrugged. The middle brother said, "Go for it." And Martín slowly nodded in agreement.

"Okay, we'll have to leave now." El Indio said his good-byes to his father and brother. He told his sisters that they were still the most beautiful girls in the village, no matter how big the village. He hugged his mother again, and said, "We will be together soon, *Madre*. Just like you wanted."

They turned to leave. Indio opened the door and stepped out. Javy followed.

Their mother said, "Martín, don't."

10

Five miles south of the border, as we traversed a broad hill overlooking the Pacific Ocean, we were met by an unexpectedly beautiful panorama. A verdant olive orchard crowned the ridgeline and dipped toward the ocean for what seemed to be forever. The orchard appeared ancient, a swath of gnarled agriculture lifted from Pompeii or Constantinople. But this was midmorning in early November on the western edge of Tijuana. The North Pacific's deep autumn blue contrasted with the tan earth and pale green acres of trees. The Coronado Islands, blocky monuments once called the "Gates of San Diego Bay," loomed on the horizon as if viewed through a telephoto lens. The combination of the rugged islands, the expanse of ocean, and the rolling orchard completed one of the more striking rural scenes I'd glimpsed in California. It rivaled any similar parcel in Santa Barbara or Malibu. But the true reason the olive orchard came as a shock was that Oscar Romo had been navigating toward the headwaters of probably the most desperate and polluted of Tijuana's urban slums, Los Laureles Canyon.

Romo had wide features, a handsome sprawling smile, and a tanned, bald head. He walked like a cowboy but spoke like Ricardo Montalbán. Driving his pickup truck along a dirt road past shanties and businesses with dogs barking from their rooftops, he'd been pondering his national affiliations out loud—a complexity he continued to mull over. He was born in Mexico to a Basque father and an American mother and, while young, was sent to study in Spain. Almost by accident, he said, he found his first adult job as a United Nations diplomat in the service of Mexico. This placed him in posts all over Latin America and the Caribbean. When he finally arrived in Tijuana, he decided he'd had enough roaming and stayed. Now he lived in a rather ordinary San Diego suburb and worked for the Tijuana River National Estuarine Research Reserve, a federal outfit that managed a big chunk of the American valley.

"I have an identity problem," he said. "In Mexico, the people call me 'gringo.' In the US, they call me a Mexican. In Spain, they don't know what I am." He shrugged, lifting his hands from the wheel.

As soon as we passed the orchard, its green sweep could be easily dismissed as a mirage. Because we next came upon denuded land and what looked like a down-market junkyard. Then, rounding a final curve, we stopped at a dirt road that descended into Los Laureles. Immediately before and below us was a thicket of shanties. You might think of Rio's favelas, of blue tarps, corrugated iron—a state of suspended construction. We couldn't see the ocean anymore but looking north over the rooftops, we could see the skyscrapers of San Diego rising like crystal formations on a salt pan. Los Laureles often drew comparisons with Tijuana's original migrant slum, Cartolandia (Cardboard Land), and, in fact, was one of the reasons *cartolandia* had become a generic term for such places. The construction techniques, growth patterns, dynamics, and rhythm of life were all the same. A man familiar with the canyon told me, "People move here with nothing, and as soon as they get something, they leave." Many, however, became stuck between the gully's sheer walls. They constructed foundations of car tires. They built shacks that clung to the crumbling hillsides. They built lives. Romo knew an elderly couple, Chinese nationals, who had traveled to Mexico with extended family. They'd intended to cross illegally into the United States. But for unknown reasons, these grandparents had been left behind. Possibly, they couldn't swim or hike or climb. Now, speaking only Mandarin, they eked out lives in Los Laureles alongside Mexicans, Hondurans, and Guatemalans.

This place had long compelled Romo. His first visit, in the 1970s, came as a lark. He'd read Father Juan Crespí's journals of the 1769 Portolà expedition rather closely; this was the group that established California's mission system. And from his reading, Romo pinpointed the party's entry from Baja into Alta California as having gone right through Los Laureles. The party had planned to rendezvous with the oceangoing portion of the expedition at San Diego Bay, which was in clear view. At the time Romo became intrigued with the Portolà story, he worked as a junior diplomat and was charged by the UN with documenting migrant culture along the border. But at that time there weren't yet any migrants living in the canyon. It was just too remote. Romo's interest in the route taken by the founders of California was purely recreational. He hoped to find a conquistador helmet, maybe, or some telltale artifact. One of the ranches between central Tijuana and the ocean was owned by Señor Soler, the communist. Romo went to the Soler place and struck a deal with a ranch hand to guide him into the canyon on horseback.

"Back then, it was beautiful," Romo said, as we stepped out of the pickup. "I have pictures of this looking green and lush. I took the main canyon on horse, but it's not certain the Portolà expedition came that exact way; there are many subbasins."

"Did you find anything?" I asked.

"Oh, I wish," he said with a wide grin. "No. If something was there, it would have been very difficult to find."

Romo's current stake in the canyon was less romantic. He worked as a "watershed coordinator" for the American wetland that lay at the end of the drainage. Down there in the green flats, the reserve and state parks staff toiled to restore wetland habitat that had suffered years of degradation—the major cause of which was this unplanned, underdeveloped slum. Gravity set the rules. Los Laureles's headwater is seven hundred feet above sea level. The wetlands two miles away are near zero. The residue and refuse of everything that goes on in Los Laureles eventually ends up in the United States. Juicy red tomatoes are one example. In the summer, tomato plants—along with green tomatillos and melons of all kinds—spring wild from the soil on the American side, the plants' origin seeds having passed first through people and then through Los Laureles Canyon as sewage, and finally into the United States as runoff in the same dirty soup carrying trash and car tires.

We stopped near the dry headwater because Romo wanted to point out a steep hillside that appeared nearly bedazzled with reflective emerald and metallic colors.

"See the trash sliding down that hill? That's hospital waste," he said. "It's huge; there are layers and layers."

It was composed of bandages and syringes, and bags of fluid. Romo had once placed transponders in the trash, and for over a year he followed their signals down the drainage into the United States. I noticed a skinny dog with some kind of spinal condition nearby. I asked about creatures getting into the biological waste.

"Yes," Romo said. "That too."

Across the canyon from the medical dump, we could see the back of a *maquiladora*, a factory that supplied goods to the United States under NAFTA's free trade agreements. Here, manufacturing waste spilled down the hill as if the factory were a giant truck that had simply backed up to the canyon and thrown the tailgate down. At a site below the dumps, developers had scraped the topsoil off a few acres of hillside and advertised the sale of lots. This caused a number of problems for Romo. Primarily, all of that topsoil had been tossed into the streambed, and would clog the fragile American estuary as soon as the winter rains arrived. The silt from another such site destroyed twenty acres of wetland in a single night. Secondly, those developers didn't own the land. They provided a nice-looking but fake paper deed, and because of a loophole that pitted the federal government against the city, nothing could be done to stop them.

A pragmatic man, Romo was concerned about the lack of sewer and power infrastructure at the site. The settlement of Laureles had begun, coincidentally, with the installation of a pump station at the bottom of the canyon. The men who built the pump station assembled homes at the work site and stayed, but did not develop their own infrastructure. The slum has been creeping up the canyon ever since. In an effort to reduce untreated sewage flow into the United States, Romo approached the Mexican government to develop a plan. The government agreed to install a sewage system at a cost of $1,000 to each household. That cost was presented as a loan to the families, which no one believed would be repaid. It was difficult work for Romo, and considering all of the unpaid loans, it was a feat he didn't think he could repeat. So when Romo noticed the new development, he walked into their little real estate shack and said he had some questions about the lots. For example, where would the water, sewer, and electricity come from?

"Oh, don't worry," said the salesman. "The old residents, they had the same problems farther down in the canyon. Then this crazy gringo showed up, and brought sewer to all of the houses. It's no problem here. We are certain that as soon as people start building, that crazy gringo will come back, and do the same thing here."

"I am the gringo," Romo said. He placed a hand on his chest.

We drove down the canyon road. It was often hard to discern from the colorfully painted houses—lime green, purple, canary yellow, sky blue, and brown—but one or maybe two walls of many of them consisted of repurposed garage doors. The wood for the remaining walls often came from demolition projects in the United States as well—recycling at its most direct. But beneath all of this, there was also a kind of geologic recycling program.

"I found a shark tooth this big," said Romo, spreading his hands to indicate an object the size of a tin can. "Right in the street here." In fact, fossils emerged from the crumbling ground with the same frequency as old car batteries. This was an ancient landscape formed by the big one—a flood of epic scale unleashed when a glacial dam in the interior fissured and broke at the end of the last ice age. The force of the water deposited sediment in layers of cobbles and tan- and copper-colored earth. If you wanted a fossil, Romo said, "you just have to spend one day here. With a bag." In fact, one could simply snag a plastic bag tumbling along the road, and then wade into the archive.

As you descend into the canyon, the hillsides grow steeper, so that it becomes more of a V shape than a basin. The shanties climb the pitched walls in ever-creative ways. It becomes dense. This is a barrio people are afraid of—me included. Maybe it's the claustrophobia and the poverty, the smell of burning plastic. I've passed by the bottom of Los Laureles on the ribbon of the International Road innumerable times. I never fail to gaze into the visual clutter of Laureles and experience something—an awe, a dread. But in the heart of Los Laureles, I found it hard to sustain those notions under the same sunny sunshine that falls on San Diego, bathed in the same sublime temperature, with families milling about, working on cars, or playing with children.

But there was one place that still gave me pause.

At a certain point, the road is the river bottom. Portions of this thoroughfare are paved, but the pavement is still riverbed. Where a subbasin called Alacrán—Scorpion—joins Los Laureles, two legs of the drainage meet at a bend in the road, doubling the potential water volume. Homes are built right alongside this section. In dry weather it doesn't look like much. Yet old carpet, diapers, and ice-cream wrappers buried in the road's weedy shoulder tell the story: this section can become a torrent. During a big rain, it separates the older settlement from the dry road up and out to the south, trapping residents in various sectors of the canyon.

In January of 2010 rain had been falling for four days when a thirty-three-year-old mother named Rocío Méndez Estrada realized that she and her children could no longer stay in the plywood shack they'd moved into just months earlier. The dirt floor was becoming muddy with seepage. This was at the base of Alacrán, and Méndez feared the shack would flood. She'd had a fight with the father of her two youngest children—the man who'd built the shack and paid the $115 rent on the plot—and in response, he'd simply walked off into the storm. So Méndez gathered her children and made a hasty retreat. But the rain continued, and Méndez realized she'd failed to pack needed medicines and clothing. She then asked the father of her eldest child to help her return to the shack and collect some things. They approached the bend in the road in a white Honda Civic. Riding in the car were her three children: Aramis, ten; Tifany Virginia, five; and Hector Jorge, just a toddler. The adults parked outside the shack and left the children while they dashed in. Even though it had been raining for days, while Méndez and the man stepped away from the car, a flow threshold was exceeded somewhere upstream, and a flash flood swept through the canyon. The water lifted the Honda from its parking place and the children were washed away. "I ran behind the car," Méndez told a reporter, "but the current was too strong."

Tijuana firefighters discovered the empty, crumpled Honda first. The body of Aramis was discovered later that day, just inside the border. But Tifany and Hector had vanished. Locals and Tijuana firefighters hunted for them on the Mexican side. In the United

States, a number of agencies, and a group that aids lost migrants called Desert Angels, searched the river valley and wetlands. A dog handler also joined the hunt. But they found no trace of the children for over a week.

Along with trash, some of the more distinctive items that wash into California's Border Field State Park are plastic baby dolls—the kind with the flickering lashes and bright eyes. The toys are so numerous that migrants who pass through the area have taken to placing the dolls' heads in the wispy trees that line the river. The impulse is almost certainly sparked by humor, but the effect is spooky, especially for uninitiated horse riders and dog walkers. People who work in the valley are aware of the dolls, so when Desert Angels volunteer Ricardo Esquivias Villegas and his dog Loba came upon a pile of storm trash, the searcher at first thought Hector's body was yet another toy. The two-year-old was half buried in trash, and his body was so damaged his sex couldn't immediately be determined. In the meantime, a migrant walking through the wetland spotted another body farther into the park. The crosser called relatives in Mexico, who called the Tijuana fire department, who called the San Diego lifeguard service, who alerted the searchers. They scoured the area, described to them fourth-hand, but quit as it grew dark. Tifany's body wasn't recovered for another four days. The county medical examiner's office took three weeks to officially identify the children. In that period, the Méndez family was still hopeful they might find the boy and girl alive because several other Tijuana residents had disappeared in the storm. The two nameless bodies could have belonged to another family.

I'd associated this tragedy with the canyon for a couple of years. Each time I thought of Los Laureles, I pictured the place where the Méndez car washed away. I imagined a precarious dirt embankment, a parking spot on a steep incline, a suspect river crossing. But when Romo and I neared the spot, the humdrum bend in the road, although fatally misplanned, both surprised me with its banality and spoke to dangers in plain view.

But this was not the place we'd come to see. Another, more like a portal into an alternate reality, lay at the end of Los Laureles, where the canyon's trough and two walls crossed an imaginary line and became Goat Canyon and the United States.

Just south of the Alacrán-Laureles juncture the road was blocked. Someone was pouring more concrete. So Romo pitched his truck up a steep road onto the eastern mesa and into a neighborhood called Mirador. Suddenly the badlands were behind us and we passed through a middle-class neighborhood with sweeping views. Chattering school kids in crisp white shirts and dark blue uniforms occupied streets and corner shops. The houses looked substantial. Green lawns rolled curbside. As we made our way to the edge of the mesa, the neighborhood literally fell away. Romo parked on the last street. We walked out to an empty dirt lot that ended in a sheer promontory and found ourselves on a piece of earth that dropped off on three sides. I tested the ground with a slight stomp. It felt like walking a plank. Across the canyon from this point rose the shadowed western wall of Los Laureles. The sound of water thundered up from below. This was the International Road and its stream of traffic heading to Ensenada and points south. Our vantage highlighted the fact that the main highway traversed an earthen berm—from the eastern wall of Laureles, where we stood, to the western one. The road and its dam-like base artificially separated Laureles from Goat Canyon. Underneath the road and the dam ran several culverts, each tall enough to walk through.

In 2007, Romo had begun to notice something down on the flats in front of the culverts that provoked his imagination. What he saw led him to dream up a tour of sorts. Romo decided he would attempt to guide a group of American citizens south from Goat Canyon into the culverts and then up into Laureles—a reverse migration with the intent to bring awareness to the disparities between the two countries, and their interconnectedness. Colleagues described his proposed project as political theater. When he approached Mexican customs and US Border Patrol officials, both sides scoffed. Romo is no slouch in the world of diplomacy, but mostly he is persistent. "I worked on the paperwork and permissions to the point that someone high up became amused," he said. As Romo readied one hundred US passport holders to cross into Mexico, he spotted Border Patrol agents chuckling at the sight of his bookish migrants. The Mexican federal government sent out customs agents to process the Americans' passports as they popped up from the culverts, and "in the only instance of its kind, the culvert became a legal border crossing," Romo said.

Tijuana police cars with flashing lights were also present. The scene drew onlookers. Passing motorists and pedestrians on the International Road yelled:

"Arrest those bastards!"

"Get the illegal aliens!"

"Deport the fucking gringos!"

Arms folded, Romo beamed in the retelling of the event. His grin spread as if the whole thing centered on a private punch line. His political theater had garnered an Associated Press story that was picked up by newspapers around the world. If former Tijuana mayor Jorge Hank Rhon hadn't been arrested on charges of illegal arms possession hours later, Romo's crossing would have grabbed even more attention.

And the thing he'd seen there, on the flat ground before the culverts, time and again—that mysterious activity which had inspired his plans and might have been a measure more bizarre?

"Yes, that was the staging area for the bikes," he said. "You would see two dozen, three dozen people waiting on bicycles, waiting for the signal." Romo looked at the sky in thought. "Whoever did it the first time knew that it was a good strategy. On foot, you're in bad shape. The bicycle is a very inventive and creative way because you can do in minutes what would take hours."

We turned our backs on the canyon and began walking toward Romo's truck. I pictured the migrants he'd described, waiting for a signal. I imagined a wave or a whistle. The cyclists' feet leaving the ground and finding the pedals; sprockets and chains engaged; balance in momentum; the dark maw of the culverts admitting a pinprick of distant light; the tunnel vision; the awful, damp smell of the pipes. And then they were gone; they'd left my imagination and rolled into the very same portals that carried silt, sewage, appliances, refuse, lost and mislaid items downstream.

"Some of the bikes are still around, you know?" Romo said, as we drove away. "You can find them in Goat Canyon. I've been tempted to take a bicycle myself. I've seen some nice ones."

11

"So, do you think he's really coming back?" asked Juan.

The *enganchador* sat with the *guía*, Javy, at the bar of the Chicago Club. It was hot outside. The bar was dark, cool, and empty. They sipped golden-brown Cuba libres—a cola-and-rum drink invented on the heels of Cuba's liberation from Spain. American GIs brought the Coke, Cubans the rum. The magic concoction seeped up into Dixieland and spread north and west with the rumrunners of Prohibition. Untold gallons of rum passed through Tijuana.

"Shit, I don't know, man. He picked up twelve thousand dollars crossing those *pollos*. What would you do?"

"His whole family is already set up on the inside," Juan said.

"That too," Javy said. "He'd be back by now. Los Angeles is only two, three hours away."

"So, how did you guys leave it? Indio just said, what? 'Thank you for your services and good-bye'?"

"No," Javy sighed. "It was pretty emotional at his mom's house. She didn't want him to go. But he had to get the *pollos* to Los Angeles to get paid."

Heading north wasn't as easy as simply hopping on the freeway. There were permanent Border Patrol checkpoints at San Onofre on the I-5 and before the city of Temecula on the 805. Vehicles were stopped by agents who peered into their interiors. For reasons unknown to the *polleros*, these checkpoints were periodically closed. The smugglers could scout the situation in a number of ways, yet regardless, six Mexicans in a small Toyota wasn't going to look good. This was the reason, Javy said, that he'd been left behind.

"Indio gave me some money and said, 'See you in Tijuana.' He also told me to get to work and, whatever . . . 'see how many you can get.' So I took the chance. I picked up two couples and they're waiting in the room right now, probably wondering what the fuck is going on."

"Indio asked me to get bicycles," Juan said, "a lot of them. I bought twenty for a hundred bucks. But he asked me to get them before he crossed and, you know, saw his family again. If Indio doesn't come back, what the fuck am I going to do with all of those bikes? I can only ride one at a time. Right, *cabrón*?"

The *polleros* ordered another round and watched an apathetic dancer. A flashy-looking couple entered the bar, followed by another man. The boys observed the trio but when the couple sat at a booth, the other man continued toward the bar. This man wore sunglasses indoors, which caught Juan's eye, and he seemed to be walking toward them.

"*Que onda, compas?*" he addressed them, then slouched backward.

"Indio? What happened to you? Have you gone *loco*?"

This took Indio aback. He straightened. "What do you mean, Juanito?" he asked, spreading his hands.

"Look at you," said Javy. "Those clothes you're wearing, and the Nikes. You're all baggy." Javy and Juan burst out laughing. "Where are the huaraches?"

The sides of Indio's head were nearly shorn and the hair on top was slicked back with gel. The style somehow made his features sharper, cheekbones higher, more indigenous-looking. His T-shirt was big and loose, making his forearms appear short but broad. The sharp creases and cuffs of his chino pants revealed that they were a brand-new pair.

"You are an overnight *cholo*," Juan said.

"Enough," Indio said. "I bought clothes for you guys too." Javy and Juan looked at each other. "No shit, a cab is waiting outside. Check the back seat."

They changed on the street while the *paraditas* ("standing ladies") in miniskirts and heels, the Chicago Club bouncer on his stool, and the guys at the taco cart watched. Then the boys sauntered back in. Javy looked at his reflection and said, "This *pollero* is really handing shit out."

In place of the bus station recruiters sitting before their Cuba libres in the bar-back mirror of a second-rate strip club, the boys now saw three hip-looking borderlands *cholos*, the factory creases of their large T-shirts hardly visible under the colored lights.

"Looking at ourselves in the mirror, with the cool new threads," Juan later admitted, "I swear we were on cloud nine."

Indio met Solo at the Tijuana bus terminal in early 2006, just two months after the first bicycle crossing. He immediately whisked his childhood *amigo* into the heart of the city. They shared the little room in the Zona Norte; they ate meat tacos on the street. And the new *pollero* initiated a tutorial in *la vida de la frontera*. Indio purchased their first cell phones. These had a walkie-talkie option, which they used to abuse each other: *Cabrón*, they'd say. *Pinche cabrón*. And for his *campesino* friend, Indio picked out a pair of black tennis shoes with white stripes.

"If you wear huaraches in the city," he explained, "when people look at you, that is all they will see."

Solo had assumed that Indio borrowed the money he'd wired, and he felt a daunting obligation to make good on the loan and bring

Indio back into standing with whoever could part with such a substantial sum—but Solo quickly learned the truth.

His lessons began with recruiting at *la línea*. Indio coached Solo on how to approach possible clients and offer their services. Their language, Indio explained—their words and the slow, resonating intonation of the farmlands—was their advantage. These were their people.

"They have a desire and you can help to fulfill it," he said, before warning, "But still, *amigo*, the *pollos* won't trust you completely. Be mindful. When your pet dog catches rabies, you share a history with the creature, you love this animal—but at that point your interests split," Indio said.

He then introduced Solo to the business at the bus station.

But here, a couple of city cops looking to snatch up some *pollos* themselves spotted the dopey peasant farmer in the strangely new tennis shoes. There was nothing a corrupt cop liked less than competition. The police arrested Solo under suspicion of recruiting migrants. He was taken to jail. After thirty-six hours in a dark cell that smelled of urine, he was placed before a judge who questioned the young man from an elevated bench. Noting his dress, his simple speech, his recent arrival in Tijuana, and the fact that Solo carried not a peso in his pockets, the sun-spotted magistrate concluded that Solo lacked the wherewithal to work as a human smuggler. Charges were dismissed.

El Indio, however, lectured his friend. "Pay close attention, Solo," he said. "The border is chaos. Our business is about intuition and precision—about reaching in and pulling something out. You need to know what's coming before it arrives."

One day Indio recruited two migrants, and he and Solo took them to the canyons. His gang had cultivated more entry points—some of them hidden in plain sight—and Indio wanted to familiarize Solo with the layout. This was also an opportunity to instruct the *pollos*. Being on the ground was the key to his operation. El Indio didn't arrive to work a shift: he inhabited the landscape. On this occasion he took the group to the western turnout at Summit Canyon. To the south, the tin-roofed hovels of Los Laureles climbed a canyon wall in increasingly untenable perches. The architecture of necessity always created a frayed aspect along the passage of the International Road. Below, on the other side, at the base of the dam-like ridge that held the road, was only desert and an anemic dirt track, which, at that distance, looked as pale as a dry streambed.

Indio had indicated this path to the clients, and he'd begun to describe the benefits of the route, when they noticed a white Ford pickup approaching from the city center on the International Road. A man drove, but the passenger-side window framed the face of a woman—the slender aspect of whom immediately drew the eye. Both the driver and the woman appeared to contemplate the smugglers' small group. But the truck continued on. Indio resumed his instruction. Moments later, however, the truck passed by in the opposite direction. A concrete meridian separated them from the traffic. Later, the Ford again dipped into the saddle of the canyon road. This time, it came to a stop in the turnout. A man in a light-colored Stetson stepped out and approached Indio's group.

12

At the foot of Avenida Revolución is a five-way intersection, the odd-numbered tail of which is a broad footpath that leads through to downtown Tijuana. Anchored at two of the intersection's opposing corners, a monumental silvery crescent—something like the Gateway Arch in St. Louis, Missouri—loops into the sky overhead. Steel suspension cables rise from the corners to meet the curvature at intervals, giving anyone appraising the monument from the highlands an impression of a spoked aluminum wheel. At ground level, the arch is surprisingly easy to miss. Its action is too lofty. It is said to be the gateway to Latin America, but a pedestrian could slip underneath without noticing any distinct change; Latin America really begins hundreds of miles north in Los Angeles—the arch is just a formality.

At the southeast corner of the same intersection stands another set of arches made of aged brick and tile, a flourish reminiscent of an early California mission. About fifteen feet tall, these arches don't appear to have a function either—their patina leading one to suspect that they were purchased from some decaying hacienda and stationed here to support a foundation myth for Tijuana. Both monuments—one to an idealized Mexican future and one to the country's past—stand at the intersection of Avenida Revolución and Benito Juárez.

And yet, this is one of my favorite places in the city because of the noisy third element: all of the troubadours, mariachis, and whole bands for hire that blow their horns in and around the ruined arches. They play into the traffic and into the noise, their suits bristling with ruffles, epaulets, and medallions, their arms cradling the shapely wood bodies of guitars, fiddles, and string basses. Horn players carry their glinting brass low, like sidearms ever ready to be raised and blasted into the street. I admired the whole idea of artists pacing, preening, and charming clients. But passing the intersection at Avenida Revolución again, and laying eyes on the city's congregation of professional mariachis, what I liked most was the idea, despite the violence and loss of the region's tourist economy, that all over the hills and valleys of Tijuana, fiestas and weddings and *quinceañeras* needed real mariachis, and there they were, leaning against the arches, just waiting.

I met Dan Watman at the big yellow *farmacia* where tourists used to buy their Viagra and recreational pain pills. We walked through the colorful, empty commercial maze that funnels visitors to the footbridge over the concrete Tijuana River and toward Avenida Revolución. We passed the arches while a mariachi group choked in ruffles played "Por Ti"—"For You"—and we kept on walking through to downtown.

At a street corner that reminded me of 1970s suburbia—the mom-and-pop stores with their faded corrugated paneling and bright but brittle plastic lettering—a honey vendor sold gooey chunks of honeycomb from a blue plastic bin. The man fought off bees still at work while, with the flourish of a magician, he stuffed the golden combs into black plastic bags. Two pesos each. There were stands selling leather belts and wallets stamped with the names of Mexican states and emblems that glorified professional truck drivers. Taco-cart workers assembled a great variety of dishes for people who stood around as if at a wine tasting, plates elevated, looks of inward discerning on their faces. Intersections held crosswalks in the form of Xs painted right through the center. And on a red light, they brimmed with pedestrians. The city appeared to be bursting at the seams with kids, teenagers, guys and girls in their early twenties—on buses, in school uniforms, hanging out the doors of minivan taxis.

In the quick-hit coverage of Tijuana's troubles, this emerging population bubble was rarely reported on. The *Los Angeles Times* did publish one story about a massacre in a private home, after which the first people on the scene were school kids let out of class down the street. In navy uniforms and knee-high socks, they tiptoed through the battered house full of gory crime-scene curiosities and the recently deceased. Yet it was never outright acknowledged that many firsthand witnesses of the war for America's drug corridors were children. They'd known no other city, no other reality. That an entire population was coming of age during a conflict with no real fronts, no political identity, ever-shifting alliances, and no end date was a hard reality to wrap the mind around. But their youth could also help explain the resilience. New art, music, ideas, and businesses sprouted in Tijuana during every period of relative peace. The young people's desire to push their city forward even took them into the streets. On one occasion, a group threw a birthday party for a giant pothole. They brought cake and a piñata. "Tijuana: where our potholes age in years," they sang. Within an hour, a city truck arrived to fill the cavity. If the violence was to have any lasting opposition, the kids were it.

Watman and I found a diner whose walls were painted the same light green color as the *chilaquiles* it served. Otherwise, it looked like any similar place in small-town California—deep booths, cash register up front, big street window. I'd contacted Watman for the same reason I'd tracked down ecologist Greg Abbott, farmer Jesse Gomez, and reporter Janine Zúñiga: I was looking for witnesses. Without any idea of where the bicycles had originated, or who had arranged their crossing, I sought individuals who, I hoped, might each produce some new piece of the story—maybe without even considering its significance.

Like photographer Maria Teresa Fernandez, Watman was a creature of the marginal space along the fence line. As a young man he'd become enthralled with foreign languages, especially Spanish, which lured him from California's Central Valley south to a university in San Diego. Afterward, he taught Spanish at community colleges and made frequent trips to the closest place he could engage in his passion, which eventually pulled him across the line to live.

Around that time Watman began to take his Spanish students to Friendship Park—a binational space surrounding the 1851 border monument, and a stone's throw from where the security fence meets the Pacific Ocean. The paperwork he'd need to fill out to actually take his students into Tijuana was daunting; some colleges even prohibited students from traveling there. So these meetings at the fence seemed the best go-around. He invited people he knew from the other side as well—a group of volunteer lifeguards who worked the stretch of beach at Las Playas were the first. The idea was simply to have his students communicate with someone *en el otro lado*. For the students, however, the sensation of meeting another's eyes through the pylons was more than a novelty. The fence offered both the security of dark sunglasses and the intimacy of face-to-face conversation. There was butchered Spanish and battered English, and a lot of hand gestures.

The encounters were meant to be a school exercise, but Watman saw something else during the encounters that compelled him: people from different worlds, who likely would never have passed a sentence between them, making each other's acquaintance across the divide. Whatever it was that charmed him, Watman soon dropped the college students entirely. He wanted anybody and everybody, as dissimilar as possible, to come to the fence and stumble through a conversation. He came up with ideas to lure disparate parties. There were bilingual salsa dance lessons attended by people on either side. There were concerts, yoga classes, poetry readings, and sign-language meet-ups. The event that drew my attention was a binational trash pickup. Watman arranged for a kite maker to teach attendees how to make kites from their trash. The images of a blue sky filled with the bright metallic colors of junk food bags and candy wrappers was transformative. I didn't know what it was blotting out the iron border fence with all of that color, but I liked it.

"There was a place that was designated for cross-border communication [Friendship Park], so I honestly didn't think it was a big deal," Watman said. Still, he did believe his work to be activist in nature. And he called these meet-ups "actions."

The events that hardened Watman's resolve began in 2006, when the Department of Homeland Security began building the "triple fence." The initial development occurred in violation of the 1969 National Environmental Policy Act, among others, as the contractors began grading the mesa east of Smuggler's Gulch. Because the construction would eventually wall off Friendship Park with an eighteen-foot-tall fence, from perches in the county and state parks, Watman began to film work he thought to be unlawful. This sparked one in a series of incidents in which Border Patrol agents detained him.

Watman was most famously detained in 2009, when he aided fellow activist Reverend John Fanestil in giving Sunday Communion to Mexicans through the fence. The passing of wafers that signified Christ's flesh through the pylons was considered a customs violation. Though warned, Fanestil continued to give Communion at the fence. One Saturday, 120 worshipers, students, and human rights activists gathered on the American side. On the Tijuana side were churchgoers and Opera de Tijuana members, who planned to sing through the service. Sheriff's deputies and an anti-immigration group called the Minutemen arrived; the latter engaged the group with emotional protests of their own. The Border Patrol literally drew a line in the sand before the wall. There was pushing and shoving. Agents readied tear gas and guns loaded with rubber bullets. Fanestil and Watman linked arms with forty others and marched toward the fence. The Opera de Tijuana members began a requiem mass. The Minutemen blasted counterprotests through bullhorns. The marchers advanced on the line in the sand. Fanestil was ordered to drop the Communion items, wafers and all, and place his hands behind his back. Authorities seized the reverend. Watman and the others marched on—until a sheriff's deputy grabbed Watman and dragged him off.

During this period of heightened tensions, as Watman regularly hiked the fence line along the canyons and out to the beach and Friendship Park, he began to notice the abandoned bicycles alongside trails. Like Maria Teresa Fernandez, he could only note their number and consistency. Other than the bicycles' presence and their tracks, nothing was left behind that might explain the situation.

My interest in Watman had to do with the fact that he was on the ground. Maybe he'd seen something he didn't know was important. He was also a cyclist, didn't own a car, and rode his beater everywhere he went. Maybe he pedaled alongside migrants on these roads. Importantly, Watman lived in Tijuana. He knew its bike culture. So when he agreed to meet and visit some bike shops in the city, I thought I saw a crack in the wall.

The first shop happened to be in the Zona Norte, a short walk from downtown. The late San Diego novelist Oakley Hall described Tijuana as being "suffused with a feverish neon glow." These few blocks along Coahuila are the source of all that light—bars, brothels, hostess clubs, and hotels that rent by the hour. Billboards announce just about anything you'd desire: better teeth, a straighter nose, companionship, legal counsel—as Edward Abbey once wrote of another desert town, these blocks are "a throbbing dynamo of commerce and pleasure." An evening around Christmas is a particularly rich time for a visit. The streets and medians are decorated like the Rose Parade while prostitutes smile and wave from the sidewalks. People in cars travel through, but here, the city is the pageant.

During the day, and up close, the reason for the Zona's fish tank atmosphere of neon and darkness becomes clear. Crumbling curbs, cracked pavements, municipal projects halted midway through. Opportunists loiter. The homeless slump against walls. The Zona is corralled by both the international border and the river, and the people who haunt both margins linger among the populace.

We turned onto a sunny street that hosted a permanent rummage sale, crossed a wide, empty intersection, and stopped at a concrete-and-cinder-block cubby. There was no door. Inside was a pile of greasy bike parts. On the sidewalk, a guy with a hip haircut and ear piercings leaned back in a chair. An old man wrenched on a ten-speed a few feet away. This was the bike shop.

Watman happened to need a part for his mountain bike—the nut to a headset—and his query offered a mild opening to our investigation into illegal migration.

"No," said the clerk, "I don't think we have that part. We only have what you see here." He nodded at the pile inside the doorway. The structure was about six feet square. There was nothing on the block walls. The parts pile looked like an art installation. A cyclist rolled up and the old man hopped to greet him. The young clerk just leaned. There seemed to be nowhere to start but the beginning.

"My friend here is looking into the people who cross the border by bicycle," Watman said. "Do you know anything about it?"

"Oh, at *la línea*?" the clerk said. "I don't think they do that anymore."

He was talking about a short period of time when entrepreneurs had manipulated a loophole in Customs and Border Protection rules by renting kids' bikes to those who waited to enter the United States on foot. That line can take two to three hours, or more. But by parting with five bucks, pedestrians could saddle a bike, split the lanes into vehicle traffic, and coast right up to the customs booths meant for cars and motorcycles. After presenting their documents to the agent and passing through, the riders delivered the kids' bikes to couriers on the US side, who wheeled them back into Mexico. Per mile traveled, this might have been one of the most lucrative rental agreements going. The business boomed. It even generated a feature in San Diego's weekly—this is how annoying the inexplicable lines were. Eventually, however, CBP officials were able to close the loophole. But the far-traveled fun and fame of this bike rental business really muddied the waters for me. When I asked about crossing the border via bike, the most likely answer was, "Ah, yes, five dollars. Ha, ha, ha." Everyone enjoyed getting away with something.

Watman and I explained the other method of crossing by bicycle to the shop clerk: the dangerous, illegal kind. The bike shop operator looked nervous. He said, "No, I don't know anything." His storeful of worn parts couldn't suggest otherwise.

Watman mentioned another shop on the west side of town, in Playas de Tijuana. So we flagged a cab that had just deposited some gentlemen at a gentlemen's establishment, and we slipped out of the Zona Norte and onto the International Road. The cab climbed Russian Hill, descended into Smuggler's Gulch, traversed a ribbon between Spooner's Mesa and the neighborhood of Mirador, and then dipped again with Los Laureles—the whole roller coaster. But in truth, I was being shunted along by my own interior diversions, peak and trough; I rolled through our conversation with the shop clerk in the Zona Norte and the flawed thinking that had led me there. Following the parts seemed like a good idea, at first. But I should have anticipated the *Tijuanenses*' genius for keeping any sort of moving contraption alive; that this question of tracking replacement parts, and thus estimating the size and duration of the phenomenon, could not prove so simple. Manufactured parts were not necessarily replacing broken and missing parts. Brake levers are made of bent metal, right? A problem easily solved by an old man with a hammer and a thin piece of scrap. I'd seen it happen in transmission shops and front yards that served as tire stores. New parts were in the eye of the beholder, and happy was the man who engineered his own way down the road.

I decided to visit the next bike shop only to obey the inertia of this investigation. The cab then crested the last summit and tipped down toward the bullring and the shimmering Pacific—and the sight of the blue ocean washed everything I'd been thinking away.

13

The first rule of the gang: don't ask any questions.

What, when, why—each worker did a job, but only Indio understood how their positions meshed to drive the operation, the exact challenges they faced, and why they seemed to be getting away with the impossible. This compartmentalization, he told the crew, was a part of keeping the business secure. The secrecy seemed over the top to them, as they were all taking risks together. But as his lifelong friend, Solo knew Indio's methods to be part and parcel of his personality—only time seemed to uncover Indio's thinking. To needle him with questions was pointless. So when the curious white pickup passed to the west, to the east, and circled back—and Indio's demeanor divulged nothing—Solo remained silent. These border people were strange in ways that couldn't be explained by any clipped answer he might receive from his *patron*.

"Hey you, *cholo*!" the driver said, stepping out of the cab of the truck. He addressed El Indio squarely. He drew near, the ground crunching under his boots. "A minute of your time." The man opened his palms in a knowing way.

Indio nodded.

"I am looking for a *joven* called Pablito," he said. "You may have seen him—a nice, hardworking guy from Oaxaca. Wears huaraches. Just kind of starting out in the *pollero* business."

"*Hola*, Roberto," Indio said, the shadow of a smile at the corners of his mouth. "How are you?"

Solo stood to the side with the migrant couple, to whom he'd been talking. They looked ill at ease in the presence of the strangers.

"I am good today. Thank you for asking," Roberto replied, not overly engaged. "I was just out, you know, surveying the field. I've been hearing all over town about this new guy they are calling El Indio. I understand he's discovered some crackpot way of passing people over—something of a mystery. Then I remembered a friend who spends a lot of time in these *pinche* canyons. I once heard him called Indio, yet I thought it the mistake of an ignorant person."

"There's nothing to survey here, *amigo*. I'm only enjoying the view with some passersby."

Roberto looked about. He pointed. "Ah, and what is that over there? You're crossing *pollos* on bicycles?"

"No. People around here, I guess they like exercise." Indio shrugged. "Cycling is good for that."

"Rentals? I see you've brought Solovino," he said, pronouncing the whole of the nickname, which in Solo's case, no one ever did; but the integrity of Roberto's information was unsettling. "Well, I've also brought a trusted associate. She's got a keen eye for the truth. She will know what's happening here."

Roberto turned to the pickup and waved to the woman. When she stepped out, she was nearly as tall as Roberto, but slender. Her long dark hair hung almost to her waist. She wore a short skirt and wedge-heeled shoes. She looked too young to be with the older coyote but maybe his stature attracted such advantages.

As she approached, Roberto said, "Pablo, I would like to present my sister Marta. She is my right-hand man in this business."

Her face emitted an olive hue, with just a dusting of freckles over the bridge of her nose. She didn't wear makeup but her lashes were naturally long and her lips a warm, light mocha—a quality that made her teeth appear startlingly white. The woman offered the *pollero* a familiar, wry smile, but nothing more.

"*Hola*, it is an honor to meet you." He stepped forward with an open hand. "I've done some business with your brother and am honored to meet the sister of a valued friend."

Marta didn't take the hand. "You are El Indio," she said.

"That's what they call me here in Tijuana."

"And you're passing *pollos* on *bicicletas*."

Indio said nothing. A gust of sea wind tugged at Marta's hair. Roberto's gaze was fixed in the distance. The conversation seemed at a momentary impasse. Solo sensed the approach of dangerous information. He gathered the migrant couple and ushered them away from the road and up the canyon slope, lest they hear what was said and become afraid.

In their brief acquaintance Roberto had noted Indio's inclination toward two basic postures. He tended to squat—on a hillside, for example—his left forearm resting on his left knee while the right elbow was propped on the right knee, the hand braced under his jaw. This was the shape Pablo had taken when Roberto had first noticed the boy, the posture of the canyonlands observer—and the form Roberto had expected to find him in when he and Marta set out looking for him that morning. The other stance was as straight-backed as a telamon, with his left fist wedged at his hip. It was almost as if the one posture aided the Oaxacan's decision making while the other was the result of a confident choice having been made. And the latter was the stance of the man Roberto had nearly missed at the side of the International Road, the one who stood with an assistant and two *pollos* he apparently had no intention of selling to his old *jefe*.

"I take it as a compliment, *amigo*," Roberto said, filling the silence the young man had a habit of cultivating, even during negotiations.

He hadn't told Marta, but Roberto had met with the ten other *polleros viejos* of Tijuana. At issue was the rash of false coyotes and unprepared guides who led crossers to silent deaths in the eastern wildernesses. It was true what the authorities alleged: that, come trouble, the *pollos* paid the price as their custodians darted for cover. The older coyotes considered clients personal guests, not offal for the desert floor. You pass a father today, they believed, tomorrow you pass his son. Their business depended on trust, gained by delivery on the promise. Considering the situation in this light, the eleven rendered a harsh decision: a death sentence on freelancers who did not adhere to the ethos and drew unwanted attention to the trade. Under the guise of search-and-rescue volunteers, a squad of mercenaries had already been assembled in Tecate.

Then Roberto caught wind of this new *pollero*, El Indio, who was said to be using Roberto's same words and treating his clients with the same consideration. He wanted to support such behavior in newcomers, but given the council's recent decision, Roberto could not hitch his reputation to an unproven wanderer of the fence line.

He indicated the migrant couple who stood a ways off with Solo. "Have you offered them food and drink?" he asked.

"Yes."

"I am glad to see that some of the young still do."

Marta inquired, "Are you going to cross these *pollos* now, in daylight?"

"I have before, yes. But not right now—I'm training my guy."

"So the business is growing."

Watching Indio, Marta said, "Brother, you mentioned a desire to grill some *carne* today. And there were some things you wanted to discuss. Why not invite this *pollero*?"

Roberto was not exactly pleased with the suggestion. The location of his home was not a point to be traded among the bus station riffraff. But Marta did not do things just to do them, so he allowed the remark to pass. This recruiter would know better than to accept.

El Indio said nothing.

"If your associate is not going to cross these people right now," Marta pressed, "he might have time for lunch."

Roberto huffed.

She turned to Indio. "You will join us?"

"Yes," he said. "I would like that."

The *pollero*, who until this encounter had always appeared raggedy, in a thin windbreaker and worn sandals, jogged on new tennis shoes to confer with his assistant. Solo was dressed likewise, but waiting with the migrant couple, his deference to the boss was clear. Roberto was more than familiar with the postures of those awaiting orders.

The second rule was: follow instructions exactly. It was a commandment that Solo had no problems with. In the village, failure to follow instructions might mean losing a crop, going without food, or water. The third rule, however, was to keep your opinions to yourself. It was a good rule for the others, the *ganchos* and *guías*, but Solo had known El Indio since he was called Pablito, a boy who'd never seen a paved street or a two-story building. And with this sharp-eyed pair who'd arrived in the truck, he sensed an ambiguous yet protracted danger.

"Who are they?" Solo asked as Indio jogged up.

"That is the powerful coyote I told you about—and a sister of his. I've never seen her before."

"What do they want?"

"They want to take me to his house."

"Is that safe?"

"I don't know."

"They seem strange."

"I know."

Solo nodded toward the migrants. He raised his brows.

"*Señor y Señora*," Indio addressed them, "my assistant here will take you to a hotel where you'll be able to prepare yourself for the crossing tomorrow. Solo will make sure to meet all of your needs until that time. You've had a chance to see the layout, and if it is not to your satisfaction, or if you have any doubts about your abilities, we can pass you on to another *pollero*."

"No," said the man. "We want to do this."

"Do you know why I drive this old Ford, Indio?" Roberto asked. It was the first time he'd used the nickname, an offer of respect, now that the *pollero* had taken on employees and had allowed them to address their *jefe* in this way.

"Why do you drive this pickup?"

El Indio had followed Marta onto the truck's bench seat. Roberto stepped in on the driver's side. He tore onto the International Road. They turned around at the entrance to Playas de Tijuana, near the Comercial Mexicana, and sped back east toward downtown—each roadside shack a flashing pixel of color.

"As you know, I could buy any kind of vehicle," Roberto said, "but this is the best possible for several reasons. It is old, white, dirty, and dented. There is not a piece on its exterior that shines, not even the chrome. The tires are just good enough, but not any better. There are no fancy rims, no seat covers, no accessories. The radio is not worth turning on, much less stealing. This is the best truck in the world for me because here in Tijuana, *amigo*, it is invisible."

"*Sí?*" Indio asked.

"There are so many *pinche* pickup trucks in Tijuana that this one, even if you did see it, you wouldn't remember it. It blends into the dusty streets—forgotten the moment it crosses one's sight. I could park in front of your house and you would fail to describe it. And there is a lesson in that. There is no need to go to extremes in hiding oneself, when one can walk about visible to the world, but never perceived and never remembered."

"Don't listen to him, Pablito," Marta said. "It's his way to rant as he drives around."

"Why do you call him Pablito?" Roberto asked Marta. "He goes by Indio now."

"I don't want to call him what you call him," Marta said.

"Oaxacan, what do you prefer, Pablo or El Indio?" Roberto asked.

"I don't mind either." Indio shrugged. "The village was so small, I almost never heard my family name said out loud. Now, I can see that having a couple of names is good."

In even the poorest hamlet, a family name had value. A place where it didn't, well, Marta and Roberto weren't willing to consider it.

"The other thing I want to tell you about this pickup," Roberto said, "is that the outside is dirty but the engine is spotless. I will never push at the gas pedal and not feel the horses." Already traveling about fifty, Roberto hit the gas and they felt the untapped power. "And the windshield's clean. Always clean. If your tactic is invisibility, you need to be alert. You need to be quick and you need to see everything."

They crowned the top of the road that spilled into downtown, which sat like a pool of dusty mercury between mountains and hills. Roberto switched lanes, braked hard, and pulled into the parking lot of a liquor store. The buildings here were brightly painted, some with murals. On the wall across from them were the words VIVA GIGANTE.

"What do you say we celebrate with some cold ones?" Roberto asked.

"Celebrate what?" Indio said.

"The fact that you are crossing people yourself now. You've graduated."

Roberto drew a wad of money from his pocket.

"Allow me," Indio said. In the close proximity of the truck's cab, he turned to Marta. Roberto had been watching their alternated glances in the rearview mirror. Now they were face to face.

In an elevated diction, Indio asked, "What kind of beer would you like, ma'am? Tecate?"

Roberto didn't like this. "I want Corona," he interceded, waving the bills.

Marta shrugged; it wasn't her fight. Indio cracked the door, stepped out of the truck, and walked into the shop.

"What's going on, Marta?" Roberto said.

"With what?"

"The invitation."

To him it had come out of the blue.

"You need more skilled workers," Marta reasoned, "and he's obviously sharp." After a moment she added, "And I like him, he's nice."

Roberto had introduced Marta to many associates her age, some good-looking and some well off. Others had come by the house. But she hadn't shown any interest and she hadn't really dated since coming to Tijuana. Maybe it just wasn't yet a part of her mind-set, he'd thought. Now, for the first time, Roberto allowed himself to wonder if this was the kind of guy who interested her—a *cholo* in baggy clothes.

"This guy? The mute?"

"He's contemplative."

"He's a *pollero*."

"No, he's a coyote now, like you. Besides, you said that you liked him too."

"I liked him as a recruiter. Now I don't know."

Martha tsked. "He's good. You saw how he was with his people."

"That's my teaching . . ."

"Quiet. Here he comes now. That's your beer he's carrying—he wanted Tecate."

Roberto turned the key and opened a set of wood doors. As they cracked open, Marta, Indio, and Roberto were promptly met by Roberto's two young sons—one just slightly taller than the other. Each had his father's lean face, but with toothy smiles. The boys were followed by Roberto's wife. She was handsome with a bright and hardy disposition that was immediately perceptible. She cradled their baby daughter in a swaddle of blankets, which she lifted to her husband. Roberto took his daughter into his arms, and his wife turned to Indio.

"Welcome," she said, smiling, and then, when Roberto failed to make introductions, added, with a wagging finger, "These two have no manners. I am Mercedes, Roberto's wife. Everyone calls me Chedas."

"*Mucho gusto*," he said. "My name is Pablo."

"Yes, I've heard about you, Pablo. Please come in."

"It's not a question of manners," Roberto muttered upon entering. "Guests are here such a short time."

Chedas frowned. The older children were used to meeting strangers, and greeted them with just mild curiosity. For the Oaxacan, however, the house must have been something of a wonder. From the outside it looked like a regular, if not more substantial, suburban home. But to the right of the entry stretched a dim hallway with a surprising number of closed bedroom doors. It drew no comparison with his family's one-room shack, or the solitary space he inhabited in the Zona Norte.

Roberto divined Indio's curiosity. "This first bedroom is mine and my wife's," he said. "It's not the biggest, but I find it easier to be close to the front door. The nearby rooms belong to the children and the family. The others are for the clients."

"How many rooms are there?" asked Indio.

"Would you believe that we started with three? But now I am ashamed to say. It seems obsessive."

"I couldn't tell from the outside."

"No? That's good," Roberto said. He gestured toward the light-filled hallway to the left of the entry. Chedas and the children passed through. Marta was no longer with them. Indio followed his host as the house opened into a living room to the right and, to the left, a kitchen that stepped down onto a backyard. An older woman was busy at the sink, and next to this was a squat, clay bread oven.

Roberto touched the arm of the woman at the sink and introduced her—loud enough for Chedas to hear the formality of his speech—as his mother, Lupita. She offered a nod in the reserved country way.

A large portrait mounted on a kitchen wall dominated the room. Set in a gilded frame, the photograph presented Marta sitting straight-backed with her hands in her lap. She wore a traditional white blouse that parted at the neckline, revealing defined and sleek collarbones divided by a smooth jugular notch. The slight swell of her bust was covered in pleated cotton and embroidery. Her bare arms were sinewy and strong. As a child, she had known the out-of-doors—a condition also responsible, possibly, for the tiniest of freckles across her nose. But it was her eyes, looming equally dark and bright like a variety of minor gem, and the thick and ropey braid of her hair draped over her right shoulder—a deep brown epaulet—that distinguished her status as ranchero royalty. If the portrait had been staged by the baby of the family to please her parents and bolster the family's claim to a dignified, pastoral heritage, the effect had been realized.

From the kitchen door, Roberto and Indio could see the lady from the portrait, now seated with an old man at a picnic table under the shade of a stately ficus tree. As they stepped out into the yard, Marta watched. The man had been reading aloud from a newspaper but as Indio approached, Marta tapped the man's arm. He looked up.

"Father," she said, "I would like you to meet an associate of Roberto's. His name is Pablo."

"It is a pleasure to meet you, sir," Indio said.

"Oh, and you as well, son," he said, setting the paper aside.

"Father, why don't you show Pablo your garden? I'm going to help Mother." Marta turned to Indio. "He's very proud of his piece of Sinaloa."

"You can see everything there is from here."

Marta stood. "Well, tell him what you have growing," she said, walking off to the kitchen.

"You have potatoes," Roberto offered with a wave.

"I have broccoli, carrots, cabbage, radish. Different things, depending. Right now there is some lettuce and cilantro. Soon I'll plant corn."

Roberto's cell phone rang. Excusing himself, he rose, and stepped off to a corner of the yard to take the call. California's Central Valley harvest was coming on, and it was a busy time.

Marta and Lupita were visible at work in the kitchen, and Roberto stood close enough to the men to catch a phrase here and there. The patriarch was a fantastic storyteller, a natural gift the man had possessed long before he could read. Roberto knew this because his father had taught himself to read and write from his own children's primary books, even as he aided them in their schoolwork. When Roberto observed the old man with the newspaper, it was not a terrible leap to wonder how much of it he was reading, and how much he interpreted from clues on the page. But Roberto knew well the story now entertaining El Indio—a parable that varied only in its purpose. When Roberto was young, things were quite difficult. But with a keen mind and a string of fortunate years, his father doubled and tripled the size of the ranch and the family prospered. By the time Marta grew into a lithesome girl, what was required of her wasn't work so much as chores. One Saturday Marta petitioned her father to let her attend a party. He agreed on one condition. At sundown, the livestock returned to the pens to feed. All that was required to keep them in for the night was to shut the livestock gate. Marta's father asked her to return early from the party and close the gate. She promised. But on waking the next morning, the family discovered the gate open, Marta asleep, and their animals feeding on a neighbor's corn. Later, the neighbor sent an invoice for the damaged crops.

Only a raconteur could weave a comic tale from such a thread. Yet with the slightest nuance, the father's intent varied: sometimes to depict himself as a man who could afford to treat his animals to the neighbor's corn, but often to paint Marta as decorative and feckless. Maybe, in this instance, the tale was meant to warn Indio of her nature.

Lupita soon stepped out with a plate of *cueritos* snacks, salsa, chili pepper, and limes. Marta returned with four open beer bottles and joined the men at the picnic table. She caught the gist of the conversation and immediately contested her father's rendition. Indio questioned the father on aspects of the story Marta disputed. In his body language and talkativeness, Roberto saw Indio changed. He wondered if this was what happened when one plied a wanderer of the fence line with food and drink.

Roberto's call went long. But he soon found himself remembering an incident that had occurred not long after the episode with the livestock gate. From a distance Roberto happened to observe Marta saddle a pony. Her head didn't reach the animal's withers. But the girl pulled herself to a mount, anyway—then she galloped, and horse and rider jumped the very gate she'd failed to close a week earlier. And two things struck him: one, that Marta had developed such a skill at all, and two, that she seemed to harbor no concern for a boundary of any kind. Was she forgetful, or defiant?

After Marta came to Tijuana to live, she expressed a desire to accompany Roberto on his rounds. He said no. She refused to accept this answer and pointed out that his trade accommodated women, and had even made a few infamous. He wouldn't budge. Over a number of weeks, Marta nagged and cajoled and finally, becoming angry, she demanded to know why he would not allow her into his confidence.

Roberto said, "Because I can't trust you to close the gate."

The reference stung.

It didn't, however, curb Marta's desire. She made herself useful by hosting and managing the clients who stayed at the house. On one such occasion, when Roberto was out making preparations for a crossing, an important *mayordomo* and his workers began to drink heavily on the patio. They became rowdy and then disrespectful. Marta knew that the *mayordomo*, as the informal boss of migrant workers on a large-scale farm, held a lot more leverage than an average migrant. But she put her foot down anyway. She said, "Men, you need your wits about you. No more drinking or you won't be crossing tonight."

The *campesinos* laughed off the threat and turned their bottles up—sending out for more alcohol. When it was clear that they weren't going to stop, Marta walked into the house, entered the guest quarters, and, on her own accord, hefted all of the farm workers' things out to the curb. Then she called for two taxis. When they arrived she asked the drivers to load the bags and instructed them to drive this group to the river—one way only. She re-entered the house, stepped out to the patio, and finding the men flat drunk, she informed them that their ride to the border was already waiting outside, and that they needed to hurry. The men filed out and jumped into the cabs, which lurched through lamplight, past street dogs, and into the dusky night.

Roberto, who returned prepared to load up his clients and move out, discovered a house empty save the family. "Where are my *pollos*?" Roberto asked. Forthright and with a clear conscience, Marta described what had happened, and added that his clients could be found down by the river, should he choose to look for them.

Roberto enjoyed the little episode; it showed decisiveness and pluck, elements he could use on the job.

"Mother," Marta hollered toward the kitchen, "some music?" A minute passed. Then the low piping of La Sonora Dinamita rose from the house. The father huffed.

"She always plays Roberto's favorite," Marta complained openly, even as her brother rejoined the group. "I prefer mariachis. They're perfect for every occasion—parties, weddings. Even a funeral. When I die, I want mariachis. Not in black either—I want them dressed all in red."

"I would like one single horn player," said the father. "And I want him to play 'Una Flor para Ti.'"

This time, it was Roberto who huffed.

"What would you like played at your funeral, Pablo?" Marta asked.

"Well, mariachis seem good. But I would want them to play a special *corrido* about an average guy who leaves his village without any idea where he will end up. He is simply collaborating with chance. He sees jungle. He sees mountains. And he arrives in a strange city where, by some piece of magic, he meets very special people who take him away in an invisible pickup truck and he finds himself at a fiesta eating *cueritos* and drinking beer and making up bullshit songs to be played at his funeral."

The group laughed.

"I change my mind," said the father, slapping the picnic table. "I want that same song played at my funeral, because, really, it's about me. I left my tiny village in Sinaloa, you know, a place I'd never left before, and I ended up in this strange city, eating these snacks, too."

"Father," Roberto said, "you were a fifty-year-old man, and I drove you myself, and I told you where you and Mother were going—to a house I prepared for you."

"The story is the same," he said.

Setting a tray of uncooked meat on the table, Lupita asked Roberto about the grill. "Oh, yes, of course," he said. "Indio, help me set this thing up." They retrieved a charcoal grill from around the corner of the house and pulled it close to the table. Roberto grabbed a bag of briquettes. Indio lifted the lid and removed the grate.

"So, how many *pollos* are you crossing?" Roberto asked him.

"A few here and there."

"I hear you crossed eight one night."

"Yes, we crossed eight."

"If you crossed eight, you can cross sixteen. What's the holdup?"

"Bicycles, man, they're hard to come by in the city."

"Marta could help you with that. She's very resourceful."

"Roberto," his mother called from the kitchen. "There is somebody here to see you."

Roberto stepped out of the backyard. He was gone awhile, and he returned to see his wife and sons at the table, as well. It was normal for the family to want to gather, and he hated for the unpredictable nature of his work to affect it, but this business couldn't wait. "I have some things to take care of," he announced. "Get the grill going. If I'm not back soon, save me a plate."

The group said their good-byes. And Indio manned the barbecue.

Roberto was absent for longer than he would have liked. And he returned to a house that was full of music and light. In the kitchen he stumbled upon Indio. Laughter erupted from the patio.

"What are you doing?" Roberto asked.

"*Amigo*, just helping out a little," Indio said.

"Listen, I've been wanting to talk to you. I have more business than I can handle; it takes me away from the family. You've proven that you are more than an average *pollero*. I need someone like you in my organization. What do you say?"

"*Gracias* for the compliment." Indio touched his chest.

"So what's your answer?"

Indio took a breath. "You know better than I that there are no friends in this business. I would rather remain good friends, because, well, who knows?"

Roberto scanned Indio's eyes. They appeared a bit glazed. Maybe he was simple, the Oaxacan, and Roberto had misread him. Roberto could only assume that Indio meant no disregard. It was a matter for another time.

"I respect the way you conduct your business," he said. "We'll keep our friendship."

"Thank you, Roberto."

"Now let's finish that beer."

Roberto stepped out of the kitchen and Indio followed. The group was still chatting and laughing. The kids ran about. Tiny white Christmas lights filled the ficus like sparks. Paper streamers radiated from the tree to the house.

"There he is," said Marta, beaming at her brother.

"What's this?" asked Roberto. "So lively." He could see that he'd missed a special little party. Then Indio rounded the table and sat with Marta, their sides touching and their arms dipping below the table in a way that suggested the holding of hands. Roberto sat slowly—he'd missed something indeed. He looked at Chedas, who smiled, and then to his father, who merely shrugged and raised his brows in bemusement.

Roberto hoisted his beer and reached across to Indio. "Well, bottoms up, brother."

Later, Roberto admitted, "That moment actually affected me quite a bit. My sister and I had been inseparable partners. But I held my feelings in. I saw a beautiful little twinkle in her eyes, an expression I had never seen before. In the coming days, as well, Marta became a different woman. She laughed and sang and made jokes with the whole family. The more time that passed, the happier she looked."

14

The broad streets of Playas were sunbaked, the atmosphere made granular by the mist and salt-laden air. The grainy, flickering light projected onto the dirty cab window gave one the impression of a sixteen-millimeter film—of homes painted in pastels, yards gated and walled, everything passing in a Mediterranean kind of slumber. The more opulent the neighborhood in Tijuana, I noted, the fewer the people outside. Dogs idled in the road; brown pelicans looked like miniature posted sentries. It was the mirage of a California beach town in the 1970s. The cab pulled around a gentle curve in the road and up to a glass-fronted shop. I could see the bikes inside. We stopped. A trace scent of rotting kelp marked us about three blocks from the ocean.

The glass door chimed, too loud for the size of the shop, and the ringing added to a buzzy claustrophobia I felt stepping in—bikes were wedged into every inch of floor space and hovered in racks above. The customer was left a shin-wide runway to a small cul-de-sac in which to stand. Light leaked between bike frames in the window, recalling a view from inside a jungle gym. A hard silence settled. The smell of the sea was replaced by the vapors of rubber and lubricant. Watman and I, only just acquaintances, fidgeted in our awkward proximity to each other. Muttering, Watman decided that maybe what he wanted was not a replacement part for his beater but a new bike, and he started to look around by moving frames aside, peering at a certain model and then moving more frames.

"*O-la*," I said, hoping to conjure a shop person. "*Hola*."

A man stood up from behind the glass counter four feet away. I realized he'd been bent down there working on a repair. Light-skinned, with a kind of sickly pallor, he wore his brown hair slicked back. His green eyes seemed surprised—leery, maybe, of obvious outsiders. "Can I help you?" he asked.

"My friend is looking for a mountain bike," I said. I had meant to say "used" but they were all used. The clerk looked over at Watman and indicated options, each difficult to get to. Metal clanked.

"I see you're doing repairs. Do you sell spare parts?" My Spanish had the quality of being both formal and limited—like a parrot's.

"Yes." He shrugged and pointed out another mountain bike in a corner.

"To groups, or individuals?" I asked.

"Just to the people who come in," he said.

Standing there among the bikes felt like standing and talking to strangers from a waist-deep pool without the cocktail to lend a purpose. Watman paused in his search. He emitted this "Eah-mm" sound that Tijuana intellectuals use to begin a sentence and said, "We're looking for stories of migrants who cross the border on bicycles."

Watman could be blunt. At times, his manner suggested that a decision had been made: conversational niceties were inefficient, and so they were out. But this bike mechanic was a source we were trying to develop, one who may have abetted criminals. And sensing the motive of our visit prematurely exposed, I saw no choice but to hazard the next obvious question.

"We thought maybe you sold parts to migrants on bicycles," I said.

Something illuminated the man's green eyes. It was as if he recognized a person, or something, behind us. I followed the gaze but caught only the door.

"I don't know anything about it," he said. His lip raised to reveal stubby front teeth—a smile.

"There were many people crossing on bikes," I said. "Right there at the border. And this is the closest bicycle shop. Some of the migrants needed help with their bikes because they were not new bikes."

"And you look like a good mechanic," Watman said, pointing to his repair job.

"I don't know anything about people crossing. But if I did . . ." He paused, and looked up. "I just don't know anything."

He shook his head. There was a silence. He gave the smile again.

And I took this as an outright admission. "You know something," I said in English.

"Sorry," he replied. He spoke English, and he knew something. "There are a lot of stories around here," he added.

We stepped out of the shop and into the airy, sunny, empty street and I experienced a dopamine spike as if I'd latched onto a prize sailfish with my naked arms. But then the fish gave me the slip. I could see it out there, jumping and bucking in the great blue. They say addicted gamblers get a bigger jolt from the "almost win," the four-out-of-five cherries dropping on the slots and the fifth just tipping, but no dice, which is a loss, but as highs go, way better than winning, which is run-of-the-mill. You win, so what? There's nothing left to hope for. But a near loss, now that has possibilities.

The shop mechanic's weak smile and disingenuous denial came as the only admission I'd found to date that the bikes emerged from Mexico at all—that they hadn't just dropped out of the sky onto the Kimzey Ranch. Even as he denied knowledge of or involvement with the bicycle migrants, I knew he knew.

"He knew," I said to Watman. "He knew something."

"Yeah, it sure looked like he did."

It wasn't until we'd walked a couple of blocks into the streets of Playas that I realized all I had now was a feeling—and when that waned, I had nothing.

Watman wanted to visit a man he called El Negro—the Black—whom he knew from his work at the border. The Playas bicycle shop was only about a quarter of a mile south of the border fence, the border monument, and Friendship Park. As part of his efforts to save the park and revitalize interest in the monument, Watman was in the process of establishing a native species garden on either side of the fence. It was meant to be "binational." To accomplish this, he traveled between the two countries and worked either side of the iron pylons on alternating Sundays. This was a delicate feat, because even to pass a seed across to the other side would have antagonized the Border Patrol agents who sat nearby in jeeps—and these officials had the ability to terminate Watman's access to the park without explanation.

As potent a symbol as it was, the garden was a humble little plot. Perimeters of cobblestone framed juvenile Shaw's agave, wild sage, and bright orange California poppies. The agave was the same dark green species that border commissioner Bartlett illustrated when he visited the marble obelisk in 1852. If the transplants took, it might be the first instance in fifty years that the native bloomed on the mesa. But this coastal desert is deceptively brutal; the young plants needed help. When Watman wasn't available to water them, he relied on a friend who worked at the municipal bathrooms. This was El Negro, a deportee who, I gathered, held a lot of cachet for a guy who traded folds of toilet paper for five pesos each.

When we arrived, there were actually two people outside the bathrooms, the man and a round-faced woman. Both looked to be in their fifties. They sat in white plastic chairs on either end of a small table set with candies, single cigarettes, and other knickknacks for sale. In their laps they held small handmade looms. The man was busy knitting a long white scarf while the woman put the finishing touches on a black, red, green, and gold beanie—Rasta colors. She looked up from the hat as we approached and kicked the man under the table. He lifted his head.

"Daniel, where have you been?" the man said. "I watered the garden on Tuesday but I didn't hear from you."

"Ah, I know, *amigo*," Watman said. "I got caught up with moving again. *Como estas? Bien?*" Watman turned and gestured toward me. "This is a friend of mine."

"Negro," the man said, leaning over the loom, a board with nails on it, and offering a weak handshake.

"*Mucho gusto*," I replied. The woman buried her head in her work, noticeably uninterested. I didn't say anything more. But Watman picked up with their plans for the garden, and Negro listened while knitting the scarf. It was easy to assume he'd been nicknamed for his mole-colored complexion. His skin was both dark and bright and contrasted with his angular, Caucasian-looking features. His beard of a few days grew thick with ample white. His dress pants and shoes I took to be overly formal until I noticed their wear.

Though it was sunny, the wind turned cold. On the plank boardwalk, a vendor pushed a display of pink, purple, and blue cotton candy in a wheelbarrow. I didn't see any customers on the beach. In the past I'd known Playas de Tijuana as the setting of summery beach days—sizzling taco carts, cold beer, frozen mangos, and flip-flop tans. The winter months muted that color and emptied the sand-blown streets. In the vacancy I caught the impression of a shuttered amusement park.

Watman asked El Negro, "Hey, do you know anything about migrants crossing the border on bicycles?"

"Oh yeah man, that is some funny shit," he said. "The bikes right there by the Comercial. It's really something because the *polleros* wait and watch for *la migra* to pass by and then, boom, they would just go, man. Vroom, straight there."

"How much do the bikes cost?" Watman asked, as if he were thinking of going over and picking one up for himself.

"It doesn't matter how much is the bike. The bike is not for sale. The coyote give it to you for crossing."

A thin, older man with a bowl cut ambled up. "*Que onda*," the man greeted El Negro.

"*Que onda*," Negro responded absently.

The bowl cut sat down against the wall beside the bathroom worker, but didn't greet anyone else, simply looked around as if this were his break-time sitting spot.

"I remember this time," Negro said, "I was down there at the fence where those guys did that work. The Border Patrol, he drives up to the fence and he says—because you know, sometimes we're just talking shit with the Border Patrol, there's no one else around to talk to—and he says, 'Hey man, don't you guys have recycling places over there in Mexico?' I says, 'Yeah, why do you ask this question?' The *migra* guy points at all of the bikes they had there. He says, 'Well, why do you Mexicans just dump this good scrap metal here next to the fence?' Man, I'm telling you, that Border Patrol didn't even know what the coyotes was doing, man."

He addressed the bowl cut. "*Oye*, Juan. You remember that bicycle-crossing shit, right?"

"Yeah," said Juan. "El Indio."

"El Indio," Negro said. "That guy is famous around here. It's a good business, that shit."

"So the bicycle crossing was organized by one person?" I asked.

"Organized? That shit is professional."

"Well, my friend here," Watman said, indicating me with a thumb, "is writing about the bicycles."

On hearing this, the bowl cut pushed himself up and slipped away. The woman looked like she wanted to roll up into a ball and hide under the beanie she was knitting. El Negro sat back in his seat, turning cold. He shot a look at Watman.

Sensing the moment evaporating, I asked, "Is this 'El Indio' around? Can I talk to him?"

"You are never going to find that person," Negro said, dropping the nickname entirely. "That person is probably in jail. We won't see him again."

15

It seems odd that a story about a gift—the possibility of a new life in a new and prosperous country—begins with a thief, but in some ways this one does. One of the first suppliers was a bicycle thief named El Maneta—the Handle. He believed that vehicles were, possibly, the perfect objects to steal because they were simultaneously the desired item and the means by which to whisk it away. In the latter attribute, bicycles were both nimble and silent. El Maneta liked bikes and enjoyed his work. He stole and stole until there was nothing left to steal and then he sold the machines cheap because they were hot—which is a win if, and only if, like the Handle, you value your time at nothing.

But then there was a kid named Angel who, like a species of condor or cougar, roamed at will through the entire border region. He'd crossed the boundary before he could comprehend what such a designation meant, and he'd gained permanent residency in childhood through no action of his own. Now, however, he frequently crossed the line on weekends to visit his girlfriend in Tijuana. His roots spread north too. He had a cousin who worked for the Los Angeles Police Department. And in the summer of 2006, El Indio smuggled another of his cousins into California mounted high in the saddle of a bicycle. The instant this cousin from the south arrived at Angel's home and spilled his dangerous little story of crossing, Angel's entrepreneurial spirit sparked on the tale's straightforward surface like a phosphorous match in gasoline.

Angel liked bikes a lot, always had. And because his cousin in the LAPD had turned him on to the Southland police auctions—during which departments unloaded merchandise taken into custody for any number of reasons—Angel knew where to get a lot of bikes cheap.

According to the Mexican cousin, this bike coyote's services were in big demand, but in Tijuana at that moment, so were bicycles. For reasons unknown to the migrant, two-wheelers had all but vanished from the streets of Tijuana. The cousin did sense, however, that the high price of his crossing, $4,500, had something to do with the disparity. And, he added, he hadn't even gotten to keep the expensive machine he'd crossed on. He'd had to leave it—a pretty horse set to run wild. In this scenario, Angel saw a perfect little triangle of low risk, solid profit, and supreme pleasure.

He could buy large batches of bicycles in what were called "lots" at auction for peanuts, then ferry them across in his van to be traded to this coyote for some real money. He and his firecracker girlfriend would then take that money down to TJ's nightclubs, and trade it all in on a goddamned good time.

"So on my next trip I went looking for this El Indio," Angel said. "I just dropped the nickname. At that time, he was not a hard dude to find. We started to talk, I mentioned a cheap price. We came to an agreement, and I started to bring him bicycles every weekend."

Angel thought that what he was selling to the operation was bikes, but what he really delivered was a method.

Indio's brother Martín also had a friend in the United States who'd acquired residency. But this was no real financial boon to the friend, as he'd been laid off from a series of low-wage jobs and living expenses were high. What really stressed Jimmy out, however, was the fact that his mother, in Mexico, was battling cancer, and the radiation treatments she required were expensive. The truth was, if Jimmy couldn't pay, his mother wouldn't receive treatment. Working odd jobs, Jimmy was squeaking by, but his financial situation, he believed, was killing his mother. Jimmy confided the intense stress he felt to his close friend Martín.

Martín confessed something to Jimmy as well. "My youngest brother works in the business of crossing people over from Tijuana." He added, "I also help out with some driving sometimes. The money is good, and my brother really needs people on this side—especially if you have a driver's license."

"No," Jimmy said. "No way. Absolutely not. I had to jump through a lot of hoops to get my papers, man, and I don't want to lose them."

"I understand, *amigo*. The people at home aren't too happy about my decisions either. But everything has a price."

Jimmy was certain that he wasn't going to work for Martín's coyote brother. He still believed there was a chance to make a decent living in the United States. Should he be deported for trafficking migrants, he knew he'd be hustling just to make Tijuana's minimum wage: fifteen dollars per day.

About a week later, Jimmy received a call from his sister, who was helping to care for his mother in Veracruz. She told him that their mother wasn't doing well, that she wasn't receiving the radiation treatments because of the family's inability to pay for them. "They're not even going to keep her in the hospital," the sister said. "They're going to leave her out on the steps if we can't pay the balance we owe."

Jimmy's appetite withered to nothing. He couldn't sleep. He paced. He ransacked his mind for a way to help his mother with the treatments and the bills. Finally he went to see Martín.

"I guess we got no other choice than to get you working," Martín said, and he withdrew his cell phone to dial Indio. The brothers discussed the open position and Jimmy's qualifications. Martín said, "Yes, he's a really good friend," and he summarized Jimmy's predicament. Then he handed the cell over.

"Hello," Jimmy said.

The voice said, "Come down to Tijuana right now."

"The thing is, I would like to do that. I want to start working with you right away. But I have an immediate expense that I need to find a way to take care of before I go anywhere. I can't get stuck in Mexico without making sure I got this bill paid."

"How much is it?" Indio asked.

"Fifteen hundred dollars," Jimmy admitted.

"Give me a name and address for the wire transfer."

"Excuse me?" Jimmy asked.

"Your sister will receive the money today. You start now. I'll be waiting."

Before hanging up, Jimmy received an address in Tijuana, a city he didn't know. He put a few things together, drove south, and crossed the border. Asking locals for directions, he found the area and then the seedy row of shacks where Indio "was waiting in a closed room."

"I knocked. El Indio came out. I introduced myself," Jimmy said, "and that is how we met."

That was the interview.

Indio directed Jimmy to an address on Olympic Boulevard in Los Angeles. In an industrial area there, he met a Mexican and a *gavacho*, or foreigner. They were waiting with an eight-ton cab-over truck. It was something like an enlarged U-Haul—and it was already packed to the brim with bicycles. The men handed Jimmy a sheaf of paperwork—a manifest, proofs of purchase, and documentation that designated these bicycles as donations to Mexican charities. This allowed for an expedited importation process and a duty waiver. The men also instructed Jimmy to drive the truck to a weigh station, where he'd receive another stamped form. He followed their directions; then he pointed the truck south.

"El Indio told me that there would be a Mexican customs agent waiting for me at the border inspection, and that this man knew everything. He would make sure that there weren't any problems," Jimmy said. "Of course, I was nervous. I didn't really know what was going to happen, or if what I was told was true or not."

The end of the I-5 freeway at the border funnels the traffic into tight lanes divided by concrete medians. Once in, there was nowhere to go but forward. Any number of cameras captured the entrants. It felt like running a gauntlet. Jimmy understood what it meant to cross that line—he would be subject to the Mexican judicial system, and he'd be deemed guilty before he ever glimpsed the flashing blue lights in the rearview. But before he knew it, Jimmy heard the click-clack of tire grates as he drove over the boundary. A Mexican official immediately waved him over to an inspection area where another armed agent directed him to park in a stall. He waited there, and watched as a panel van loaded with mattresses was rifled through. Drivers paced uneasily outside their vehicles. Eyes darted in the presence of agents. The officials began to pull each of the mattresses out of the van, turn them over, and tear the fabric. An agent of obvious rank appeared at Jimmy's driver-side window.

"Documents," the man said.

Jimmy handed the sheaf of papers to the agent.

"Please step out and open the rear door."

He did as he was told and rolled the aluminum slider up. The men beheld a nest of wheels, spokes, cables, reflectors, and frames.

"Okay," the agent said slowly. "Everything seems in order. Are you nervous? You look nervous."

"No, I'm not nervous," Jimmy said. "I'm just trying to donate some bicycles."

"That's a lot of bicycles to donate."

"We have big hearts for the children of Mexico."

"Big hearts? Ha! I'm just messing with you, Jimmy." Then the agent pointed toward the exit. "Those police cars over there are waiting for you."

"I don't understand," Jimmy said.

"Those are your policemen."

"Mine?"

"Look, get in the truck and pass out of the inspection area. Those policemen are here to provide security and escort you to your destination. It's the only way possible."

Jimmy felt he had no choice. He stepped into the truck, sparked the engine, backed out, and crept toward the exit. He didn't slow but looked over as he came to the police cars. An officer made sharp and direct eye contact. And as he passed, their vehicles pulled into line behind him. One flashed its lights, sped forward in an adjacent lane, and then merged in front. Jimmy followed this vehicle along the International Road as it paralleled the rusty fence, and then up an incline where they took a turnoff to Russian Hill and the neighborhood of El Soler. The lead car drew the caravan through a middle-class neighborhood and stopped before an unassuming single-story ranch house. There were no neighbors in the streets or in the yards. Only the last shuffles of hastily closed curtains signaled anything other than a vacant suburban street. The front door of the destination house opened, and the *cholo* from the ramshackle room in the Zona Norte walked out.

Jimmy learned that he was not the first to make a trip, that he was a replacement for a driver who'd broken his foot playing soccer. So he felt fortunate to be doing the work. He was paid $1,000 a week, which allowed him to keep up with his mother's treatments. And because he made only about two trips a month, he had a lot of downtime. But soon Jimmy was directed to destinations farther and farther afield: Phoenix, Albuquerque, Denver, El Paso, San Antonio, and Houston.

"Whenever I'd arrive, there would be two or three people waiting for me with the truck already loaded. I'd be given the paperwork, and we'd look it over. My job was to drive."

It wasn't until 2007, when Jimmy was assigned to pick up an empty truck in San Diego and drive it to some isolated stretch of highway in the Mojave Desert, that he learned he wasn't alone. At a solitary turnoff boasting an all-night 76 station, Jimmy met a second driver whose truck full of bicycles had broken down. They shook hands and began transferring the load. They joked about how nice it was to be able to roll the product rather than carry it and they marveled at some of the bikes among the mess of them. On the road, underneath the black desert sky, this driver mentioned to Jimmy that there were others, like El Junior and Yony. They'd talk sometimes, on meeting like this, but not much: How was the last trip? Oh I got a flat at such and such. Broke down in Gila Bend. And Jimmy's mind gathered a picture of quiet, unnoticed ghost trucks traversing the great western night, as smooth and silky as drips from a leaky faucet, draining America's bicycles south.

16

The scene is grainy, black-and-white. The crumbling tenements, piazzas, and arches of postwar Rome form the backdrop. A sudden downpour blankets the Porta Portese market as Antonio Ricci and his young son Bruno reach the square. The boy pulls a woolen jacket over his head. Water streams from the brim of Ricci's hat. Wheeled carts laden with bicycle tires and frames for sale are packed and rolling away with vendors. Bent over handlebars, casual shoppers begin to cycle away, too—the whole market a school of fish darting for cover. Ricci's head pivots right then left; he is seemingly the only man with two feet on solid ground. His attempt to examine each of the fleeing bicycles signals his misfortune. The Fides single-speed on which his young family depends has been stolen. There is no money for a replacement. There is no job, no rent money, without the Fides. A fortune-teller advises Ricci, "You'll find the bike quickly, or not at all." Everyone in Rome knows exactly where stolen bikes end up—in parts at the market. But on Ricci's arrival, bicycles scatter like possibility in the wake of his own personal torrent.

Since its release in 1949, *The Bicycle Thief* has commanded a top-ten position on any serious list of cinema greats. Director Vittorio

De Sica chose nonactors for the leading roles. The man who played Ricci was a factory worker named Lamberto Maggiorani. The son Bruno was played by Enzo Staiola, a little man-like child the director found selling flowers on the street. There is one incidental scene in which Bruno, trying to cross the road on foot, is nearly run over by cars, twice. This was a real clip of Staiola caught by an astute cameraman. These players weren't acting. At poignant moments Maggiorani levels a gaze of utter exposure, evoking a silent survivor of Europe's grinding postwar recession. It feels real because it is. Maggiorani struggled to find work long after the filming wrapped.

Watching the film again in the 2010s, it seemed a little too familiar—the universals of hope and personal isolation in economic conditions wrought by a mad, wheeling world too big to understand. I pressed pause frequently. I stood. I paced. I saw myself in Ricci. And I returned to the narrative of *The Bicycle Thief* specifically, and only, because right there on its surface was another universal experience, one repeated every two and a half minutes in America alone: missing bicycles.

In England's Selby train station, a man wearing a high-visibility vest like those of other rail staff stepped up to a crowded rack of bikes. He disabled the lock on one, threw a leg over its saddle, and casually pedaled off. Neither the man nor his actions were noticed until police reviewed their security footage. The man in the fluorescent orange vest with bold reflective stripes happened to be the British Transport Police's most-wanted suspect in bicycle thefts across Northern England.

In July of 2012, looking to stanch a rise in cycle thefts, San Francisco police took the extra-normal step of responding to suspicious online ads. They followed leads through layers of informal sales—which eventually brought them knocking on the door of eighteen-year-old Irving Morales-Sanchez. "Officers said they found eight bikes in his kitchen," reported the *San Francisco Chronicle*. "A search of two storage lockers he was renting in Oakland turned up 106 more bicycles, 80 tires, and a frame." Morales-Sanchez's public defender claimed it was the family business—the restoring and reselling of bikes, that is. Family members said they didn't know the bikes were hot. Reporters following the case seemed to enjoy pointing out that San Francisco bike thefts dropped precipitously after Morales-Sanchez's arrest.

In 2006, a North Vancouver man established Bike Rescue, a not-for-profit organization with a mission "to locate and return lost or stolen bicycles." Founder Gordon Blackwell purchased bikes in shady parts of town at rock-bottom prices. If no legitimate owner claimed the bikes in thirty days, he sold them at near market value "to fund the operation." In 2009, Canadian Mounties raided the Bike Rescue facilities and seized 153 cycles. Blackwell himself was arrested in January of 2010, after which he pleaded guilty to fencing stolen property. He was out on parole in 2012 when Mounties, operating on tips, again discovered twenty grand worth of high-end bikes and parts in his new residence. Blackwell told media reporting on the case, "You know, you guys are going to undo all the good I do."

That summer Alyssa Chrisman rode her Giant touring bike 4,179 miles from sea to shining sea—a North Carolina-to-California run. The Central Michigan University student had joined a group of cyclists on a fund-raising ride for an affordable housing organization. The journey was meant to culminate in the sunny beach city of Santa Cruz. But the cyclists stopped briefly in Davis, California, to celebrate the college town's famous bike culture. There, Chrisman locked her bike with two others outside the Bicycling Hall of Fame and stepped in to learn a famous bicycling lesson. When she came out, her Giant was gone.

There is something cosmic about the completion of a bike chain's cycle through gears and sprockets—the full rotation of the tire, the endless looping and traveling only to return to the point of departure—that makes the bike a fabulous vehicle for irony.

During World War II, the automobile assumed total dominance of American streets, and bicycles were increasingly considered toys. Since then, there have been two major moments in one's trajectory via machine: when your training wheels are taken off, and when you dump your bike altogether in favor of a car. But there is also a rarely acknowledged third universal that occurs between losing the training wheels and gaining the car, and it is the loss of a well-loved bicycle. Death, taxes, and missing bikes.

In various ways, most of us are complicit.

At twenty-four, I attended a party thrown by a popular friend. It was loud and crowded and fun. The crew knew a lot of people from a lot of dodgy places and they were all there having a good time. Late the next day, almost as an afterthought, the host, Derek, called around asking if anybody had ridden his bike home. It was an average black beach cruiser distinguished only by the menacing character of its patina. The flat black spray job and rusted spokes and nicks and wear made the bike look like it belonged to the neighborhood creep. None of Derek's acquaintances admitted to borrowing the bike, and as he was leaving town for a few weeks, he didn't have time to go looking for it.

A couple of days later, I was driving my squeaky '68 Mustang up a residential hill in another part of town when I ran out of gas. I parked the car, popped the trunk, found the familiar red gas can, and started walking. A block down the hill, my eyes happened to peer into a fenced yard, and I saw what looked like Derek's beat-up cruiser—its nicks and wear. I set the gas can on the curb. I gazed right, then left, and jumped the fence. Snatching the unlocked bike by the frame, I hoisted it over. With a pop from the ankles, my feet lifted, following my hips, knees, and shins right on over and onto the sidewalk. The downhill getaway went as smoothly as the bike's bent rims allowed.

While the cruiser sat in my kitchen waiting for Derek's return, however, I really began to think about the act. In California, there's nothing more common than an old beach cruiser. *Was* this the missing one? Or did I steal someone else's wheels with belligerent ease? If so, the act came to me, well, like riding a bike. I considered returning the hot property to the fenced yard. But I knew that returning to the scene was as dumb as committing a crime. My pretensions of righteous revenge on Derek's behalf were really beginning to deflate.

So when I heard that he was back in town, I gave Derek a call and asked him to come over. Once he was in the living room, I asked Derek—who wore, weirdly, a shimmering blue 1950s-style sharkskin suit—to have a look in the kitchen.

"Oh, you fucker," he said. "*You* stole my bike."

"Yeah," I said, relieved that he recognized the cruiser. "The second time."

I quickly told the story using my hands and elbows and arms and legs. Yet Derek seemed vaguely, amiably indifferent to the feat—even as he wheeled his cruiser out the front door. "Cool," he said with a wave. "Thanks."

It is a nothing story, really. But when I think of the somersaults of identity I'd have endured had Derek not accepted ownership, I pause. I scheme on how I would have returned the bike to its owner. Maybe this would be an even more noble gesture than liberating it. At night. Over the fence. Through the gate. Would it be more honorable to knock on the door and explain the situation? No, I've pictured the owner's face. It's not pleased. I would not knock. In fact, I likely wouldn't have returned the black cruiser at all. Too ashamed to admit guilt and too chicken to ride the bike about town, I'd have let it rust in the side yard.

More painful than imagination, however, is that my friend Derek died unexpectedly within the year. And in thinking about him, and retelling stories about him within our peer group, I've realized that as electric a friend as he was, the energy one felt in his presence came down to the fact that he was also an insanely inventive and chronic liar—a quality I don't begrudge in the slightest. But in memory, I do examine the look Derek shot me before walking out of my apartment with his beach cruiser. The weak smile tells me something different on each recall. I revise this story often—for myself, for others. But in the bedrock of the deed, I think I stole somebody's bike.

Many of the Tijuana River Valley residents I spoke with concerning the bicycles came to the obvious conclusion that the bikes were stolen from someplace, maybe by the individual migrants themselves. David Gomez noticed a sticker on several bikes that indicated they'd originally been sold by a shop in nearby Coronado, a wealthy enclave just to the north. The fact that these bikes had been crossed into Mexico and sent back to the United States with a migrant on top suggested to him that the Coronado bikes, at least, had been pinched for that specific purpose. Cars, trucks, and vans stolen along the border end up in Mexico with such regularity it's taken almost as a migratory pattern. Why would these bikes, or anything on wheels in the Southwest, be any different?

State parks ecologist Greg Abbott was convinced that the bicycles were caught in an eddy of some sort, circling through border defenses and then back again through the commercial lanes into Tijuana—riding in trucks packed with used couches, refrigerators, mattresses, and plush animal toys—in an unbroken cycle. Abbott was an old hand in Mexico, and knew it well enough to feel certain that the bikes were not from there. *Tijuanenses* liked to bike about as much as they liked to swim, which wasn't very much, by the former lifeguard's estimate. In direct observation, however, he saw only the northbound tracks of the migrant bikes' movement. Where they'd originated from, empirically speaking, he couldn't say.

Terry Tynan claimed that if he came upon a bike that exhibited a licensing sticker of some sort, he'd just "leave the bike in the dirt." He didn't want to end up with obviously stolen merchandise on the ranch. I think what he meant was, he didn't want to harbor stolen merchandise that was easily traceable. But, even as I listened to him say this—my feet in the dirt and the sun on my face—good sense told me that the statement slipped past his cracked lips as one of those obfuscating gushes interview subjects emit in an almost nervous twitch, like a squid escaping behind its ink cloud. It is human nature to talk; eventually everybody does. Terry loved to talk about his bikes but having done so, it seemed, he wanted some portion of the story back. After searching for bikes with Terry and later talking to his neighbors, I knew it was not in his nature to let a bike lie, any bike.

The sense I got from this obsession struck me as the same as when an unknown dog appears and takes up residence on your property. You've got good food and a nice spot to rest, so the dog stays. She's streetwise and knows a good thing. Months go by, and hey, you didn't steal the dog. It's the animal's own choice. You like her; maybe the old family didn't treat her so well. The fact that you never advertised finding the dog, or even asked around—the fact that you're covetous of the dog and have renamed her—is beside the point.

Yet, in Terry's growing collection, in his increasing abilities to track and scavenge and sniff out bikes, the scenario of the dog was repeated over and over. And of course, after she had hung around long enough, he didn't have a problem selling the dog either.

"To me, it didn't seem like it was that organized," said *Union-Tribune* reporter Janine Zúñiga. In conversation, she indicated that the Border Patrol didn't appear to feel that way either. In her piece,

Zúñiga quoted Border Patrol spokesman Jerry Conlin as saying, "For [migrants], it's a quicker means of getting from point A to point B on that type of terrain."

But the sheer numbers suggested something more than convenience. In colloquial shorthand, the Border Patrol calls a group crossing here or there a "onesie" or a "twosie." No big deal. But if you multiply a group of fifteen, which many observers have seen, times 365 days in the year, you get 5,475 migrants crossing undetected in one five-mile stretch of the border. Multiply this by the two and a half years it had been going before I ever caught wind of it, and you get 13,687. These are outside numbers, of course. But even at half that rate, the volume of bicycles alone presented one hell of a sourcing problem. Were dozens of migrants from southern Mexico and Central America gathering in Tijuana daily and randomly deciding to cross this craggy landscape by bike? And if so, did they then scour the city for reasonably priced wheels? After two-plus years of cycle crossings, could there possibly be any unwanted bikes left in Tijuana? How was it possible, then, that reliable bicycles were made available to the migrants on a daily basis? Could it possibly be true that a central organizing figure, or group, was stealing bikes from the United States and importing them to Tijuana for that specific purpose?

"I do remember talking to the Border Patrol about whether the bikes were stolen or not," Zúñiga said. She reported that agents inspected bikes for details that might indicate whether the vehicles had been used to smuggle drugs—in the tubing or tires, for example. No drugs were found. Then the Border Patrol researched the serial numbers on all of the bikes the agency took into custody. No evidence of theft was suggested by those checks, either. "But, yeah," Zúñiga said on recollection—she'd lived in Mexico City and knew the border culture as well—"they were definitely US bikes."

There is not a lot to learn from the serial numbers that manufacturers stamp onto the frames of bicycles. In code, some will relay the production year, the model, and the factory in which the bike was built. Each manufacturer uses a different method in formulating a serial number, so there is no set sequence. And some numbers may not relay even the basic information. Serial numbers are there mainly to reunite an owner with a lost bicycle. But law enforcement does not keep a national database of serial numbers, either of the bikes they've impounded or of those reported stolen. A private enterprise called the National Bike Registry (NBR) charges owners ten dollars to register their serial numbers online, and if a registered bike turns up after being stolen, law enforcement can access the information attached to that serial number. The NBR claims that 48 percent of stolen bikes are recovered by law enforcement, but only 5 percent are returned to an owner. This is because, they say, most owners never register their serial numbers or even write them down. Unless Border Patrol agents at the Imperial Beach station accessed the NBR archive and punched in the serial number of a bicycle registered with the NBR by an owner—in the past ten years—it is likely that number wouldn't have told the agents more than they could gather by looking at the bike itself.

At the height of the phenomenon, Border Patrol began to drive their jeeps and kilo trucks over abandoned bicycles. Rims were "tacoed" and frames bent. Some agents on foot slashed bike tires with pocketknives. The desire to disable the vehicles, and prevent their further use by a migrant, explained some of this activity. But some of it may have been born of frustration. Storage capacity at the station was maxed out, and they had no concrete way of knowing where the bikes were coming from or where they were headed. And regardless, the agents were not bike caddies. Better to wound the bikes and leave them in the dirt.

The question of theft drew me back to the Kimzey place to kick some tires and poke at Terry's pile again. This time I took a closer look at the frames. Like a raucous house party reaching its crescendo, the collection was a colorful, moving, shifting affair. You never knew who might show up—new bikes caught my eye even while I was reassessing my opinion of an old acquaintance. Plus, I wouldn't know for some time afterward, but Terry was actually storing the best bicycles in a prefab wooden shed stationed right next to the stack of motley passers-through. If I considered the shed at all, I probably assumed it was filled with manure-laden rakes and shovels, not gold. It was like a backstage party at the party, and the bikes most likely to have been registered by their owners were attending this one, coolly out of view.

Still, there were things to learn from the pile. I was looking for stickers of origin: shop emblems, school and club affiliations, municipal tags, etc. I mentioned this to Terry, and he looked at me like I'd missed something as big as the wooden shed right in front of my face. He reiterated that he'd found whole groups of bikes tagged with police auction stickers. Terry then began to list the cities and towns across the Southwest that the stickers represented. The list of police auctions sounded something like an intro to a blues song about old US 80, the Ocean-to-Ocean Highway: Dallas, Fort Worth, Las Cruces, Phoenix, San Diego. He ended with, "And someone was hauling 'em through to Mexico!"

Two journalists I admire for their love of their bicycles independently followed their own missing wheels into what was termed the "underworld" of bike theft. This included homeless encampments, drug corners, back alleys, chop shops, flea markets, and police property rooms.

Even for experienced international correspondent and author Patrick Symmes, the hustle of missing bicycles proved formidable. His initial inspiration was to attach various GPS devices to a series of bikes and observe where they ended up via his laptop computer. Symmes's technological rabbit hunts spanned the bike-crazy cities of

New York, Portland, and San Francisco. Symmes even succeeded in enlisting the aid of the San Francisco Police Department and the Portland Police Bureau, which was a bonus because, as San Francisco's Sergeant Joe McCloskey put it bluntly, "[Bike theft is] just a low priority."

Although promising, the GPS trap yielded a mixed bag of results. The first test bike was locked behind the author's apartment, but soon disappeared without a trace. The bike and GPS unit might have been ferreted away to an underground garage where the GPS signal could not reach satellites. But the unit could have suffered a coincidental failure. Or maybe the thief was on to the ruse and disabled the device. Technology has its limits. Another bike trap the author set remained locked to a New York parking meter for weeks. But as Symmes learned, the bike's mass was slowly being reduced as thieves parted it out—the brakes, the seat, cranks, etc. Symmes set a third bike trap against a mailbox in Portland. The bike disappeared two hours later. Symmes tracked it around town on his computer screen. At some point, the GPS showed the bike's movements vacillating at a slow pace along the river promenade—the Waterfront Bike Trail. Symmes feared that the reason the bike was traveling at walking speed was that the thief was trying to make a sale to a passerby. The amateur investigator wanted the thief, not the buyer. So he cabbed it down to the waterway and immediately ran into the purple Giant Yukon, and the bearded old man on top of it. Instead of trying to sell the bike, however, the man began to spout conspiracy theory. He'd been separated from his fortune, he said. He was the son of King Richard III. Symmes thought he'd set a trap for a bike thief, but now he realized that what he'd caught was a schizophrenic.

Justin Jouvenal wanted his specific black-and-gray Fuji Touring recovered, and lacking Symmes's resources, he set out into the San Francisco streets on foot. The journalist visited a back-alley fencing operation where a couple of sweaty guys sold bikes and parts out of a van. He stopped by an informal but well-known market in the parking lot of a Carl's Jr. drive-thru. There, he was offered a steal-to-order service. If Jouvenal named the bike he wanted, it could be his. But he didn't want someone else's Fuji. Suspecting that his ride was in the process of being parted out and sold as a Franken-bike, Jouvenal visited an open-air chop shop in Golden Gate Park, where squatters tore bikes down and swapped parts to disguise their identities. The tactic blurred the trail for theft victims. Finally, he was introduced to the SFPD's stolen-property facility at Hunters Point: "[Lieutenant Tom] Feney ushered me through a metal door to the warehouse and then swept his hand through the air as if pointing out a beautiful panorama."

Jouvenal looked over "a cache of stolen bikes so big that it dwarfs the stock of any bike store in the city." And yet, the warehouse did not contain his beloved Fuji.

In a 2014 survey of everyday cyclists conducted in Montreal, researchers at McGill University reported that 50 percent of their subjects had been victims of bike theft, and that many active riders had had their wheels pinched more than once. To give an indication as to the size of the market, a 2011 FBI fact sheet listed 189,428 bikes reported stolen, a number up 4.2 percent from 2010. But these were just the reported thefts. The cycling advocacy group Transportation Alternatives in New York City claimed that actual thefts were more likely four to five times the reported figure.

"In America's rough streets," wrote Symmes, "there are four forms of currency—cash, sex, drugs, and bicycles. Of those, only one is routinely left outside unattended."

The economic journalists at the website Priceonomics, however, considered that the financial upside for bike thieves seemed "limited." Analyzing bike theft using conventional economic theories—risk vs. reward, for example—Rohin Dhar asked, "Is the juice worth the squeeze?" His conclusion: "The illicit bike trade isn't a very easy way to make a lot of money."

In major cities, most cyclists know at which locations their wheels are most likely to get pinched. And most people know where hot bikes are sold cheap—in places like the Porta Portese market in *The Bicycle Thief.* These days, victims also know to check websites like Craigslist and eBay, where stolen bikes increasingly turn up. With a bit of investigative work, Jouvenal found a chop shop, fencing operation, and street market for stolen goods. Police also know where these activities occur, but because bike theft is not a law-enforcement priority, there is a low probability that criminals will be caught. Despite the princely sums fetched by a few high-tech bikes, the act of stealing one is often considered a misdemeanor and is rarely prosecuted. There's just not much squeeze.

But because there is little risk, the activity is more pervasive and the market is flooded, so there's not much juice either. According to the NBR, thieves can fetch only 5 to 10 percent of a bike's fair market value. In fact, the more expensive the bicycle, the lower the percentage a thief can get: "A bicycle that sells for $200 new will sell for $20 on the street when stolen, and a new $2,500 chrome alloy machine will sell for as low as $125 [or 5 percent]."

Professional bike thieves do exist. In 2012, the Los Angeles Sheriff's Department routed a trio of young men who combed websites for sales of high-end bikes. The ring posed as potential buyers and contacted sellers via the ads, thereby gaining location information. The thieves then broke into suburban garages and houses by cutting holes into the tops of garage doors, using a handmade tool to pull the release strings. A bike shop owner in Los Angeles helped the thieves fence the bicycles by parting them out, a tactic that pulls in 25 percent of the fair market value as compared to the 5 to 10 percent fetched by a complete, stolen bike.

The common narrative pushed by Symmes and Jouvenal—that the mass of bike thefts is committed by drug addicts and petty criminals—seems self-evident, apparent in what is most visible on

America's streets: bare rims chained to parking meters, broken U-locks clanging around signposts, and grubby idlers trying to pawn off suspect wheels to passersby. But the numbers required to support a full-time bike theft "underworld" just aren't there. And as Dhar pointed out, even for opportunistic thieves, bike theft is an inefficient use of criminal tendencies. The squeeze of the law may be tender, but the risk won't yield much juice.

So what is actually happening to the hundreds of thousands of bicycles stolen in the United States every year?

The US Department of Justice commissioned a series of "Problem-Specific Guides" intended to aid police departments with academic studies and policing advice on a number of crimes. In 2008, the authors of "Bicycle Theft: Guide No. 52" presented their law-enforcement audience with some humbling data, one set of which suggests that "clearance rates"—the rate of successful arrests in relation to a given crime—for bicycle theft can be as low as 1 percent. That's only arrests, not prosecutions. To place this dismal rate into context, the clearance rate for bank robbery is as high as 60 percent.

The guide suggests some reasons for these rates, the most poignant being that few victims can prove ownership. "The majority of bicycle owners cannot supply sufficient details to assist in an investigation. As a consequence, even when an offender is detained, the suspect may be released without charge and may be given the stolen bike on release."

And not all of the wheels in police custody are hot in the traditional sense. Cops glean abandoned bikes from the streets, impound them during routine arrests, and confiscate them as evidence in unrelated crimes. In places like Philadelphia, the city makes semiannual sweeps for bikes locked to parking meters and other municipal property.

This conglomeration of cycles in custody, piled in warehouses and property rooms, may be explained by a pattern the authors of the Department of Justice guide are clear about: "Where the quantity of stolen cycles recovered is high, a high proportion of offenders are probably joyriders." That's right—joyriders. I'm on foot, I see your bike is unlocked, or easy to unlock, and I ride your bike to my destination and ditch it to the fates—and you know what? I enjoy it. The joyride has inspired multiple films, dozens of songs, a Transformers character, a video game—and at its heart, is a theft that one engages in for something other than profit, like a fun bike ride. Wheels are "recovered," most often, because they have been abandoned. The Justice Department guide cites police recovery rates as indicators of joyridership—from 25 percent in Ellensburg, Washington, to 80 percent in Dayton, Ohio, the latter "suggesting that many more offenses were committed for the purposes of transportation or enjoyment than for financial gain."

And it's old, this thing. The following passage appeared in a 1919 article in the *Messenger Index* of Emmett, Idaho: "The theft of bicycles from the high school building is almost an everyday occurrence, but so far the police have not been able to catch the culprits. Most of the thefts seem to be committed from pure cussedness rather than to profit thereby, as most of the wheels are taken to an out of the way place and wrecked."

The incidents of casual theft are compounded by what is called a "crime multiplier." For example, your bike is stolen. So you buy an obviously hot bike off the street because it's cheap, and you knowingly receive stolen property. Or you need to get to work immediately, so you grab another bike and you're off. This is the penultimate scene of *The Bicycle Thief*: having exhausted all other options without retrieving the Fides—even when he has caught the actual thief—Ricci decides to steal a bike. But then he is caught by the bike's owner, and shamed by the growing crowd. Further, his son, Bruno, sees that his father is a scoundrel as despicable as the one they've been chasing. Of course, this is the fiction of the film. Few thieves are caught. What really happens is so much more complicated: A joyrider steals a bike and dumps it; the bike is picked up by another rider, who drops it in front of a house; a homeowner finds the abandoned bike and takes it into the garage, where it sits for years, until it's time to clear the garage, and the bike is sold at a rummage sale. Or not: The homeowner's son "borrows" the bike to ride down to buy some crack but is snatched by police. The bike is impounded. Meanwhile, the original owner has joyridden a number of bikes to make up for the loss.

"A single bicycle theft does not necessarily equate to one offense," says the Justice Department guide, "but may lead to a series of related crimes." Receiving stolen property, fencing stolen property, and vandalism are some of the obvious examples.

Partly because I like vintage bicycles, I've owned only one bike with a crystal-clear provenance, and that was the blue-and-white BMX Huffy that was stolen from me by local toughs and, I was later told, smashed down an anonymous manhole. But to complicate matters to a cosmic scale, I'll agree to what the statistics allege:

I didn't rescue Derek's bike, I stole your bike. I gave your bike to Derek and let him walk right on out the door with it. He probably sold the cruiser for drugs. What's more, long ago when I was just forming as an independent person, just learning my multiplication tables, you stole my little Huffy even though it was too small for you to ride, and, for fun, you stuffed it down a manhole. Some poor sap of a city worker probably found the Huffy down there in the sewer, pulled it from the shit pipes, washed it, and turned it over to the police, who sat on the cycle for a while before selling it at police auction. And now, decades later, it looks like a couple of migrants from distant Michoacán or Sinaloa have illegally crossed the US–Mexico border on your and my bikes both. Not only are you a thief, you are complicit in human trafficking.

17

El Indio, Javy, Juan, and Solo prepared to pass nine *pollos* through the little canyon across from the Comercial Mexicana. It was about ten on a weekday morning. The blue sky was striated with the last bands of a tropical storm that had withered and diffused hundreds of miles away. The air still hung thick with scents of the southern latitudes. Indio's crew had progressed to crossing in broad daylight as long as all of the other factors came into agreement. The high visibility left an even tighter margin for error, so they arrived earlier than usual. Each bike was double-checked, and the migrants seemed eager.

East along the fence, a tan-colored pit mine defaced the west side of Bunker Hill. It didn't seem so much like a pit, rather as if someone had cut the rounded hill with a cake knife and taken a piece. The border fence looked dangerously close to falling in with the sage and scrub as trucks withdrew more and more cobbles and dirt. The access road that served this operation also dipped down into the canyon, almost to the *polleros*' camp. Betraying its scarce use, however, the rutted track dwindled and died out before it reached El Indio and his band of gold miners.

At about 10:15 AM, a white-and-blue Tijuana police truck entered the access road at the dirt excavation. It was not an uncommon sight.

The *polleros* knew that cops often chased *vagabundos* and *indigentes* up the hill. The hurry-scurry was entertaining but not dramatic—like obese terriers loping after lizards. But this particular vehicle slowed at the entrance, and then descended toward the fence. The smugglers caught the faces of a familiar officer and his female partner. This pair sometimes brought bicycles they'd snatched from riders they'd stopped on minor infractions—leaving the commuters to hoof it. Indio and his workers paid $100 for each of these stolen bikes, and considered it a pretty good deal to receive a bicycle out of what was essentially an extortion situation. They could easily have gained nothing and still had to pay. Locally, the cop was known as Gordito—Little Fatty. He was chubby, the partner even more so. Along with the bikes, Gordito sometimes brought *pollos* he'd stolen off of area recruiters. He received $150 for each of these. The victimized *enganchador*, in order to smooth business relationships, was also paid by Indio, receiving $100 for each of the *pollos* stolen and delivered by Gordito.

The police truck stopped at the end of the track. Gordito and the female officer stepped out and walked into the declivity where the *polleros* waited. Gordito rested his hands on his gun belt the way a man might hold the rails of a rowboat in risky seas. The woman proceeded with outstretched arms while gazing at her feet, a fat lady balancing on a line. Their dark uniforms could not mask the darker marks in the armpits.

"*Hola, muchachos*," Gordito called, his breath heavy and short.

The timing was particularly bad. If he'd come about some *pollos* he wanted to sell, it was too late to check them out. And if he'd brought bikes, they weren't really needed. But today there was an altered demeanor in the partners.

"*Buenos días*," Indio said.

A second police truck then pulled to a stop on the shoulder of the International Road above. Two policemen emerged from the vehicle. Standing at the guardrail, they had a direct view of the action.

"No *pollos*?" Indio inquired of Gordito. "No bikes?"

"You've got to come with us today," the cop said.

"We are about to do some work here."

"Maybe them," he said, indicating Solo, Javy, and Juan, "but not you."

"What's up?"

"You failed to make arrangements with the chief."

"We've been doing business with you."

Gordito shrugged. "He doesn't know that."

The bikes were already on the other side. The time was right for the crossing; a moment more and the white-and-green *migra* truck would descend Bunker Hill for the shift change. In one swift action, Indio and the migrants could be cycling away from these cops and their entire union of corruption. It was a plan they'd rehearsed, but for some reason, Indio did not make this move.

"Okay," he said. "So, I come with you, but my guys stay here, right?"

"*Está bien*," the policeman agreed. His shoulders slacked.

While the rest stayed put, Indio began hiking up the gravelly slope to meet the cops. When he reached them, Gordito said, "Now, please turn around."

Solo, the guides, and their migrants watched as Indio obliged.

"On second thought," Gordito said, pausing to address his partner, "I believe the *pollos* should also come with us."

She nodded in agreement.

"For what purpose?" Indio asked.

"They are worth something to the other *polleros*."

"Who will only sell them back to me," Indio said. "Let's say we cut out the middleman. I'll pay you for them now."

"That will work too." Gordito shrugged.

The partners led Indio to their vehicle and ushered him in, before squeezing into the cab themselves. Solo watched the truck make a jerky multipoint turn, its tires burdened in the wheel wells as it trundled up the track. The other policemen had vanished from the roadside.

That evening, El Indio strode into the Chicago Club. Both poles were occupied by dancers; the music bumped loud with the tinny brass of norteño music. Vinyl booths overflowed with patrons, waitresses sashaying among them. Juan, Javy, and Solo lounged at the bar—not like celebrants but after-work grumblers.

"Indio," Juan roared when he spotted the boss approaching, "you got sprung!" He flagged the bartender. "A beer for the inmate!"

Solo stood and grasped his friend about the shoulders. "*Amigo*, when you were arrested, I thought, shit, we weren't going to see you again. The Zona room was already so lonely, I couldn't stand it."

"I wasn't arrested," Indio said.

Solo straightened. Indio let the embrace fall from his shoulders. He looked at the gang of men backed by colored lights and dancers. The rollicking music, the party, suddenly seemed estranged from this interview. There were no friends here. "Did you guys cross the *pollos*?" Indio asked.

"Yes, of course."

"Every one of them."

Solo hesitated, but said, "When we met Martín for the pickup, he asked about you. I couldn't lie."

"Lie about what?"

"The arrest, or whatever," Solo said.

"Gordito and the lady? They came on an errand, a courtesy."

"And the handcuffs?" asked Javy.

"For their protection, *cabrón*."

"Indio, you think that fat bitch is afraid of you?"

"At the time, I don't know. But now, definitely. The chief and I came to an agreement."

The veteran coyote known as El Sombra confirmed the situation. "When El Indio was working," he said, "you could see the lights from the police cars stopped on the side of the International Road. Absolutely no one could approach the area. I don't think the president had the security El Indio did."

Of course, this was not exactly true. Known operators like El Sombra were granted access. And it wasn't long before a recruiter whom Indio had met at the bus station along with the very first of his Tijuana acquaintances—such as Javy and Juan—arrived with two migrants he apparently wished to pass. The duty of managing *pollos* had fallen to Solo, and so it was not without interest that he observed the arrival of this odd troop. The *enganchador* nodded to Solo. But on greeting El Indio, his demeanor bloomed.

Indio's old comrade said, "Look at you, *amigo*, the hero of all of the bus station workers. You know that, right? The way you've come up."

"*Gracias*, Chino," Indio said. "It's good to see that you are well."

He was called Chino not because he was of Asian descent, as the name might suggest, but because of his curly hair—a nickname derived from the curls of an ancient Mayan pig. This recruiter was several inches taller than Indio and wiry—the amiable sort of drug user who had a habit of standing closer than was acceptable on the frontier. The men he brought with him were filthy. They stood off to the side like a couple of overly lean mongrels.

"I never would have recognized you in these fancy clothes," Chino said. "You look like a success, really. That kid I met at the bus station would have seen a guy like you and run the other way. Am I right?"

"That was a long time ago," Indio said, waving off the appraisal.

Solo had not yet arrived in Tijuana during Indio's time at the bus station. So he did not know the breadth of Indio's acquaintances. He tempered his suspicions of this recruiter. But what the man said was true: Indio did appear transformed. The influence of the borderlands hung about him like a cape. And lately, there was something more. It couldn't be summed up in fashion alone, but there were clues. Marta preferred a decidedly urban look on her man, and along with his baggy blue jeans and spotless tennis shoes, he now wore a gray fedora that Marta had admired in a shop window. It held a rooster's feather in its band.

"Not that long ago, no, not at all," Chino said. "Your belt too, that's a nice belt."

It was a light blue mesh belt, a style worn by military. This one was clasped by a slender silver buckle. The end of the belt hung along Indio's left hip in the fashion of the time. Also a gift from Marta, the buckle was inscribed with an "I."

Indio raised a hand to rub his nose, a signal that the appraisals were over. "What can I do for you, Chino?" he asked.

"Your man, he hasn't greeted my *pollos*," Chino said. "Must be new."

The smugglers looked at Chino's men and noted their soot-smudged and scabby appearance. Solo didn't have to guess that the men lived in the river.

"Those *pollos* don't check out," Indio said.

"These are good *pollos*, quality customers," Chino said. "They have people on the inside. Tell your worker to make the calls. Where'd you get that one, anyway? I mean, people skills are a must in this line of work."

"I've known this *chavo* all my life," Indio said.

"Okay, *amigo*. Instead of the usual $150 each, give me $280 for the two. That's a discount."

Solo shook his head. Indio verbalized the sentiment. "I can't help you today."

Chino bent his elbow and tapped the underside to indicate a cheapskate. "This is not the village. Give me $250."

"I don't want them."

"*Cabrón*. You're in Tijuana now. Give me $180."

Good, hardworking *migrantes* could be found all over town and this man had brought two drug addicts who wouldn't check out. Indio said, "Get out of here."

A light came to Chino's eyes. He began chuckling. He put his hand on Indio's shoulder and then embraced him. Indio pushed back, but the two men stumbled as if joined in a sack race. The more Indio pushed, the more unstable they became. Chino cackled. The pair wobbled and fell. Still, Chino would not let go. The gray fedora tumbled, went bowling away. It was not violence, but it was not friendly. Solo jockeyed about them but hesitated to intervene. Chino convulsed in titters and snorts. "I need this one, Pablo," he wheezed. "I need the favor."

Indio finally broke the embrace and sprang to his feet, his fists seemingly clinched before he landed. "This is not a bus station game," he said. "This is serious business."

Chino, on his back now, raised a slender arm, pointed, and said, "Ha. Look at your hair, *amigo*. It's combed so perfectly. Ha, ha." He caught Solo's eyes. "Where is Pablo de Oaxaca? He would do me the favor."

Solo remembered Chino's *pollos*. He looked but they were gone.

Without notice, the policeman appointed to guard the highway stepped around Solo and Indio—his club was already drawn. He began to beat Chino, producing a wallop like a dropped sack of rice, each blow making the same inconsequential sound. Chino didn't resist, but cried in a way that was almost laughing. The cop finally put the curly-haired recruiter on his stomach and, squatting, dug a knee between his shoulder blades. He drew one noodle-like arm at a time and applied the bracelets. And without a word, the officer dragged the recruiter up to the police car parked along the International Road.

Solo bent to fetch the fedora. He picked off foxtails. Indio didn't even dust himself but watched his old comrade, now kicking his way up the desert slope in the clutches of the cop. The scene had a blown-through quality, a miasma like the moments following the passage of a dust devil. It was up to each man to reconnoiter his frame of mind. Solo handed the hat over. Indio held it between his wide hands—seemingly in contemplation as the police car tore away.

"Chino was right about the clothes," Indio said finally.

"What do you think is going to happen to him?" Solo asked.

"Something bad, probably." He let several minutes pass. Indio reached into his baggy jeans pocket, removed a cell phone, and dialed. "Yes, this is Indio," he said. "Bring your prisoner back to me."

Maybe Chino spread the story of his release and Indio's forgiveness. Maybe Solo let it slip in the Chicago Club between dancers and Cuba libres. Or possibly it was the men from the river who likely watched from a hidden distance. But it was an oft-repeated story. The tale of Chino's aggression and eventual pardon—his release from certain torture—beamed through the smuggling community. Chino was troubled, but well liked. All agreed that he deserved everything he got. The fact that El Indio offered a simple forgetting of the slight won him the esteem of the *malandros*. Rather than demonstrate the weakness of a leader unable to twist the knife, in the fast-developing narrative, Indio's gesture represented strength such that he could afford a kindness in a place where few kindnesses went unpunished.

In his version of the tale, Roberto's summation was this: "My brother was beginning to shine like no one else before."

18

Two men followed at a distance as Maria Teresa Fernandez and I made our way up a thin dirt trail along the fence line. The route was steep enough so that, at times, we looked for notches or footholds in the climb. At one of these places, I stopped to offer Fernandez a hand, and that's when I noticed the men. This was on the Mexican side of Bunker Hill. And the rusted metal sheets of the wall built during President Clinton's Operation Gatekeeper rose with us. The Pacific Ocean, its line drawn on the horizon and the expansive arch of the western sky, comprised an entire gradient of pale blues. Below, to the south, was the International Road and the neighborhood of Playas de Tijuana. To the north, the russet colors of the Tijuana River Estuary rolled into the United States.

"I don't know, Mateo says it's up here. Somewhere in this section," Fernandez said.

I'd have imagined the fence line to smell of the white and yellow chrysanthemum flowers and the potent native sages that carpet these hills. Or, maybe, of nothing at all. But up this close it smelled of people—an animal musk with the odd whiff of something worse. The panoramic views, the pillowy brush, the open space, and the sea breeze were all dislocated by this trace scent. It dawned on me: so much went on here that went unseen, part of this border edifice had to be constructed in the mind.

We reached the graffiti that Fernandez wanted to photograph; any change to the wall offered her a challenge, like documenting sandcastles before the tide came in. Metallic silver and blue, the rounded, indecipherable graffiti letters took up more than a panel of the corrugated iron. It must have taken some time to create. And there were a lot of forces ready to chase the spray can artist away—thieves, thugs, police. Fernandez moved about, clicking images with a silent efficiency. When I turned to look, the men on our trail were still a ways off, but gaining. I could see only that one wore a red shirt and the other a dark shirt with white pants.

"We have all of the states of Mexico represented on the fence," Fernandez said, pointing as if to a passing crowd. A faded mesh of place names stretched the length of the fence. There are thirty-one states in Mexico. It seemed possible that each was repeated a thousand times. Personal names and dates—recorded by people who had soon crossed, or who had hoped to—were also etched and tagged onto the oxidized iron. Up close it looked like the leaves of a guest registry. IVAN WAS HERE—14/4/11. There were the origin countries: ARMENIA, CHINO, SAN SALVADOR. Also listed was what they thought of themselves. POLLOS PUTOS. And what they saw of their antagonists. AHI LES VAN LA MIGRA.

"Do you know those men?" I asked. This was her beat. I figured she'd know.

"What men?"

"Down there. They've been following us."

"Oh, no. I don't know those men."

We continued along the wall—a word most border people use interchangeably with *fence*. The corrugated iron sheets that make up this portion of the boundary once served as interlocking, temporary runways in Vietnam, and found a new life welded together in a sixty-mile run. You can't see through the metal, which would suggest a wall. Border Patrol agents ruffle at this word. The agency prefers the word *fence*, and their spokespeople admonish others to use it as well. I suppose *wall* conjures obvious and failed reference points: the Wall of Jericho, the Walls of Troy, the Berlin Wall, the Great Wall, Hadrian's Wall—that chain of embankments Romans built to keep barbarous Englanders out of England.

I've often thought that our boundary line could use a richer handle, something like Hadrian's. Mexicans call it *la frontera*, or *la línea*. Novelists T. C. Boyle and Joseph Wambaugh named it, respectively, the Tortilla Curtain and the Imaginary Line. Both good, but neither epic to the scale of the boundary. Our border operates as a screening process for motivated laborers—something like a temp agency that separates the good from the bad workers with a mud run—while also acting as an instant cost inflator for prohibited goods, starting with untaxed cigs and alcohol and moving through to people, narcotics, and exotic zoo animals. Maybe this was the point that Border Patrol was trying to make in differentiating *wall* from *fence*. As a wall, it was doomed to failure. But as a fence, it was a great growth engine for border-enforcement jobs.

It's hard to disagree that *fence* sounds neighborly. And it did begin as a fence, this wall. Its history as such might solve the naming problem. The first barriers were mere cattle fencing. And though Richard Nixon launched Operation Intercept, a mandate to search every person and car entering the United States through ports of entry, during his administration five thin strands of barbed wire separated San Diego from Tijuana at the border monument. Since Jimmy Carter, however, each successive president has left us with a new layer to the edifice, something like the legacy gift of a presidential library. "Carter's Curtain" was chain link. Ronald Reagan extended it, and built migrant detention centers. Bush Senior intercepted migrants at sea. Clinton's contractors were kind enough to weld the metal runway sheets in a way that aligned the corrugations horizontally, creating great foot grips and handholds so our neighbors could pop on over and talk to us anytime. Bush Junior's gift wasn't so generous. It was eighteen feet tall. He also paid a lot of our money for high-tech surveillance towers that corroded, failed in high wind, rain, and dust storms, and went blind in the fog. Obama pulled the plug on the failed "virtual fence" in 2010. Still, he continued to fulfill 580 miles of the triple wall mandated under the Secure Fence Act—this, as if metal-cutting equipment did not exist in Tijuana. There are sections of the Bush fence that boast more holes and patch jobs than a freight-train-load of hobo pants. Obama's legacy might be in the sky, however, as he unleashed the age of drones.

The two men were now quite close. We made eye contact. One was old and one was young. Fernandez and I paused to gauge the situation. Then, at the bottom of the trail, a third man wearing dark clothing appeared. This figure seemed to be advancing at an accelerated pace. We waited.

"*Hola*," the older man said on approach.

"*Buenas tardes*," answered Fernandez. "Are you crossing?"

The men caught their breath. "We're trying to cross, yes," said the older man, "but not now." He nodded down the trail at the dark figure.

"*Policía?*" asked Fernandez.

"*Sí*, El Gordito."

They knew him, or knew of him. This pair wasn't following us but escaping the short, fat cop. Tijuana's municipal police extort money from migrants with such regularity, it didn't occur to anyone present to mention exactly what it was the policeman wanted on this hilltop.

"Have you crossed before?" Fernandez asked.

"Yes, we've both been inside. I was in Michigan. I have a daughter there now. I'm trying to get back to her."

His partner added, "I was packing onions in LA, but then I got deported. If I can get there, I can get my job back." They both looked down the trail. "Okay," the young man said with perfect American pronunciation.

"Okay," we said in turn. "Okay."

"*Buena suerte*," offered Fernandez with a low wave.

The migrants turned and hiked toward the crown of the hill. Despite the close and painfully slow chase, there seemed to be many avenues of escape. The men could turn down into Los Laureles Canyon. They could make for the International Road. I didn't worry about their flight from this solitary cop until I saw another uniformed man pop up from the east side of Bunker Hill, a dark figure holding a radio. The migrants looked to be in a pickle, one that appeared well rehearsed. This is when the migrants turned toward Clinton's rusty old fence, climbed the corrugated metal ribs, and threw themselves over. They were gone.

El Gordito caught up to us fast. He was sweating and panting, the uniform bluer than I'd thought, more significant, and pressed. The badge was real. His expression focused. Those goddamned migrants had part of his pay in their pockets, I was sure of it. When Gordito's feet crunched down on the earth we shared, he muttered a curt "*Hola*."

"*Hola*," I replied.

"*Buenas*," followed Fernandez.

Meeting at the top of Bunker Hill, the two policemen conferred for a moment. Their quarry had called their bluff. What could have been some easy pocket change was now the problem of *la migra* and the United States. Who knows, maybe they'd see those fucking *pollos* once they got caught, processed, and deported back to Tijuana. Then one of the policemen pointed toward an open patch on the Mexican slope. A man, presumably homeless, was either sleeping or dead on a mat of greasy blankets. I'd noticed his camp earlier but took the man's lack of response to this police presence as a sign of impunity. And maybe it was. The police descended on the man and pulled him to his feet. His body language failed to register concern. One cop held the man's hands behind his back while the other rifled his pockets. They came up with nothing, and left the man to his ink spot on the side of the tan hill. I turned to see Fernandez snapping photos of the whole shakedown.

El Gordito's *compadre* passed back over the hill, and the fat man himself approached us on his descent. He wore sunglasses and no expression. "Be careful with that camera," he said to Fernandez. "There are thieves and criminals about."

"Okay," she said. "But what did you want those men for?"

"For assault," he said.

Fernandez shook her head, and tsked. So much compassion seemed compressed in her slight frame that to be judged by her was to be guilty. Gordito didn't give the gesture a thought; there was money to be made in this town. The air then ripped with the arrival of *la migra* agents on muscular quad motorbikes. First one then another pulled to an idle just on the other side of the fence. The sound of their engines reverberated through the metal. Nothing was visible to Fernandez or me, but we knew our friends were now in the crosshairs of the *jalapeños* as well. And soon to be caught, surely. This was the most enforced portion of the border. The sun had risen to high noon, leaving nowhere to hide. Depending on the migrants' records, detainment could mean anything from a short return trip to a year or more behind bars.

But the quads shot off to the east, and the hilltop went quiet. After a while, we turned to make our way back down the trail. The navy-blue bowling pin figure of El Gordito waddled down the route with a swift familiarity. Soon, he was out of sight. We took our time. Fernandez snapped some shots. I made notes. The bullring in Playas looked like a saucer I could flip a peso and a wish into. Around a final curve, we watched as the cop drove away in his *camioneta*, his little truck.

The home of Mateo, the man who had sent Fernandez up here to photograph the graffiti, then came into view. The house was a converted semitrailer parked in a kind of stair step notched out of Bunker Hill. It was a dirt mine. And if the excavating progressed any farther north, the billion-dollar border fence would cave into the operation. The house was parked on a level patch. From there, the terrain continued to descend in low undulations to the ocean. It wasn't readily apparent that the house was a truck trailer because its additions and outbuildings had altered its shape into a sculptural construction of white blocks. If it had been parked outside of MoMA, the house would have received serious artistic critique.

"When I first came to the border to make pictures," Fernandez explained, "I wanted to photograph homes built of unique materials. There are so many in Tijuana." She came upon a home in Colonia Libertad that used President Clinton's corrugated iron as the back wall of a multiroom house where three generations of the same family lived. Technically, US soil extends three feet south of the wall. Some members of the family slept with their heads in the States and their feet in Mexico. On either side of this compound, neighborhood people gardened at the wall in the way you'd beautify an ugly backyard fence—succulents, tomato plants, and fruit trees. Across from the wall was a small market called Pasadita—the Little Crossing—where essentials for a strange commute might be purchased.

The photographer continued to encounter people who made portions of the wall their homes but, as if at a juncture, her artistic vision skipped tracks. She'd wanted to make art out of these creative houses, but like many people who got too close, she became ensnared by the fence. Now, all she wanted was to document life along this strange line.

Still, Fernandez kept in touch with the friends she'd made while photographing their odd houses, Mateo especially. He would alert her to new artworks on the fence, and importantly, he would accompany her. She'd had rocks thrown at her. She once slipped and fell down a steep decline. So Mateo's companionship was much appreciated. In return, Fernandez brought food and clothing for his family. She took their portraits and framed them for the house. Yet while she'd delivered some gifts when we first arrived at the semitruck earlier that day, for reasons unknown to me at the time, that friendship was not directly perceptible.

Mateo had wide-set teardrop eyes like those in an ancient Egyptian portrait. His face and mouth were also wide and his half smile revealed teeth spaced like fence posts. Fernandez had introduced me as an *amigo*. We shook hands; he barely gripped mine. I could see that he wondered what an American was doing here next to his truck trailer, the pit mine, the border fence.

"My friend is curious about the *pollo* business, the one that used bikes," Fernandez said.

"I hear they worked from this lot right here," I added, and I pointed to the gently sloped land just below the truck trailer. It was so close a position to where we stood, I imagined one might have caught their conversations in drafts.

Mateo nodded and said, "That work is their job, not my job. It's bad business to explain other people's jobs."

He looked around and found what he was looking for—the fat cop sitting in his pickup at the side of the International Road. Then he mentioned to Fernandez, "You two should go look for the graffiti you're interested in."

As we made our way back down to the truck trailer, we came upon the older migrant we'd met earlier on the hill, the one who had followed us and, along with his partner, jumped the fence. A magician, here he appeared back on Mexican soil. The man beamed as we came near.

"We thought, for sure, you were caught," Fernandez said.

"No," he said with a chuckle.

"How did you get away?"

"I just ran along the wall, on the other side, to down there. Then I jumped over."

"*La migra* came for you."

"Yeah, I saw them," he said.

"Where is your friend?"

"He went the other way. I'll see him later."

We walked together toward the trailer and Mateo stepped out. He grinned as well. "El Gordito is gone," he said, shrugging, an apology for his curtness earlier. "I don't want any problems with him, because he knows me, he knows I'm always here." He then congratulated the migrant on his escape.

"*Sí, gracias,*" the man replied.

"Gordito used to sell *pollos* like him to the bicycle coyotes. Down there." Mateo indicated the lot. It was empty now, and covered with spring flowers. "Sometimes he would bring bikes to sell too. But always, he wanted money for allowing the migrants to pass over."

This was the same lot El Negro had described as a base for bicycle crossing—where he stood when the Border Patrol agent approached on the other side, spotted the bikes, and asked why Mexicans didn't recycle waste metal. When I considered the site in Los Laureles Canyon that Oscar Romo discovered, a picture of a diverse enterprise revealed itself. This explained why each ranch and farm on the American side received its share of the abandoned wheels. I gathered that this lot was a secondary site, yet since it was located across the street from the supermarket, Comercial Mexicana, it was the one that everyone knew about.

Mateo became grave and asked, "Do I have your confidence?" He looked at Fernandez. She nodded. "Okay. After I first arrived here in late 2006, I started seeing some movement, at night. The bikes came in trucks and they put them down in here. They brought the bikes ready to go. I think bicycles from *el Norte*, but they were used. The *polleros* brought exactly one for each of the *pollos*. Every day, I saw the trucks coming with the bikes and *pollos*. Every kind of *bicicleta*—kids', mountain bikes, *turismos*. All kinds of people. They passed *migrantes* every day, even in winter."

"Were the crossings steady, or did the numbers of migrants go up and down?" I asked.

"One year was extensive. I think 2008—it was very, very busy. And at that time I believe they were making rounds with the same bikes that went to the other side, because you wouldn't find any bikes in Tijuana. It seemed like that was a problem. This is when Gordito brought some bikes here to sell to the *polleros*. Maybe they didn't work, I don't know. I don't think the *pollos* had the money for him, or they didn't want the deal. Because one day Gordito and his partner cuffed the *pollero*. They must have come to some agreement because the next day, the *polleros* were right back here with a load of *pollos* and *bicis*."

"Do you know the *polleros* personally?" I asked.

"No," he said. "They worked there. I worked here."

"Have you heard of a man called El Indio?"

"There are a lot of *indios* around here," he said.

19

"We came to Tijuana in February of 2006 and we didn't know anyone in Tijuana and we didn't have anyone waiting for us here, or on the other side either," said Leti, a twenty-one-year-old woman traveling with her friend Julia. "I think, like all poor Mexicans, one has the tendency to want to get ahead, to pull yourself out of the poverty hole," she said.

Being young, they had also come for the adventure, just hoping that God would be on their side. At first Leti and Julia camped on the streets in the Zona Norte, a common staging point for *migrantes*. "I would sleep for a bit and then Julia would, so that we could watch over each other. Those were really hard times for the two of us. But after wandering around and getting to know the place for a good amount of time, we made a friend there in La Zona."

His name was Tomas and he worked as the parking attendant at an unassuming hotel that catered to the Zona Norte's visitors. He was stationed in a glass booth that stood adjacent to the parking lot entrance. Being fixed on that busy street, Tomas was seen as a point of communication. Neighborhood people dropped by, leaving Tomas with messages, information, and gossip.

"He was funny and nice," said Leti, "and Tomas seemed to have connections. We talked with him about our situation, and he told us that if we wanted, me and Julia could stay in his room."

The space was very small, but the women immediately rearranged things to accommodate themselves. Their plan was to stay with Tomas while he looked for a way to get them across. The handsome parking attendant had mentioned a number of acquaintances. One was a friend's boss, a man he called El Indio, who passed migrants of all types. Tomas said he would try to speak with this man, to ask if he could do a special favor in this instance, because the women didn't have any money. It wasn't common, he said, but *polleros* sometimes did deals. And most didn't mind helping out a couple of girls, especially ones as sincere as themselves.

"Only a few days after we moved into the room," Leti said, "some guy named Juan showed up. He had five *migrantes* with him, and he said he wanted to keep these people there with us, and that Tomas would know why. But when Tomas came back to the room just before sundown, he looked at me and at Julia, and was like, 'What's up with all of these people?'"

Leti described the man who'd brought them. Tomas made some calls on his cell phone. "A little later," she said, "the famous El Indio appeared."

The women were surprised to see that the head man was so young, just a few years older than they were. He met their greetings with a clear, pleasant expression. His bearing was confident, somehow magnified by an inner reserve that seemed at odds with his youth.

Yet, Leti said, "even he—El Indio—asked, 'Why are these people here? Whose are they?'"

Tomas answered: "I suppose they are yours, *amigo*. Juan brought them."

Indio made a phone call himself. Before Tijuana, Leti and Julia had never lived in a house with a telephone, let alone a place where everyone carried phones in their pockets. They watched Indio as he stepped out and conveyed orders into the device. Soon afterward, a van arrived. El Indio and the driver ushered the migrants into the vehicle and then they all sped off.

"Seeing how efficient and confident he was there at the house," said Leti, "me and Julia decided to go down to *el Cañón de los Laureles* with Tomas. And I tell you, we were able to see the way that man worked. It really was a whole affair—people running this way and that, talking on the phones, and sometimes yelling in panic." In her singsong voice, Leti mimed the workers. "'What do you mean I didn't tell you that, man? Next time pay more attention! Okay, okay, anyway . . .'"

Leti felt a burst of excitement when El Indio gave instructions; suddenly the dream seemed real.

"Follow the person at the front of the group, the one guiding—that was emphasized the most," she said. "And it was really cool when the *gancho* went to distract *la migra*. Right away the agent guy rushed down and chased after him. With that, the guides, the migrants—*todo*—took off flying to the inside. One straight line. A minute later, they just disappeared from view."

The next day, the women woke early and returned to the canyon alone. They found El Indio in a rush—one of the workers had forgotten water for the crossers.

"I said to El Indio, 'Give me the money and I'll go to the Comercial to buy it.'"

Without a word, Indio thrust a wad of pesos into her hand and turned back to his work. The women ran off toward the International Road and the blocky, bright orange supermarket—hustling there and back, over the rough terrain, as fast as they could. They bought small individual bottles instead of the gallons they'd seen the day previous. El Indio commended the decision.

Leti offered the *pollero* his scanty change, a gesture that seemed to surprise him. In response, Indio said, "Tomas explained your situation. Let me see what I can do for you."

Leti said, "If you have someone who can give us work over there, we'll make payments to you weekly, I promise. If you please help us out, we won't let you down."

El Indio made a gesture suggesting that she should be patient. He went back to his business. Not long after, he approached the women. "Listen, one of you is going to the other side right now. Who wants to go first?"

Communicating via imprecise shrugs and hand signals, the women came to the conclusion that Julia would be the first to leave.

"From the time I sat down on the bicycle, preparing myself," she said, "I had this strong feeling, like, *this is something I never thought would happen to me.* When I saw the leader beginning to take off, my whole body started trembling. I couldn't believe it, *me*, trying to cross by bicycle into the United States! And the pace became fast really quick. By then my body was really shaking, all-out adrenaline. In the distance, on top of a hill, I could see a *migra* truck. I was scared. But maybe it was the fear that kept me going, kept me from blacking out. That first burst was really tiring. I felt lightheaded. I pedaled as fast as I could go. Then, around ten minutes after we tore out of there, the guide slowed down to gather the group. It seemed like we *all* were falling apart. Some of our riders were covered with dirt from crashing. I fell too—but you'd just get right back up and start again. No one could wait or help anyone else. A guide was there in the back keeping an eye out, but really, no one can ride your bike for you. It was each person's responsibility to either keep going or stay behind."

Down a dirt track, the group reached a thicket of bushes that signaled the river and wetlands just beyond. They entered a trail that revealed itself only once the guide waved the first riders through, but the ground became too soft and soggy to continue. The guide ordered the migrants to dismount and leave the bikes.

"We just threw them down," Julia said. "Then we ran for about five minutes until we reached a road. There, the people who were going to pick us up were already waiting."

Solo made it known to the new workers that El Indio was bringing in a professional to handle general management, as well as some supply and cash-flow issues. This person was to be obeyed as if Indio himself had made the orders. Further, Solo said, Indio would be scaling back his own trips to the inside.

"But as you can see," Solo added, "we have more migrants than ever. We'll be running more trips per day. This means more opportunities to make money."

A man nicknamed El Cholo had been deported from the United States, and like El Indio, he had walked the borderline from the mountains to the sea looking for an opening. After a few days, he began to go hungry. Then he came upon a group of *polleros* staging a crossing from Los Laureles.

"That's where I met El Indio," Cholo said. "He gave me food when I was just starving. He said, 'Why don't you go ahead and help that guy over there fixing bicycles, right near the border?' He paid me well—a decent guy like him, it motivates you to work."

El Ruso—the Russian—had also been deported after getting caught up in some shady business. He said he was conflicted because he wanted to live as an honorable person. But without a voter ID card, the only work he could find in Tijuana was the illegal kind: selling drugs, smuggling drugs, robbing for the police, and killing for money. For him, pitching in with El Indio's gang was not only a lesser of these evils but, frankly, also a means to survive.

Solo, El Ruso, and El Cholo had arrived at the canyon a few hours early one day and were working on a pile of bikes near the fence. Cholo squatted on his haunches, helping Ruso adjust some brakes.

A nondescript white van with tinted windows appeared on the access road above and rolled with the creeping sound of granite gravel being crushed under weight. At the end of the track, it slowed, made a three-point turn—its big engine bubbling like a race boat's—and then backed farther in.

"Whoever gets out . . . if you get a bad feeling," Ruso warned Cholo, "jump the fence. We can come back later."

"Okay, *amigo*."

The men heard a door slam before they saw the driver. Around the side of the van stepped a tall, dark-haired woman. She wore black sunglasses, a light tank top, and a short skirt.

"Is this bad?" Cholo asked.

"I can't tell," said El Ruso.

Solo couldn't be sure where Marta's arrival placed him in the pecking order. He didn't intervene or even acknowledge that he knew the woman.

"Gentlemen," she said on approach, "what are you doing?"

"I'm working on these brakes," Cholo said.

"And you." The woman indicated El Ruso. "What are you doing?"

"I'm also adjusting the brakes."

"Is this your job? Or are you men just tinkering?"

"No, we are bicycle mechanics."

"So this is a business? And, maybe, the boss has a phone you can call him on?"

"Yes, that's true."

"And how are you paid?"

"In dollars," Cholo said.

"But are you paid by the week, the day, the hour?"

"No, we are paid by the bicycle."

"So it is in your best interest to repair as many bicycles as you can, as fast as you can?"

"Yes."

"Then why are two men working on one bicycle?"

Cholo held up the one pair of pliers. "Because we have the one set of tools."

"Someone has a cell phone, right? Between you, there are six hands, six ears, three mouths, and three phones."

"One phone," Solo said.

"If you don't have something, if something doesn't fit, if it can't be done in time with the resources you have, the only thing you have to do is communicate that need and more will be delivered. Correct?"

"*Sí*," the men said.

The woman turned on a heel and walked back to the van.

"Run?" asked Cholo.

"No," said Solo.

The lady opened the rear van doors, and then waved at the mechanics. "I have little burritos and soda here for you. Which would you like, orange or purple soda?" She smiled. "We have both."

Although Marta's arrival wasn't a surprise to Solo, he felt the men standing next to the van with their sodas and wrappers of food—himself included—looked like grammar school kids scolded by the teacher. He said the woman could be charming and energetic one moment, and bark orders like a general the next. It was difficult to argue or even defend oneself because what she said was usually accurate. Her field observations were uncanny.

"That presence brought out in us—I don't know if it was fear or respect, but we all paid closer attention to the work," Solo said. "Marta had eagle eyes. She wouldn't treat you badly, and she never arrived with nothing in her hands. But when she turned up, someone would always look and say, 'The boss is here.'"

20

I received a phone call from Ben McCue, the environmentalist. "You're not going to believe this," he said, sounding incredulous. "Terry Tynan's sold all of his bikes."

Already, the border bikes were streaming out of the valley in the silent steady way that floodwaters recede into the ocean. Greg Abbott trucked bikes abandoned in the state park to AMVETS—a veterans' service organization with a chain of thrift stores—as well as to the Salvation Army depot, where they were repaired and sold to the general public. The Border Patrol gathered as many as could be stored for evidence, and agents sometimes dusted the bikes for fingerprints, but when storage space maxed out, they handed the bulk of them off to Richard J. Donovan Correctional Facility's refurbishing and donation program. The Gomez family conferred bikes on Father Joe's homeless services organization, as well as on a number of young Mormon missionaries. Scavengers scoured under bridges, culverts, and washes. Tynan hawked bikes at the swap meet, and on his property, and finally, McCue claimed, he'd sold out to a single entity that happened to be in desperate need of dirt-cheap bikes.

For my part, given the lack of a comprehensive bicycle registry or any type of paper trail, the only real way to track the bicycles was to follow their travels hand to hand. And so, after fielding McCue's call, I immediately drove south. Approaching the last exits before the border, I turned off into the Tijuana River Valley, where Monument Road flickered by in a pastoral blur. I crossed Hollister and pulled onto the dirt lane that led into the Kimzey Ranch. And sure enough, next to the barn, I found Terry Tynan poking around what remained of his bike party. He idled, as if sweeping up the confetti. Just about all of the bikes that rolled were gone.

"What happened?" I asked, shutting the truck door.

Tynan still wore his dirty INTIMIDATOR baseball cap. The Marlboro Lights poked from the breast pocket of his white T-shirt. He kept a full mustache but the salt-and-pepper scrub of his unshaved beard was catching up.

"Sold 'em," he said with a grin.

"To who?" I asked.

"To Hollywood!"

"Hollywood? How did that happen?"

"Well, it's not really Hollywood. But it is a movie studio out there in Kearny Mesa: Stu Segall. My friend works there and he said they needed bikes, a lot of 'em. He knew about my bikes, and . . . we made a deal."

Terry visually wiped his hands clean of the bicycles. McCue had been right, I couldn't believe it. This was not a hoarder's tendency at all. I'd misjudged Terry.

"They bought a few at first, the studio did, a while back. Then they wanted more, and then they wanted all I had. Their guys had to make regular trips with a twenty-four-foot stake truck. They got most of 'em."

I looked around. The leftover bike parts and frames at our feet and in small heaps were a sad sight, like the final, dwindling hours of an estate sale—Grandma was dead and no one wanted the chipped teapot she'd loved.

"What do they want with all of your bikes?" I asked.

"Not mine, ha, not anymore," he said. "My friend says they're shippin' off all over the country. He says they're going to be used in war-training exercises."

"What do bikes have to do—" I began to ask, "What does a movie studio have to do with war-training exercises?"

"Uh, here, you should talk to them. I'm fuzzy on the details." Terry withdrew his cellular phone from his pocket. He hit the speaker function, presumably so I could join the conversation. "I'll put you on to Eric Kiser, you know, my friend who works there. Hold on."

"Hey Terry, what's up?" the voice said.

"Hey. I got a guy down here, a writer, and he's looking into the bikes. It's a good story, and, uh, I told him about selling the bikes to you guys. And he was wondering what you all are doing with the bikes."

"You know what we're doing, Terry," the voice said.

"Well, tell it to him," Terry said. He handed the phone to me.

"Hello," I said. "Eric?"

"Yeah," the man said. "So, okay. You're a writer?"

"Yes. And you bought Terry's bikes."

"You bet, the studio did. And we're looking to buy more."

"Well, it's good news for Terry. But that's a lot of bikes. What do you need them for?"

"So what's your angle on this? Just about bicycles?"

"That's the plan," I said.

"Okay, that sounds all right. So what we do is build hyper-reality training facilities for military applications. If you were to walk through our facility, you'd see the sights and hear the sounds of Iraq or Afghanistan. We've got open-air markets and fishmongers in the streets. We've got live actors playing locals, as well as insurgents. There are pyrotechnics and ambient sounds. What it is . . . it's the magic of Hollywood applied to war training. Soldiers—marines, army, or whoever—they come in here to train, and it desensitizes the men on what they're going to come across in the field."

"And how do bicycles fit in to all of that?"

"Terry's bikes are integral to the set dressing. You've got to imagine, these are poor countries, so they ride bikes. Now, we're building these RHUs—that's Relocatable Habitat Units—and we're shipping them to vital army, navy, and marine bases. The set dressings go with them—across the country. The military is benefiting from the bicycles Terry there is fishing out of that swamp. It's pretty impressive, actually."

"Sounds like it," I said. "I'd like to see the facility."

"Well, uh—so you say you're writing mainly about bikes, right?"

"Yeah, I want to follow the bikes wherever they go."

"You get my number from Terry, and we'll set something up. Now, if you'll hand me over . . ."

I gave the phone back to Terry. He clicked the speakerphone off.

"Some writer, I told you," he mumbled into the phone. "I don't know, he just showed up one day with another guy, one of them enviro-dudes. Likes bikes, I guess."

He listened for a bit, then huffed and clicked the phone shut. He pulled the cigs from the shirt pocket, flicked one from the pack, fished in his jeans for a lighter, and lit up. When he exhaled, Terry looked up to the mesa top and the switchback trail where the first bicycle and migrant had come from.

"Your friend says he needs more bikes," I said, breaking the silence. "What have you got to sell?"

"Uh, not much," he said, raising his arms, encouraging me to have a look around.

"Do you think the migrants will just keep on coming, dumping more bikes?"

"Actually, no. I think it's done. I don't know if I will have any more bikes to sell. The whole thing, all them Mexicans, just dropped off."

"Dropped off?"

"It slowed considerably, and then just stopped."

"It stopped? Why?"

"The Border Patrol workin' with Special Forces or black ops—that's what I think. They sent operatives into Mexico and rounded up all them coyotes. Stopped the whole thing."

"You think Special Forces violated Mexican sovereignty to capture some illegal bicyclists."

"That's one way to explain it."

"How do you know?"

"I talk to Border Patrol around here," he said, pointing his cigarette around the valley, and added, "But they didn't tell me that bit about Special Forces. It's just what I think. Obvious, if you ask me."

To my surprise, Eric Kiser agreed to give me a tour of the facility at Stu Segall Productions. On the phone, he colloquially called their training facility "Baby Baghdad." And a week after my visit to the tree-studded, riverside Kimzey Ranch, I found myself standing on a sidewalk out front, amid a colony of orderly business parks that lined eastern San Diego's Ruffin Road. Stu Segall Productions' seventy-thousand-square-foot complex was unique among the corporate HQs only in that it was gated. A chain-link-and-oleander-shrub perimeter obscured most of the view from the street. At the gateway, I could see only the guardhouse and a couple of broad, windowless, concrete buildings. From the looks of things, they could have made just about anything inside. Movies wouldn't have been my first guess.

A squat man maneuvered a tan-and-white golf cart around the side of the main building. He careened through a looping turn and brought the cart back to a succinct stop just inside the gate. If the cart had been a Camaro, it would have slid to a powerful halt—and the man behind the wheel held himself in the manner of a driver who'd made such an entrance. He then threw the guard shack a thumbs-up and waved me through.

"Eric Kiser, vice president of manufacturing," he said when I approached. "Get in. I gotta take this call."

I sat down on the cart's bench seat. The VP withdrew the vibrating cell phone from a belt holster and began offering one-syllable responses to the caller. Kiser was in his forties, I guessed. His wavy brown hair was sun-streaked and parted on the left. He wore a trim, light brown beard and his thin features sported a touch of sunburn. Oddly, his head looked small on top of his bulky shoulders and stocky frame. Maybe it was the narrow, tinted eyeglasses that created the impression.

We wheeled between the nondescript buildings, through a parking lot, and then approached what looked to be a mothballed commuter jet. Next to the airplane stood a wood tower with the business half of a helicopter protruding from its upper deck. Vertical tracks on the tower, I presumed, raised and lowered the copter. Kiser put the cell away, and, as if changing character, he began what seemed to be as thorough a tour as he'd offer anyone. He delivered specs on the jet and the helicopter. The lingo flowed rich in abbreviations, acronyms, and military jargon.

"What is OPFOR?" I had to ask.

"That's Opposing Force."

"And this is a TV studio?"

Understanding that I was at a loss, he said, "We are Hollywood. Nothing is too much of a stretch. We can do anything. We've got scent replicators that can reproduce the smells of dead corpses and feces. We have simulation rifles that produce an honest sensation of recoil. Former military consult on our designs. Local Arabic and Persian speakers write signs and help us with authenticity. We just made a meth lab, and we got our own meth lab experts. We can re-create the 'rotor wash' of a Black Hawk, and the sea spray off the bow of a destroyer. Here we are, right through this way."

As if entering Disneyland by the back entrance, we approached an arch made of a shipping container set across two low buildings.

The container was light green with a logo that read WAN HAI—the name of a Taiwanese shipping line. The top and sides of the container were dressed in the accoutrements of a ship—marine ladders, hand railings, life preservers, portholes, a smokestack, and a control room. If kids had easy access to shipping containers instead of cardboard boxes, the play ship produced would be the same. Then, passing underneath, we emerged into the sunlight again and were confronted by a bizarre and squalid little hamlet.

Like the set of a cowboy flick, Baby Baghdad had a one-dimensional quality to it. Plywood paneling, simulated brick, tile facades—all were painted to suggest age and wear. Arabic script splashed across the walls, the work of an imaginary tagger. Clothing was strewn on washing lines. Cables suggesting electric and telephone service passed roof to roof. A few items looked just out of place enough to impart the surreal—a plastic palm tree, a broken lawn chair, a stereo speaker, a spare tire, a rusty Weber barbecue. The ground was littered with plywood chips and asphalt shingles.

"We just held a marine training exercise," Kiser said. "This ground cover enhances the perceived threat environment, it gives the semblance of exploded IEDs—that's an improvised explosive device. Check this out," he said, as he walked toward the kind of concrete divider you might see on a freeway meridian. Kiser bent and picked it up with one hand. "Foam," he said, smiling. "Almost as light as air."

When he lifted the block, I caught the blue frame and bright aluminum rims of a beautiful little ladies' Peugeot called Urban Express. It leaned against a set wall in the background, and sparkled as if it were new. Up close, I could see its registration stickers. Someone had valued the bike enough to register it, which few people do, and here it sat missing a front tire. I then spotted a black Murray BMX, with red grips, white cranks, and a white sprocket. I could see that it had once been thoughtfully customized by the BMX rat who owned it. It still bore muck from the Tijuana River wetlands, as well as two flat tires and a rusted chain that curled around the frame like a garden snake.

"Terry's?" I asked.

"Roger. Those are just a couple of Terry's swamp bikes. There aren't many left here. The bikes are being sprinkled all around the country—China Lake, California; Boise, Idaho; Fort Chaffee, Arkansas. It might sound funny, but the bicycles are just as important as the paint and facades. This is pre-deployment training, and hyper-reality means as real as possible. The bikes give the sets a sense of movement and commerce. Plus, the soldiers, actors, crew—hell, everybody loves riding them."

"How did it come to you? How did you know that Terry was sitting on all of these bikes?"

"Just visiting the ranch, going horseback riding," Kiser said.

I couldn't envision this Kiser character and the ranch family son, Terry Tynan, trotting along together, enjoying a sunset jaunt.

"And Terry told you how he came into them?"

"Yeah, the Mexicans," he said.

"Now they're headed to restricted military bases all over the country."

"Roger."

The dispersal of Terry's "swamp bikes," I assumed, had everything to do with President Obama's November 2009 order of a temporary "surge" in Afghanistan. Thirty thousand additional troops were being prepared for deployment at that moment. The common refrain was that few of these young Americans understood much, if anything, about their destination. I stepped around three-hundred-and-sixty-degrees, taking in the hyper-realistic training facility, and I couldn't have named any one country the set might resemble. It had the flimsy and hodgepodge quality of a third-world fever dream.

In a window cut from a plywood facade about twelve feet up appeared what I took to be a mannequin insurgent. It wore a headdress and a baseball player's goatee. Its skin was a coffee brown. On closer inspection, I noted its red-rimmed eyelids, furrowed eyebrows, and a gaze that looked both sad and irate. The figure held a grenade launcher that drooped like a macaroni noodle. There was another insurgent with the exact same face and goatee, the same belligerent stare, but this one was bald, his shirt burnt orange, and he held an AK-47 assault rifle. I couldn't shake the comparison no matter how long I looked—the foam-sculpted insurgents reminded me of Yogi Bear, the chinless cartoon character; the furry one who loved picnic baskets, inhabited Jellystone, and was tailed by a sidekick named Boo Boo. On spring-loaded mounts, Yogi Bear popped up in windows proffering semiautomatic rifles and explosive devices. Soldiers in training were meant to obliterate Yogi Bear on sight.

"Excuse me for saying this, but the sets look kind of one-dimensional. Kind of shabby," I said. "Are they convincing to soldiers?"

Kiser didn't register insult in any way; on the contrary. He said, "We provide the sights, sounds, and smells of warfare, but like a TV show, the sets need to change quickly. The materials need to be light, and because they get damaged, they need to be cheap. It's all down to the lessons Stu Segall learned in Hollywood. He's the real patriot here. He doesn't do all of this for the glory. He's one of the good ones. I would take a bullet for the guy."

This declaration of foxhole loyalty from an employee caught me off guard. "Are you former military too?" I asked.

"That's a negative," he said.

Kiser led me out of Baby Baghdad and into the broader studio lot. Suddenly, as if we'd walked through a curtain, I spotted studio workers commuting building to building on the saddles of bicycles. There were bikes leaning against fences, parked outside mobile office units.

The workers of movie magic wheeled from one narrative into the next. In this way, I understood where at least a few of the serviceable bicycles of Baby Baghdad had slipped off to. They'd careened off the war set to other scenes and other lives. Later, I'd learn that many a worker desirous of a certain model had pedaled them homeward. The wounded, almost always, were left behind. Anyone skilled enough to fix a flat, I thought, would have made off with that pretty little Peugeot.

As we walked, Kiser busily explained some of the products that had emerged from their work in military and police training. One item was called a GETFO, which officially stood for Get Forces On/Off, but for people in the know it meant Get the Fuck Off. It was like the mobile version of a fireman's pole that aided soldiers in exiting the seven-ton transporter trucks. It seemed simple, but in war contracting, he said, "branding is everything." Another product was called a BUG-V, short for Ballistic Unmanned Ground Vehicle. This was a full-sized foam reproduction of a car, taxi, or light truck mounted on a remote-controlled undercarriage.

"The BUG-V can be used in various exercises: vehicle checkpoints, sniper training, or urban warfare," Kiser asserted. "Soldiers can literally blow a BUG-V apart with up to fifty-caliber rounds, and after, just sweep up the little pieces."

In person, the BUG-Vs looked awfully misshapen, as if they'd melted unevenly in the sun. Their spray-paint jobs furthered this perception by lending their soft surfaces the waxy, colored finish of a Spider-Man birthday cake. When the sad and angry coffee-brown foam insurgents were placed behind the wheel and sent rumbling across a desert landscape, I wouldn't have known whether to laugh or to shoot.

Outside a big, open warehouse we encountered a head-high, onion-domed minaret, probably ten feet in diameter. It had been painted a vibrant Easter egg blue. The artifact would eventually cap a mock mosque in a mock village meant to replicate Islamabad—and was destined for who-knows-what base in backwoods America. At the moment, it was just a chunk of petrochemicals with its paint drying in a Southland parking lot.

Inside the warehouse, a few real-life artisans buzzed about a workplace full of woods, molds, and paints. It resembled a cabinet shop. One man wearing an army-green T-shirt and camouflage pants stood at a desk with a large, marbled side of beef set before him. At first glance, the meat looked blurry. This was because it was really foam. Taped to a board at the back of the desk were photos of real cuts of beef. The artist eyed the photos and used a delicate brush to apply the last strokes of rippling white fat. Impeccably detailed fake fish were laid side by side on beds of fake ice. There were crates of light green cabbages, dark cucumbers, brown potatoes, golden onions, and red peppers. White rice and black beans spilled from plywood platters. In a corner I spotted three Yogi Bears leaning, forgotten, against the shop's fire extinguisher. Each possessed the same red-rimmed eyes and hackneyed face, but different beards. The human, mostly male artists followed Kiser's tour with an ear and an eye, but worked as steadily as elves.

Kiser then led me into a back room that was absolutely packed with fake weaponry: Claymore mines stacked like plates, mortars like a pile of yams, grenades arranged like storefront pomegranates. Plastic AK-47s and M16s hung on racks covering an entire wall. I supposed a boy might have seen in that room a wonderland of playtime possibilities. It was if the weapons of green plastic army men had become, like boys eventually do themselves, fully grown. But the close quarters, the chemical smell, the sight of so many phony weapons destined for simulations of wars with ever-shifting endpoints and illusory goals became repellent. I stepped out of the warehouse.

Our last stop was a cluster of rooms that sometimes posed as an Iraqi restaurant, sometimes a hospital, and sometimes a meth lab. With a finger, Kiser lifted a teapot from a crate of them.

"Guys out there want too much money for, basically, junk," he said, dropping the teapot. "When a contract says we need to buy two hundred beds, we need two hundred beds. The military doesn't care if they look good, if they're functional, if they smell. The contract will say two hundred; the auditor will look down the list and count the beds."

"That's why you went to Terry for the bikes?"

"We needed a lot of bikes cheap. They didn't even need to roll."

The conversation at the end of the tour had cycled back to the very beginning: just a bunch of bikes, dirt cheap. But there were still too many questions the bicycles could not answer for themselves. And grasping for grasping's sake, I fired some of those questions on Kiser:

"Can you tell me the exact number of bicycles you purchased from Tynan, their makes and models, and on what dates? Do you know the price paid per unit, and what price was billed to the US government? Can you tell me what improvements, if any, were made? Can you tell me how, and how many, bicycles were shipped to each specific location? Is there any sort of retention rate, for the bicycles, at each of these facilities? Is Segall Productions responsible for resupplying bicycles should they roll out of these training exercises without authorization? Is there any way to track the bicycles if they do? Is there any sort of manifest as to the entirety of bicycles purchased by the studio and dispersed, for reasons of war preparation, around the nation and the world? How far, that you are aware of—how far, exactly, and for how long, can these border bikes travel?"

"Uh," said Kiser, "you're going to have to put that to the big man. Give him a try on Monday."

21

Marta began to spend the majority of her free time with El Indio. And though this was perhaps normal for women dating at her age, the development came as something of a surprise to the family.

"My daughter never was the type to be getting boyfriends like the crazy girls out there today," her mother said. "No, not at all. She was with her brother all the time."

Roberto, while frank about missing the companionship of his former lieutenant, granted her access to his recruiters, the best in the city, as well as various crash pads he used to house migrants. Admittance to Roberto's business infrastructure sharply escalated the numbers for the bicycle operation. But Marta's acumen in the business was something special; she had a touch that couldn't be replicated.

"More than anything," Roberto noted, "this was El Indio's big break."

And on the job, Roberto couldn't help but notice the chatter that pursued the young coyote. Established *polleros* would place important clients in his care, knowing his success rate and reputation for honesty. Plus, people just seemed to gravitate toward him. Of more importance to Roberto, however, was that El Indio had also become "the main topic of conversation at the house."

New vehicles marked the gang's rise and scale; so too did the number of unforeseen difficulties they encountered.

One day, Marta took the van to meet Juan, who, as they'd arranged, was waiting in the little Zona Norte room with nine migrants. When she arrived, eight of the *pollos* paced outside with looks of concern, while inside Juan argued with a young man in grubby jeans and a T-shirt. The young man stood in the corner, his hair disheveled and his eyes glassy. Juan stood closest to the door.

"What's up with this guy? Is he on drugs?" Marta asked.

"I don't know," said Juan. "He thinks he's being kidnapped."

"Leave him here. We'll take the others."

"All right, but his contact checks out."

"We don't need it."

"No, I have to cross," the man said in a sudden reversal. "Please don't leave me."

"Do you still believe that you're being kidnapped?" Marta asked.

"No," he said.

"Can you calm down?" asked Juan. "If you can calm yourself, we'll go. If not, you're out."

"I'm calm," the man said. His breath seemed to be slowing.

Marta and Juan ushered the others into the van. The group avoided the disturbed youth. As an olive branch, Juan offered him the choice of the front bucket seat or the final spot on the bench. The man chose the latter, which caused his immediate neighbors to grimace.

Marta navigated the van out of the Zona and headed west on the International Road. She took a turn near Smuggler's Gulch that led the group through a ramshackle slum and up a rise to the head of Los Laureles Canyon. Here the road descended into the oldest of the city's western settlements. The track became thin. It followed a dry creek bed. Dwellings encroached on the road. The van was not going fast, maybe only twenty miles per hour, when the agitated *pollo* began yelling, "Let me out, let me out."

The man lunged from his seat and pulled at Marta's arm. Juan attempted to intervene. But the jerk of her arm caused the steering wheel to turn sharply right. Marta tried to brake but lost control, and the van and its riders careened into an irrigation ditch. The van tipped and its right side collided with the bank. The migrants were thrown on top of each other as the van came to rest at a forty-five-degree angle.

The man who caused the wreck was still clamoring. "Get off of me," he yelled. Crumpled in the passenger seat, Juan looked to Marta. She was strapped in, but not completely alert. The driver's side door above her was the only option for their exit. Juan shook Marta's shoulder. Her eyelids blinked open.

"Are you okay?"

"Yes," she said. "I think so."

"Can you open your door?"

"No," she said with effort, "it's too heavy like this."

Juan unbuckled and, standing on the door beneath, he helped Marta unbuckle herself and open the driver's door. Then he supported her as she crawled out of the van.

"Is everybody okay?" Juan asked the others.

The erratic migrant began scuffling with those on top of him.

"You," Juan said, pointing at the visible portion of the man's face. The crazy *pollo* became wide-eyed and quiet. "How about everybody else?" Juan asked. "All right, I'm going to get out. Help each other and follow me."

Then Juan emerged from the van. Marta looked shaken. "Are you hurt in any way?" he asked.

"No, *nada*," she said.

The migrants began climbing out of the van and Juan stepped back to help them. He also helped the crazy man. "You need to get out of here," he said, "before the boss finds out. None of us will be able to help you."

But the man sat down on the tilted van. He put his head in his hands.

Marta collected herself with resolve. She addressed the *pollos*: "Listen up, we're going to walk the rest of the way. It's not far. Whatever your needs are, we can attend to them there. If you still want to cross, you can do that as well."

The group gathered and walked down the hill. Marta was in charge again. Juan noted only a slight tremor in her gait.

22

"Sure, I've used the bicycles," said Tarek Ahmad Albaba. "They don't always work that well, but you can mess around on them." As an actor and role player for Stu Segall Productions' war subsidiary, Strategic Operations, Albaba had traveled to bases like Camp Lejeune, North Carolina, and Fort Bliss, Texas, among others. "And yes," he said, "the bikes were always there when we arrived."

In the days after my visit to the Baby Baghdad on Ruffin Road, calls made to higher-ups at Segall Productions yielded little result. While dialing, my mind's eye pictured the yellowed parchments of their purchase and shipping records—and tangible answers to my questions block-printed upon them. I believed that an agreeable chat might result in access to those numbers. But I spoke only to a receptionist and then to answering machines. In the absence of an official response from the brass, I altered strategy. I decided to go looking for the hirelings who'd actually handled the bicycles—the people who'd wheeled and pedaled them—realizing en route that these were the very people I had been wanting to talk to all along. Like me, they were simple witnesses standing on the banks of a strange river.

Albaba and I shared mutual friends, and I knew that he'd worked at some sort of training facility on account of a story traded casually among our peer group—that, while role-playing as an Iraqi insurgent, he'd been attacked by a squad of marine recruits and knocked unconscious with the butt of an assault rifle. On coming around, he was said to have possessed the presence of mind to verbally disabuse the greenhorns as to the difference between role-play and reality. I'd heard the story before becoming aware of Strategic Operations, before I knew of Eric Kiser or even Terry Tynan. I gave Albaba a call on the off chance that his role-play had occurred at Segall Productions—as well as the improbability that he knew anything, anything at all, about the swamp bikes. And as it turned out, Albaba had ridden them for both fun and profit in distant states. He'd already been privy to some studio discussion about my inquiries. Citing our mutual friendships, he agreed to meet.

At twenty-seven, Albaba was handsome and athletically built. His parents had immigrated to the United States from Lebanon and Palestine, and had prospered. And now Albaba's own dreams of writing and producing films appeared to be coming to fruition. I met him at an airy office space—his first—astride a San Diego fishing wharf. He welcomed me in and we sat with a view of the docks, boats, and pelicans. I took out a voice recorder and placed it on the table—something, admittedly, I wouldn't have done in Mexico. The effect is often the same as withdrawing a camera only to watch smiles fade into strained simulations. Eyeing the device, Albaba described the interconnected nature of making TV and films in this backwater satellite of Los Angeles. It was a small pond. He intended to offer his contacts, as a friend—but times were tough, I should know, and jobs could disappear. "That's my only thing," he said.

About himself, however, Albaba proved exceedingly open. So I asked if there was any veracity to the story I'd heard about his being knocked unconscious by an overly enthusiastic recruit. He didn't answer directly, but instead began to speak about his hometown, Charlotte, North Carolina. His family was well integrated into the community there. They'd assimilated and built relationships. On the success of a family auto shop, the family had traveled the United States and a bit abroad. In high school Albaba played for an elite soccer team, and felt every bit the American teen he was. Then the Twin Towers were attacked. In the aftermath, slurs rained down on the family by the "shit ton." He remembered soccer games in which opposing fans and parents screamed "terrorist" in his direction. "It was a traumatic experience," he said—something he chalked up to being surrounded by nowheresville hicks. So upon graduating, Albaba wanted to get out to the liberal, tolerant West Coast. He wanted to try his hand in show business. He got an agent, and a bit of paid work. Otherwise, he filled in as an extra whenever he could. Then Albaba's agent sent him out for a different kind of role: playing an insurgent at Segall Productions.

"They told me they were looking for Arabic-looking, Arabic-speaking actors, or whatever, and the pay was decent," Albaba said. "It is acting. You are acting an Iraqi villager. And anything you can do to hone those skills and increase experience—that's where my head was at."

On the set, the difference between role-play and on-camera work was emphasized: there were no set lines of dialogue, and improvisation from scene to scene was not only encouraged but also essential. If stopped by a soldier, an actor could submit to arrest, or flee, or fight.

"You were allowed to get into it with the marines," Albaba said. "I was young and felt strong. I had martial arts and wrestling in my background. So when they said I could play, I really did play. I mean, I tossed some marines on their asses. You would hear superiors getting pissed off at the soldiers."

It was role-play, Albaba said, but he added soberly, "I really am Arab, and they really are soldiers." He heard epithets like *towelhead*, *haji*, and *sand nigger* thrown around. "I was reminded of high school, and those same seventeen- and eighteen-year-olds who have that view—and here they are now, going to war. It was scary to me. I knew that once they got to Iraq, they weren't going to treat the people with respect."

The premise of the scenario in question was that a knife had been discovered in one of the village "units." It could have been a bunker, or it could have been a house. The villagers/insurgents were either to submit to arrest and further searches or resist. Albaba found himself with a short file of marines coming at him. He could have easily raised his hands and surrendered. But he grabbed the first soldier by the pack straps and threw him to the ground. The man didn't pop to his feet as Albaba expected he might and Albaba realized the military gear the soldier wore was too heavy. So Albaba used the same technique on two following men, but now the first was up, which caught his attention, just long enough for a fourth soldier to strike Albaba with a rifle butt in the back of the head. The actor went down, but would not admit that he was out.

"These were trained marines; if I took down a few of them, it definitely felt like some sort of victory," he said. "But it was getting to the point where it was starting to hurt. They had full gear. I just stopped. It wasn't worth it."

Albaba stepped away from role-play but continued to cycle back to Stu Segall Productions for various gigs. He wanted to emphasize that as the "Shock and Awe" portion of the Iraq conflict evolved into the "Hearts and Minds" phase, the demeanor and professionalism of the troops improved, as did the sets. The bikes, for various reasons, seemed instrumental in creating that common ground. People on bikes, pedaling to market, are the same everywhere.

Albaba and I talked at length about his life and work before I got around to a question that had been needling me. "Why the company resistance to my interest in used bicycles?" I asked. "Is there some national security concern?"

"Well, kind of," he said. "They bought those bikes under the table. There's no paperwork. They didn't even know where they came from. They could be hot, probably are. And then, the studio is selling those bikes to the United States government."

In fact, they were selling them with an impressive margin. Tynan kept his best finds and sold the serviceable ones at the swap meet for twenty bucks apiece, which was still a fantastic deal for a reliable set of wheels. But then, through his connection with Kiser, he sold third-rate bikes in bulk to the studio. Segall Productions sold each of these as set dressing to various branches of the military. They were Tynan's worst bikes. And Albaba was right: they had most likely been stolen at some point. But that was not their exact status when Tynan raked them out of fields and trenches. The only crime was abandonment and existing without papers. It struck me that, with shocking speed, the border bikes had been transformed from America's stolen goods and joyrides into pennies-on-the-pound police auction fodder, then transnational contraband, then swamp trash, then something akin to the infamous $640 government-contracted toilet seats—all with little to no change in their actual appearance or operational mechanics. I realized the price of a bike has nothing to do with its ride, purpose, technology, or age. It has to do with to whom, where, and under what circumstances it is sold. It has to do with hearts and minds.

Stu Segall was well known for refusing interviews and shunning publicity. His stance may have been due to the proprietary nature of his business, or even legal troubles and controversies drummed up on the lot. But his past was almost certainly a factor. It had been described as "spicy" by the local press. Employees used the words "shadowy" and "dark." Just about every production shooting south of Los Angeles ran a portion of its business out of the Segall lot, for logistical reasons. It possessed all of the necessary equipment, as well as links to local talent and the trades. Further, the San Diego market wasn't big enough to go after, so there was little fear of competition from LA's major players. In effect, Segall Productions was the only consistent movie gig in town—and from what I'd gathered, the boss ran it that way. The lack of competition was felt primarily by the workers. They got experience on his lot, but they also got suppressed wages and no job security. In exchange, their loyalty was demanded. For good reason, few with ties to the studio talked out of turn. Yet each knew some piece of Segall's personal story.

Born just after Christmas in 1944, Segall hailed from the small seaside town Swampscott, Massachusetts. Before graduating from high school in the early '60s, he split for Los Angeles, where he enrolled in community college and took odd jobs. The transition from small-town New England to the booming liberal metropolis must have been an exhilarating one. Segall drove a forklift, among other gigs. But his most pivotal engagement during this period was a three-year stint working as a private detective. The job was an education; it seemed to give the young transplant confidence, and further, it turned out to be a chip shot into the movie business. As Segall told Bryan Senn, the author of *The Most Dangerous Cinema: People Hunting People on Film*, "I used to be a private investigator. And I ran into a guy through a mutual female friend who was a makeup artist in tittie movies, the T&A business. He was fascinated by me being an investigator, and I was fascinated by what he did."

What the guy, Ray Sebastian, did was put makeup on naked people who were preparing to have or simulate sex. Sebastian soon invited Segall to act as his assistant makeup artist on a production featuring a number of well-endowed women, and now it was Segall's turn to enhance their body parts. "You know, you have them lined up on tables, and you just went down this line and you put makeup on these girls."

According to Senn, Segall continued taking gigs as a makeup artist but he also filled other film set positions like "grip" and "generally doing whatever needed doing on a low budget movie set." A book titled *History of X: 100 Years of Sex on Film* claimed that Segall got his start "as a porn actor working for Ted Paramore," aka Harold Lime, a writer and producer whom Segall worked with in other capacities. Whatever the route to his decision, Segall told Senn that he took a figurative look around and concluded, *I think I can do this.* And on borrowed funds, Segall made his own movie in 1969. With that title, *Harvey*, Segall took up the director's chair just in time to meet what critics now consider the Golden Age of Porn.

In a hint at what was to come, the dawn of the 1970s saw a couple of productions that featured explicit sex and also received widespread release. But in 1972, when *Deep Throat* premiered at New York's New World Theater, the film was met by cultural forces that vaulted it into a phenomenon. Tagged as "porno chic," it was at once conflated with sexual liberation and the target of obscenity trials, the coverage of which only heightened its notoriety. Forty-eight weeks after release, *Deep Throat* still ranked in the top ten of box-office revenues. Then, in 1973, the United States Supreme Court narrowed its definition of obscenity from "utterly without socially redeeming value," to the current standard delivered in *Miller v. California*: that which lacks "serious literary, artistic, political, or scientific value." With increased production values, plots, and even character development, the creators of pornographic films could now argue that their products included artistic merit. Suddenly, the nation's thicket of local and national anti-obscenity laws and prohibitions was cut back, which greatly expanded the genre's potential audience. This led to bigger budgets and more creative license. The movies were now shot on 35 mm film, were shown in sit-down theaters, and every major city included a boulevard that crammed a string of such theaters into a marquee-studded parade.

Under the nome d'arte Godfrey Daniels, Segall followed his first effort with the sequel *Harvey Swings*. And using the aliases P. C. O'Kake,

Ms. Ricki Krelmn, and Arthur Byrd, among others, Segall made fourteen full-length sex films over the decade, sometimes two and three a year. They had names like *Spirit of Seventy Sex* ("a costume piece with wardrobe mostly from the Garden of Eden," reads the description on IMDb) and *Teeny Buns* ("three girlfriends discover that they can make money the old-fashioned way"). Segall directed some of the biggest names in the business, and garnered awards. And in a nod to his ambitions outside pornography, he produced and directed 1977's *Drive-In Massacre*, in which a serial killer slaughters patrons of a rural California drive-in with a sword.

That same summer, the US Department of Justice released a report on the intertwined relationship between organized crime and the pornography business. It fingered Stu Segall Associates, with offices in New York and Hollywood, as a business affiliate of Bonanno crime family capo Michael "Mickey" Zaffarano. Not only was Zaffarano president of Stu Segall Asscociates, together Zaffarano and Segall served as directors of a nationwide adult theater chain, Pussycat Theaters. Organized crime had moved into the pornography business very early on. The industry operated in a legal gray area and was conducted mainly in cash, which made it prime territory for money laundering and racketeering. According to the FBI, each of New York's infamous five families sent emissaries to Los Angeles—some with instructions to corner the market. Intimidation was brought to bear, and at least one theater was firebombed.

Zaffarano was a big guy with a broad face who had once been a bodyguard for family boss Joseph Bonanno. His father was said to have worked for Al Capone in Brooklyn. In the book *Donnie Brasco*, Joseph D. Pistone, the FBI agent who famously infiltrated the mafia to the extent that he was on the verge of becoming a made man, bragged about having met Mickey Zaffarano through one of that captain's subordinates. The meeting was a new height in Pistone's long climb up the chain of command. When Pistone dropped his undercover identity, which resulted in over two hundred indictments of crime family members, those formerly associated with the undercover agent were assassinated.

But this would not be the fate of Stu Segall Associates president Michael Zaffarano. By 1977, mafia members had also expanded into the piracy of mainstream movies. The Justice Department claimed this trend had cost the mainstream industry $700 million in lost revenue. And the Motion Picture Association helped finance a nationwide FBI sting called Miporn, for Miami Pornography, where the investigation into a clandestine web of porn distribution, racketeering, and piracy began. Some of the mainstream movies pirated included *Bambi*, *The Exorcist*, *Saturday Night Fever*, and *Jaws*. In February of 1980, on Valentine's Day, four hundred FBI agents fanned across the country to make arrests on the strength of the Miporn investigation. Agents searched the offices of Louis Peraino, financier of *Deep Throat*, and his brother Joseph C. Peraino—both of whom, according to *The New York Times*, were associated with New York's Colombo crime family. At the Peraino offices agents discovered film reproducing equipment and a number of original film reels—including, get this, a copy of *The Godfather*.

Agents also raided an office located at 1600 Broadway, Manhattan, which a report by Attorney General Edwin Meese claimed to be the New York office of Stu Segall Associates. According to Zaffarano's former underling, Joseph Pistone, aka Donnie Brasco, the Bonanno family captain fled the FBI on foot. But the fifty-six-year-old didn't get far, because he soon collapsed, the victim of a heart attack. Agents found his crumbled figure clutching a reel of porn that Zaffarano had apparently hoped to conceal from authorities. *The New York Times* reported that Zaffarano died an hour after agents attempted to serve him their warrant.

The loss of his business partner, and the upending of the industry, didn't seem to slow down Segall. And despite the fact that agents observed wanted mafia associates as guests at Segall's home in Los Angeles, he avoided entanglement in the Miporn operation. The year Zaffarano died, Segall released *Insatiable*, featuring Marilyn Chambers and John Holmes, the most successful film of Segall's career and a modern porn classic. He followed this with a sequel, more movies, and by 1984, in a nod to his founding career as an investigator, Segall joined Stephen J. Cannell Productions to produce the hit TV series *Hunter*—a police drama centered on cagey, rule-breaking detective Rick Hunter.

Segall's past almost certainly informed *Hunter*, and the fictional detective reciprocated by boosting Segall into the mainstream.

In 1991, Godfrey Daniels had graduated from a two-decade career in adult entertainment and escaped Los Angeles by establishing a studio for low-budget cable productions in quiet San Diego. The new venture found success with serial programs such as *Silk Stalkings*, *Renegade*, and *Pensacola: Wings of Gold*. But ten years later, in the wake of 9/11, the studio's business began to weaken for a combination of reasons.

In a twist of fate, the Drug Enforcement Administration's San Diego headquarters just happened to relocate to an office complex within shouting distance of the back lot. One day—the story goes—DEA agents heard automatic gunfire in the neighborhood and soon descended on the studio with guns drawn. Once there, they came face to face with "movie magic"—blank-firing weapons and actors shocked to see the real deal. In a peaceable turnabout, the DEA agents proposed that the studio mock up a training program for them. Trials in what was called the "shoot room" were successful. And with the growing wars in Iraq and Afghanistan, Segall saw his opportunity. He turned a portion of the lot into a Middle Eastern village replete with foam "insurgents," minarets, and a dingy, moth-worn look of disorder. Segall's people consulted their military contacts from dramas such as *Pensacola* to evaluate the potential for realistic training. The villages, whether intended to replicate Kurd, Persian, or Arab settlements, developed a common nickname, Baby Baghdad, and through government contracts these Baghdads were built at the most important bases in the United States. As set dressing, the studio shipped the swamp bikes around the nation. Soon, Native Americans role-playing as Afghan villagers at a Baby Baghdad in Nevada pedaled the bikes around a set weathered to look like Helmand Province. Christian Iraqi immigrants to the United States found work as Islamic extremists pretending to destabilize their former homelands. Simulation bullets flew. Pyrotechnics blasted. And the line between Hollywood make-believe and real war continually blurred.

Even in make-believe, problems arose. In 2004, eighteen-year-old marine private Jesse Klingler volunteered to play an interrogation victim on a set at Marine Corps Air Station Miramar in San Diego. According to a Marine Corps investigation, Klingler was blindfolded, bound, and gagged during the exercise. A Lebanese role player employed by Strategic Operations conducted the mock interrogation. He questioned, punched, and kicked Klingler, who was lying prone. The role player also held an AK-47. It was loaded with blanks. Guidelines required guns to be kept some distance from their targets. But maybe things felt too real. At some point, in an apparent act of intimidation, the actor placed the rifle against Klingler's body parts. Finally, he put the rifle against the soldier's right thigh and fired. Hot gases shot from the riffle barrel and ripped a hole in Private Klingler's leg. He rolled onto his side, attempting to evade further harm. The simulation turned nightmarish when the actor, apparently unaware that the gagged soldier was wounded, fired another round into the other leg. The actor then aimed at the soldier's neck, at which point marine observers intervened. Klingler's injuries ended his marine career.

According to an employee who managed a portion of the company's budget, Segall Productions was up to its ears in debt. And, highlighting the downside of military largesse, attempts to hoover up grant money from the Department of Homeland Security just got weird. Senator Tom Coburn made an example of Stu Segall Productions in his report on the "misguided and wasteful spending" of DHS's Urban Areas Security Initiative grants. The report cited Segall Productions' staging of a "zombie apocalypse" tactical demonstration at a posh counterterrorism summit in 2012. The exercise cast forty actors as the gray-faced undead who were hell-bent on capturing an anonymous VIP while authorities fought them off. The demonstration was meant to simulate a "real-life terrorism event" for which DHS paid $1,000 per summit attendee. Brad Barker, president of the security firm the HALO Corporation and the organizer of the summit, told an Associated Press reporter, "This is a very real exercise, this is not some type of big costume party."

There were plenty of reasons for Segall not to talk to a stranger poking around his swamp bikes, but given the variety of criticism pointed his way, I'm not sure he could pinpoint any particular one.

"It's embarrassing, really," said set designer Kim Zirpolo.

Along with designer Bill Anderson, Zirpolo was responsible for the look and feel of the training facilities of various nicknames—from Margoz in Fort Polk, Louisiana, to Little Kabul. By default, she also had her hands deep into procurement, buying everything from window curtains to copies of the Koran. During his stint at Stu Segall Productions, Tarek Ahmad Albaba had become close to Zirpolo. So it was not without reservations that Albaba put me in touch with her concerning the movements of what some at the studio suspected to be hot bicycles. When we first spoke on the phone, I explained my interest in her work and that Kiser had already granted me a tour of the set. As suspicious as she might have been about my motives, she expressed dismay at the thought that my first exposure to her design was the facility on Ruffin Road.

"I wanted to take Baby Baghdad, or Kabul—whatever you call it—to the next level. But Stu . . ."

She didn't need to explain. By the time I'd reached Zirpolo I'd heard plenty about the thrifty operation at Segall Productions. The odd aspect of this particular frugality, however, was that the set I'd been shown by Kiser was used as the showcase for a majority of their contracts, an example of sets that were priced in the millions—and now, a major source of studio income.

According to Zirpolo, the Baby Baghdad I'd seen was a shabby pastiche of her finished product. For example, she said, the marines at Camp Pendleton, California, had wanted a field of opium poppies to replicate such a crop in the Afghan hinterland. Zirpolo sourced container loads of plastic poppy flowers, bulbs, and hip-high stems. Then she and her crew painstakingly erected the fakes into a wind-ruffled expanse of agrarian green. Soldiers used the site to train in opium interdiction and eradication, among other uses. From Zirpolo's description it wasn't hard to imagine the Tin Man, the Scarecrow, the Cowardly Lion, and Dorothy encountering the spell-cast sea of poppies at the shore of the Emerald City—this time with soldiers stalking through the growth.

Then, Zirpolo described an $11 million installation at Fort Irwin, California—a drab town of meat stands, groceries, bakeries, and cafés. Command specifically asked Zirpolo to build an Iraqi bike shop. The theaters of war Zirpolo was asked to replicate were almost exclusively impoverished. As early as the 1890s, the bicycle was called "the poor man's nag." Even today, African politicians promise bicycles to indigent voters. Soldiers who had been deployed suggested that bicycles would lend the fictive villages a sense of commerce, movement, and vitality. The result of Zirpolo's labor was a mud-colored, two-story facade ornamented with a green-and-white striped awning. A yellow-and-white sign in Arabic ran across the shop's front. Outside the darkened doorway, perhaps three dozen bikes—mostly mountain bikes—stood in rows, their bright purples, blues, and reds contrasting with the desert village palette like gummy bears dropped in dirt. The bike shop was the only corner of the installation that truly sparkled.

For a while, a photo of the Fort Irwin bike shop dominated the Strategic Operations website. I found myself drawn into it—I counted bike frames, tires, the hoops of wheels hanging from the shop awning. Compared to the Tijuana bike stores, it was a wonder. Yet it was obvious that the models displayed were not of Middle Eastern origin. Their source was obvious, but I had to know for sure.

"Those were all Terry's bikes," Zirpolo admitted.

Even so, during our first phone conversation I could sense that Zirpolo was hesitant to reveal the details. When I asked how many bikes she'd purchased from Tynan, I received a vague and middling approximation. When I asked where, exactly, the bikes had ended up, Zirpolo said she couldn't be sure. Considering the rise in business brought on by the troop surge and the fact that Tynan's stockpile had been all but cleaned out, both responses confounded me. I continued to phone Zirpolo, however. We chatted. It helped that I wrote for a surf magazine, as San Diego is a surf-stoked city and a good portion of her studio colleagues, as well as Zirpolo herself, were devotees. I described my passion for the bicycles. I knew people she knew. Moreover, I got the impression that she'd reasoned herself out of worrying over a surfer obsessed with shitty bicycles. I wasn't a threat anymore; I was pitiable. Eventually, Zirpolo agreed to meet me at a beachside taco joint near her home in San Diego's north county.

At a picnic table I greeted the petite blonde at the heart of all of this hyper-realistic war play. Straightaway, in her rich Boston accent, she announced that she was at heart a "peacenik," and that her work was filled with jarring dichotomies. She wanted to work in the film industry but she didn't want to live in Los Angeles. Times were tough. War play was the compromise.

Finally we got to the point of our meeting. "You can't just go and get a large number of bikes just anywhere," she said, "especially for us—we're really frugal. Kiser mentioned that he had this friend down by the border, and he had good bikes. I called [Tynan] up and asked him what he could do for me." She looked out at the ocean. We watched the surf roll in. "Actually, I have a bike from him," she said. "It's a Univega from the 1970s—I've looked into its history. Love that bike more than life itself."

Lots of people admire bikes, but not often more than life itself. The weight of the sentiment struck me as disproportionate, but Zirpolo repeated the phrase. And then she explained how the bright yellow cycle was currently stranded with an ex-boyfriend in Los Angeles. She'd been thinking of asking some of her shadier coworkers to liberate it. She'd memorized the code to the ex-boyfriend's apartment complex. In Zirpolo's expression, I thought I caught the love of a bike mingling with the curls of smoke lifting from the extinguished romance. There is more to a bike than metal tubing, wheels, and a chain.

And after a long pause in the conversation, Zirpolo said, "I was conservative with you before, you know, about the amount of bikes I bought from Terry Tynan. When you called I thought, *My God, what if this is coming back to haunt us?* We are subcontracted to the federal government."

"So, you did buy more?" I asked.

"I bought more, a lot more." Enough bicycles, she said, to require at least six trips with the twenty-four-foot stake bed, and on at least one occasion, the use of a semitrailer. I asked her to describe the scene when such a load arrived at the studio—I saw a chorus line of singers, dancers, and trick riders, a sky filled with the tossing of aluminum rims, and music that mimicked the tempo of gears meshing and chains clinking.

"You're forgetting, I get loads of everything. We are salvagers," she said, curbing my expectations. There were beds to buy, pots and pans. "But when bikes come in on a load, I'm like, 'Who has tires? Who has chains?' Everyone would contribute to make them what they are."

Zirpolo appointed the studio handyman—a guy said to be Patrick Swayze's stunt double in the movie *Roadhouse*—as head bicycle mechanic. Rocking to the soundtrack of *Hawaii Five-0*, this man toiled on the swamp bikes. Later I'd learn that many workers eyed a cycle for themselves or their kids. The moment the bikes left the valley, they began to fan out in grand fashion.

It took a few more calls to Zirpolo and another meeting—something like an ongoing conversation, status report, or friendship, even—before I gleaned something of what the parchments contained. Tynan accepted cash only, so money was withdrawn from "petty" reserves, an action that obscured exact accounting. But Zirpolo, who after Kiser's introduction did the deal, said that the studio paid between five and ten dollars per bike. The studio then sold the bikes to various arms of the military, priced between eighty and one hundred fifty dollars apiece. "Sometimes more," Zirpolo said. "Sometimes we sold them as part of a bike repair business or shop, like at Fort Irwin."

At those prices, the military could have gone to Target or Walmart at retail, but the patina of age and the muck of the wetlands, I understood, had dusted the machines with a meditative squalor that was hard to replicate and tricky to value.

I needled Zirpolo as to the precise destination of each load. She said that at the beginning she created a file for every installation—the names of which sounded like cities disappeared by sandstorms. She and Bill Anderson were based out of a trailer on the lot where they scoured the Internet for cultural cues to places they'd never been. As the surge in Afghanistan ramped up and business boomed, she continued to make files but details were skipped, papers were stacked, moved, and lost.

"There were just so many places," she said with exasperation, indicating a range between the island of Guam and the state of Virginia—and as far north as Canada, as far south as Louisiana, as close as Camp Pendleton. "The only way you're ever really going to know," she said, "is by talking to my boys—the swing gang. They're the ones who placed the bikes by hand."

23

Lupita had never been happy about her daughter's palling around with Roberto and his associates, much less her direct involvement in his work. The matriarch knew the telltale signs of a dangerous business when she saw them. With the arrival of El Indio, however, her position slowly altered. She could see that Marta was falling for Roberto's new friend. A suitor was firmly in the picture, and suddenly Marta's affinity for the *pollo* business seemed more reasonable, less about wanton risk-taking and more about building something. Lupita sensed that this ambitious *pollero* was a "good man."

Roberto opened his home to the young Oaxacan. Accepting the hospitality, Indio arrived at and departed from the family compound at will. "On many occasions," said Roberto, "he stayed there with my sister, since they would come home so tired from work. On average they'd sleep just a few hours before their cell phones began ringing again. My sister would make something for breakfast in a hurry, and set out Indio's clothes. Then the two of them would hit the street."

Lupita listened to their conversation. "All the time you could hear them talking about the business," she said. "My daughter would tell him: 'That's a good idea,' 'Maybe better this way,' or, 'I don't think that's necessary, do this or that.' They would work out the different situations, they'd drink a few beers, they'd put music on, and then even *I* would start dancing with them."

The change that came over the two of them was plain to see. Part of it was the way they behaved. Roberto said he didn't believe Marta and Indio could have hidden their feelings if they'd wanted to; it all played out through their expressions. But the couple's attire began to change as well. Indio asked Marta to dress more conservatively on the job. Maybe it was jealousy. But there was also the argument that her style choices caused Marta to stick out, and maybe even attract the wrong element. Seemingly overnight, gone were the miniskirts and low-cut blouses. Marta wore pants now and sensible tops. El Indio's dress changed under her influence as well, but in his case, it was to dramatize his identity as border *cholo*. The tired black windbreaker disappeared, replaced by baggier pants, a handkerchief in the pocket, sometimes a tank top, and even the type of *tandito* that *pachucos* used to wear in the United States. His transformation into the kind of *cholo* that garnered respect *en la calle* was complete.

One day El Indio informed Solo that he would start taking Tuesdays off, but that the business of crossing *pollos* on bicycles would continue under Solo's care. For undefined reasons, Tuesdays proved to be the lightest days for the crew. Given the way things were shaping up, however, it was still going to be a tough task for Solo. He'd have to manage the team—the bike mechanics, the recruiters, the *comunicador, gancho, guía, levantón*—as well as the migrants, and give orders exactly as the boss would have wished. Indio would prepare everything Solo needed beforehand, he said, but the coyote had to take the time for Marta and himself. Solo understood; he said he was up to it.

That first free Tuesday, the couple loaded the company van and pointed it south. Out of the city, Mexican Federal Highway 1 ran like a ribbon that mirrored the contours of the coast. Waves crashed against black rock and filled the desert atmosphere with a fine moisture that diffused and softened daylight, making the jagged landscape appear rounder and everything more radiant. They motored past the Coronado Islands, their brown hummocks like breaching whales. The coastal buttes were intermittently dotted with low-rent vacation homes, shabby cornfields, and dark shacks. Long stretches of beach lay unpopulated. Empty desert lots sometimes gave way to abandoned condo developments. There were both wildflowers and a sense of urban decay. On a lone hill, a seventy-five-foot statue of Christ held his arms out to the sea. The small cities of Ensenada and Rosarito bookended a little surf-splashed fishing village called Popotla, a favorite among Marta's family. Its bay harbored a fleet of open *panga* fishing boats, and was protected from Pacific storms by a crescent-shaped point that appeared to gather up its pocket cove. The ocean could be roiling to a fury outside of the rocky promontory, but inside, the water was always sheet calm. The geology was unique, but what drew the eye was the cacophony of shacks on the ridgeline of the point, going all the way out to the last bit. Their fantastic color, their shapes—it looked as if an ancient circus had shipwrecked on the point and had decided to stay there, hosting shows by the hour. These belonged to the fishmongers, restaurateurs, and modern-day pirates of Popotla. In fact, the main smuggling business to rival that of Tijuana's *malandros* was the swarm of contraband *panga* boats that shipped out from Popotla, slipping north with the resolute persistence, and dumb-luck aim, of a grunion run.

It was common for couples and tourists of all stripes to stroll among the fishmongers and admire or gawk at the variety of their catch. Some of the creatures displayed on beds of ice appeared absolutely prehistoric. At the tip of the point was a restaurant, a wooden establishment seemingly balanced on the rocks like a dry-docked raft. It held an open deck with plastic chairs and tables adorned with flower-printed vinyl tablecloths. For Marta's family, it was a place of both escape and celebration.

Away from the house, unhitched from the workload and the secretive world of smugglers they inhabited, Indio and Marta were able to get to know each other. While neither was the type to offer unbidden anecdotes from their personal histories, over the course of their dates, those accounts became not peripheral or incidental, but somehow central and relevant.

Marta's memory of her home in the mountains of Sinaloa was still fresh, and she wouldn't have spun the nostalgic description Roberto might have conjured. Still, it was a real part of her identity. The land was rugged and they had been poor—less so as she came of age, but examples of backwardness were everywhere. Obviously, Marta didn't dress or even talk the way she did when she first came north. Tijuana had given her a dusting of modernity; her mother would say crudeness, even. But as a girl she was very serious about her studies. Her brothers and sisters called her bookish. But to Marta it was something more. She was competitive and even hinting at superiority. The ranch school was hardly an institution where overachievement was the norm, and betraying a feeling of superiority in such a small class and community was, needless to say, seen as less than generous. It was common for neighbors to lend anything needed to get by. So in the classroom with the teacher sent by the government, when the bookish girl refused to share her test answers with the other girls, great offense was taken. She was called greedy. And prideful, Marta detached from the girls of the village, a course that drew her toward more masculine pursuits.

Outwardly, El Indio's defining moments seemed as sharp as the points on a seismograph. He was simply left in the village with his elderly grandfather, and when the *abuelo* passed, the boy had to fend for himself. The decision to travel north was one of survival. His recent gains in Tijuana—well, somebody was going to do this work, somebody was going to get lucky. Why not him?

Between the points, however, were more subtle questions that begged answers—confidences that required intimacy. For example, upon arriving in Tijuana and encountering Roberto and his open invitation to cross, why didn't the young *migrante* go to be with the people he'd long pined for? Did he resent the family that left him behind? Or had time diluted his feelings? Had he simply forgotten them?

The truth was, soon after his arrival in Tijuana, El Indio had tried to cross. Three times. And those experiences had forced the traveler to be cautious of others and rely solely on himself, to become distant and inventive. Indio would explain that he'd left Oaxaca with $308.40, his grandfather's life savings. He'd heard stories about the dangers of *la frontera*, so he'd made a little pocket inside his underwear where he kept his inheritance. On the trip, he met many other *pollos*. There was one group who'd made arrangements with a coyote, and one of their number asked him if he had anyone on the other side who could pay for his crossing. It was not a lie to say that he did have people *en el otro lado*. The coyote accepted him into the group. And this figure planned to cross the *pollos* in the mountainous Tecate section called the Eagle's Nest, where they would make a hard trek to the pickup spot. Moments after they set foot in the United States, however, the travelers were beset by a gang of violent thieves. These men robbed the *pollos* of everything visible—money, jewelry, provisions—and sent them, defeated, back into Mexico. Their coyote expressed only a "*ni modo*"—oh well—and hatched a plan to cross the next night. Indio became suspicious of this man. He never even checked on who would pay for Indio. And the Oaxacan wasn't going to give the bandits another chance at his hidden money. So he slipped the operation and was soon back in Tijuana's central district. Within a day, he linked up with another group and another smuggler. But when the time came to leave, this man arrived so drunk the *pollos* refused to go with him. Later, Indio was picked up by a smooth-talking female recruiter. She had a stunning confidence and a quick wit about her. Her guides seemed competent enough, and he agreed to make the night crossing near Otay. None expected the immediate wash of lights and revving engines of *la migra*, a rabbit hunt in the brush. But Indio wasn't about to let the authorities get ahold of him. He ditched this group and ran and ran until he came out on the Mexican side again.

He started to roam around on his own, sleeping wherever he was at nightfall: up against a market, under stairs, wherever. He wandered close along *la línea* all the way out to Playas and, little by little, went along checking out the scene.

This was when he met Roberto. But by that time, he'd begun to see that *polleros* were buying *pollos* like himself at a very good price. And because he'd experienced that part of migration, he knew where the valuable clients could be found.

The *pollo* became a *pollero*. It was as if a sheep took a look around, noticed who carried the big stick, and became a shepherd himself. "My whole life I kept my dream close of having something, and, why not, of being somebody," he said.

El Indio and Marta liked to drive the smugglers' van into the tourist beach town of Rosarito. They ate, they drank. They danced to American rock and norteño music and continued their date by club-hopping into the small hours.

Roberto wasn't staying up intentionally. As he got older, he just didn't require as much sleep. And so the brother was aware of all movement in the house.

"They came back at dawn on Wednesday morning so *dichoso* and content," said Roberto. "To me it seemed like living a dream."

Lupita, who also slept lightly, noted the hour. "Everything and everybody was happy," she said. "The same goes for my husband and I—which always makes me really scared. That much happiness is related to fear."

24

In January of 2012 a low-pressure system that had formed in the Gulf of Alaska dropped down to the temperate latitudes and brought cold ragged wind, rain, and turbulent seas to the desert coast. This was the kind of rainstorm that had historically swelled the Tijuana River into a braided, roiling thing that broke dikes and sluices, turned ranchland into bogs, floated car tires by the container load, drowned livestock, polluted the ocean, and spawned flash floods of the type that had washed the Méndez children out of Los Laureles Canyon. This was the kind of storm that had brought me to the Tijuana River Valley in 2008, and the latest arrival signaled that my obsession with the border bikes had tripped into another year.

Given that I was compelled to travel to Tijuana during the storm, I admired that El Negro lived in a ship, however credible. It was perched on a low cliff above the beach. The entrance, like the rest of the businesses along that stretch across from the bullring, was level with the street. But its facade facing the ocean lorded over the boardwalk below. And this, in truth, was the only aspect that distinguished this *barco* from the other oceanfront buildings, as an artificial boat's hull emerged from the structure, black and rusting, and hung midair like a vessel embarking on an elevated plain. The bow held a port for a cannon and was topped by a decorative railing. I assumed that it had been built as part of a themed restaurant, but I could never determine if El Negro's ship was in a state of halted construction or one of decay. It turns out there is a form of construction so leisurely that it approximates atrophy. This example looked as if Noah's ark were slowly emerging from the earth. El Negro's job was to keep squatters from commandeering the ruin.

The detail of the ship and my contact's nickname—the Black—suited an increasing feeling I'd had each time I'd come to Playas, that I was slipping ever so surely, notch by notch, into a den of pirates. After that first bungled interview, I'd continued to visit El Negro at the municipal bathrooms. We discussed the myriad ways to cross. We walked the canyons. We plumbed the mysteries of my search—unfolding enough upon each visit, I felt, to chance another. The primary discoveries were, one, the widely accepted belief that the *pollero* called El Indio had built the most successful migrant-smuggling operation in the area's history; two, that he had abruptly ceased the bicycle-crossing business at the height of its glory; and three, that he'd simply vanished.

El Negro proved himself to be a particular fan of a good story. He never greeted me without a new one. And I believe he liked a tale so much that he'd momentarily set aside his strong reservations about me. Those first questions put to him in front of the bathrooms took root in his mind—as he remembered trucks with California plates, laden with bicycles, threading into the little canyon—and spurred a host of his own queries. He began poking around his contacts, and then truly researching the legend of El Indio in a slow, methodical manner that resembled investigating a geriatric's crime by visiting all the bingo parlors and bridge clubs in town. So when El Negro sent word on the stormiest day in a region not well suited for them, Dan Watman and I dropped everything and set out for Playas de Tijuana.

In the shadow of the border wall, adjacent to the lighthouse with its single illuminated lens, we visited the first set of bathrooms only to find them shuttered. Same with those on the boardwalk. The rain picked up. We hustled along the line of plywood seafood stalls, restaurants, cantinas. On a sunny day there would have been day-trippers and mariachis. Today the streets were wet, windblown, and empty.

Among the series of entries, Watman recognized and then knocked on a black particleboard door. "Negro," he hollered through a crack, and banged again. Under an awning ten feet away stood a light-eyed man with spindly jailhouse tattoos. He might have been loitering; he might have been waiting for the rain to cease. He watched us like a gecko. It was only through his eyes that I saw us for what we were: two gringos knocking on a ramshackle door in a downpour. There's a chance the spooky *güero* considered selling us whatever we were there to buy. The badly hung door then wobbled, scraped, and opened a smidge. A brown eyeball peered out. "*Sí?*"

"*El Negro esta en casa?*" Watman asked.

"*Quién es?*" The eyeball was fixed in place.

We identified ourselves. The door stuttered shut. The loiterer under the awning shifted posture. I thought he would be my next interaction. But then a husky laugh erupted inside. The groggy morning voice of El Negro commanded, "Let them in, let them in."

The doorman conceded and we were admitted beyond the black gate. The person before us was small, and he wore a yellow rain slicker. It was a fortunate item to have in the storm, I thought, and a fitting detail had the ship been in operation. After granting us entry, he quickly shoved the door closed and locked it with a chain. The interior view came as a revelation: before us was a large open area, a vaulted ceiling, and planked floors stinking of creosote. Broad galley windows the width of the room opened first upon the ship's bow and then on the stormy Pacific Ocean. Other than the distant Coronado Islands—dark shapes intermittently obscured by cloud drift—no land was visible in the entire panorama. I saw only surging waves and bands of blue showers sweeping the horizon. I nearly expected the floor to list from side to side.

El Negro emerged from a tiny room to the left of the landing. Inside it I could see a string of socks drying on a line.

"It's a rain day," he said. "You've caught me sleeping." He shuffled into his morning routine, rubbing his eyes, washing at a sink. I realized I'd not seen El Negro without the foam hat that read RECICLADOR CASTRO. I found the hat amusing—not only because it advertised a recycling center named after a dictator, but because I could picture Negro wearing it when the Border Patrol agent at the fence line, indicating the pile of bikes on the Tijuana side, asked if there were any recycling centers in Mexico. El Negro's wavy, leading-man hair with the wisp of silver running through the crown surprised me—he was not the bathroom worker in this domain. Then the doorman, Ramon, spoke so quietly at my elbow it came as a peep.

"*Mande?*" I asked.

Below the yellow slicker, he shifted his weight from foot to foot, in a state of constant preparation. He could have been eighteen, maybe twenty. He wondered if we might have some change for a morning coffee and a cigarette. Watman and I dug in our pockets for pesos. When Ramon had the coins in his palm, he opened and slipped through the door—a courier of a secret. This was when El Negro gave us the backstory; it was a tale both common and complex. Border Patrol had recently dumped Ramon on the streets of Tijuana at two in the morning, and like most deportees, he didn't know where the hell he was. Southern Mexicans plucked from a dishwashing job in, say, Newark, New Jersey, and expelled upon the seediest part of a border town with neither connections nor a plan were sitting ducks and everybody knew it. In the Playas community, people ensnared in this circumstance were directed to El Negro. He had a gift for scaring up the essentials: food, clothing, and, if not outright accommodation, at least a sense of place. El Negro had survived the experience himself and, some would say, prospered. Out of feeling for his people, he now captained the deported to safer shores.

"Tijuana is an octopus," Negro said. "If you're smart, it can hand you things. But its arms are so strong and so many—if it decides to take, you will lose everything before you know what happened."

We drew up chairs made of two-by-fours. The ship's mast—fashioned from a local telephone pole—was lying across the deck, out the galley doors, and onto the bow. The mast divided the room and forced us into an awkward huddle. Although it was mostly dry inside, as bands of the storm blew by, a pitter-patter drummed the decks.

I'd learned my lesson about asking abrupt questions in Mexico. American-style journalism acted as a kind of antidote to the truth—the more efficient and straightforward the question, the slower and more obfuscating the answer. So I bided my time. We talked about the weather.

From a corner of the ship's broad windows, the three of us could see work underway on a new sea fence that extended the border wall into the waves. A significant but temporary pier had been built along the line, and from this, a sequence of pylons was being driven into the seabed by heavy machinery.

"I tell the people," El Negro said, pointing, "it's throwing money away."

Quite literally, I believed as well, it was like pouring money into sand. The contractor that won the job had failed to take into account something every surfer knows: anytime a construction like a pier or jetty is placed in the littoral zone, sand quickly forms around it. Shallow spots make great places to surf. Already, El Negro knew of *polleros* guiding migrants around the sea fence at low tide. Some brought a change of clothes, others endured the knee-deep water. Waving at the entirety of the new $70-million-per-mile US border wall, El Negro said, "The [American] president is all the time trying to pull down the sun with his finger."

Ramon returned to the ship with a steaming cup of coffee that he politely shared with his host. He had a cigarette for each of them. As the three of us continued to talk in a hodgepodge of English and Spanish, Ramon paced the plank flooring and took calculated puffs on his cigarette and long gazes out the galley windows. It reminded me of passing time in transit. Floating somewhere out there on the storm clouds was a new life plan.

In our cluster on the ship deck, as wind and rain beat at the galley windows, El Negro finally cleared his throat before revealing the information that had brought us there. He said he'd been drinking in the Zona Norte and outside a bar called the Chicago Club, he'd run into two men he knew to be bicycle mechanics who worked for the bicycle coyote. From memory, El Negro conjured the scene of these two men working day and night, jammed in a shack lit by a single bulb, surrounded by rims and hubs and frames and cranks, all within spitting distance of the fence. As romantic as the image was, the disclosure that there were two full-time mechanics was a harbinger that told a broader story. The necessity of two mechanics suggested a number of bikes larger than I had yet imagined. It validated the possibility of tracking down delivery drivers, suppliers, etc.

I began this line of inquiry, when Negro said abruptly, "I don't know about those things."

"Well, what did you learn from the mechanics?" I asked.

"They told me where to find El Solo."

"Who is El Solo?"

"He is the brother of El Indio."

"Brother? Really?"

"No, not really. But like a brother—a friend since they were little, from back there in Oaxaca."

"Wow," I said. "And what is he like, this El Solo?"

"I don't know, just regular. Like him," Negro said, pointing at Ramon.

"You mean he looks like Ramon."

"Yeah, all the people from over there look like him."

On several occasions, Watman had pointed out the sinews of bigotry entwined in Mexican culture. The idea that all indigenous people looked alike, and that this look wasn't handsome, popped up time and again. The fact that Negro looked indigenous as well was a contradiction so common it wasn't worth mulling over. But I suspected the answer about Solo's appearance to be a smokescreen. In the past, when I'd ask about the work or job of one of El Negro's associates, he'd say, "Oh, a regular job."

I'd ask, "What kind of a job is a regular job?"

El Negro would look around and point at the closest approximation of a man doing work—a coconut vendor, a fishmonger. "Like that," he'd say.

"Really?" I'd say. "Your friend sells coconuts too."

"Sure," he'd answer. The truth was that "regular appearances," "regular names," and "regular jobs" meant that I couldn't be trusted with specific information. So right about then, I was wondering what, exactly, I was doing aboard ship.

Then El Negro stood. He walked off into his cabin and returned with a grammar school folder. He situated a two-by-four table in front of his chair, placed the folder on the table, and took a seat. He withdrew some reading glasses, put them on, and opened the folder as delicately as if it contained sheaves of papyrus.

"What are these papers?" I asked.

"These are my interview notes."

"Interview notes?"

"Yeah, my interview with the guy I'm talking about. I am a writer," he said. "Like you."

Then, El Negro began to read from the pages, and within a few minutes, maybe less, Watman, Ramon, El Negro, and I were walking along the gravelly roads of a leafy green Oaxacan village that boasted a dozen or more shacks, one tractor, one bicycle, and two small boys named Solo and Pablito.

25

In Roberto's estimation, Marta appeared a shade slender for a serious chef. Yet she moved about the kitchen with the confidence she'd exhibited on the ranch as a girl, even among colts in the stable. It wasn't austere so much as efficient. Her hair was up and she wore a dress for a special outing. But then she'd slipped her mother's heirloom apron on top. Below the trim of the calf-length dress, her ankles dipped into the kind of pumps she donned these days only for her dates with El Indio.

This was in fact a Tuesday, the one day she and Indio set aside for themselves. But on this occasion the couple had sweet-talked the entire household into treating the day like a traditional family fiesta. This required Roberto to take the day off as well. The hook had been Marta's promise to make her *chiles rellenos* with peron peppers. Marta's cooking was a treat. Roberto especially appreciated her *pintos refritos*, dark speckled beans she fried with a preparation of mustard and pepper. Even the smell that filled the kitchen from their cooking, he thought, was delicious. The beans and freshly chopped onion and cilantro provided the aroma, but the perons accounted for the flurry of activity. Though he never touched the raw ingredients himself, Roberto observed with such acute attention that years later he could describe every step Marta took in preparing her labor-intensive specialty—the golden-yellow pods opened and the reedy veins and seeds removed; the waxy skin grilled on a hot *comal*, softening the flesh and giving that smoky flavor; each pepper individually wrapped in paper and set aside for easy peeling. Marta managed the pot of stewed beef with her sinewy arms as deftly as she'd later fold cheese into the tender parcels. Finally, the stuffed peppers were closed with toothpicks and a rich tomato salsa was ladled on top.

Though Marta approached the kitchen with a characteristic precision, from the outside patio Roberto noticed something additional—something cultivated and secretive. Plans; his clients carried them in their minds like the precious briefcases they'd pop open on the other side. And he recognized the look even as he hefted charcoal into the grill and tussled with an order of *carnitas* that he'd carried into the house like a fat child. Music played from the stereo. Their mother padded *masa* into tortillas and tossed them onto the *comal*. Roberto could make out the voices of other family members in the driveway. They admired a vehicle El Indio had purchased just that week. There were many distractions that afternoon. And still, Roberto mulled over Marta's demeanor. He wondered if his instinct hadn't been tainted, maybe by wafts of a less-than-noble emotion he'd experienced in recent times. It wasn't outright jealousy—he and the entire family were happy for Marta. They felt blessed, even. But Roberto recognized a feeling of displacement. The lovers Marta and Indio commanded the attention of his entire household. All conversation touched on the activities of El Indio, his business, and the success of what was called, in shorthand, "his idea." At this moment, Roberto could hear a rather casual discussion between his own father and the young man he'd introduced to the family. And now his sister blissfully swayed to music while presiding over his wife's kitchen with a matron's confidence.

At the time of his courtship with Chedas, Roberto's people were still living far off in the mountains of Sinaloa. Tijuana was strange and new and blossoming before them. The frontier city was always unpredictable. The couple built this home from almost nothing but their imaginations. They filled it with children, relatives, friends, and strangers. And now that foundational achievement was serving as a humble stage for a more dazzling romance.

Yet Roberto's family was content, which had not always been the case. And Roberto believed that his power, in business as well as in the home, derived from his big-tent mentality. There was more to be gained by including others in one's own successes and supporting them in their individual endeavors than in jealously guarding one's little tract of plenty. He'd seen more than one smuggler chase off potential allies. So Roberto cooled his thoughts. His own time in the sun had been long and fruitful. The present belonged to Indio and Marta.

Roberto caught the cascading sounds of more guests arriving—friends and associates. His children spilled onto the back patio like small gusts destined to slam shutters and open doors. Roberto lit the coals and they came to life with a small roar. Stereo volume increased, and chatter rose to meet it. The table was set. Lupita made trips to the kitchen, returning each time with new plates of colorful snacks. And no sooner had Roberto finished preparing the grill than he spied his father at the kitchen stoop, waving his arms for silence.

"Everybody listen," the old man said. The guests turned to see the patriarch in his straw hat and plaid short-sleeved shirt. He'd stepped out of his normally reserved persona. "I have something special my wife Lupita and I would like to share. New things, good things." He looked around him and called, "Dear Marta and Pablo, come please."

Drawing the apron from her shoulders, Marta emerged from the kitchen. In view of the gathered, she was immediately shy. Indio broke from the center of the crowd to join Marta and the old man. His smile commanded his entire face—chin lifted, eyes alight. The father took their hands. The people hushed.

"Pablo has quickly become a natural member of the household, and one week ago, he came to me and he asked my permission to marry our youngest daughter, Marta. Her mother and I agreed, and more importantly so has she. So I present to you the news that Marta and Pablo will soon marry."

The guests burst into cheers. Marta's eyes widened, a girl surprised by her own dreams said aloud. Indio looked to her, willing a glance, a ray of her attention.

The food was served. Some guests sat; some stood. Each party waited and circled around to congratulate the couple, who barely had an opportunity to eat or drink. Watching the pomp, Roberto thought, amusing himself, *So my baby sister is going to be a "Mrs.," and he a "Mr. El Indio."*

"The announcement filled us with joy," he said later. "We drank beer. We drank wine. You know, we put the music up and we danced and sang."

At work on the borderline, El Indio carried the news of his engagement close to his heart. With Solo at the helm, the operation was running smoothly. Bright new workers had been brought in by Javy and Juan. Marta's network of *enganchadores* delivered *pollos* almost trouble-free, and for the time being, the group was well stocked with bicycles. Though he'd backed away from guiding migrants for strategic reasons, El Indio decided to take the next group. It had been some time since he'd connected with his brother Martín, who'd taken on the duties of pickup and liaison to distant cities. He hadn't seen the rest of his family for an even longer period. And this, likely, was a sticking point. Indio hesitated to share his joy and good fortune with his parents. He must have understood that his unannounced appearances and swift departures caused them to be guarded in his presence. He would have caught the raised eyebrows and the shrugging of shoulders. The family left a child behind in a faraway place, and now this man came and went at odd hours, always with strangers in tow. It was almost certain, had he shared his news with his mother and father, his joy would have been met by village nail biting and skeptical glances. The very nature of his work precluded the open and honest disclosures expected of a son. El Indio comported himself as if this trip were like any other, a mere business run.

He and a young guy called Apolo had the *pollos* "nailed up against the fence." This is what they called it when they put the migrants under or over the fence and ordered them to stand with their backs to the wall until the signal was given. Indio didn't like the look of their traditional point of entry. The two Border Patrol agents, each parked on the nearby mesa tops in their kilo trucks, weren't sticking to the expected schedule. "The action had gotten hot," Apolo said. Something had occurred down at Playas that was pushing independent *pollos* east. "Things were always changing," he said.

This was a busy time for Simon, *el checador*, whose job it was to divine the movements of *la migra* and keep tabs on floating migrants. Depending on the variables, Simon's report from the heights of Summit Canyon could force El Indio to choose from a few less-than-advantageous options. He might order a worker to approach privateering migrants and offer the bicycle service. Unaccompanied *pollos*, however, often did not have the means to pay. Or having crossed through the area in the past, they might have opted to chance it themselves. In this case, the *polleros* could ask the independents to hold off. But if they refused, or looked unreliable or sketchy in any way, the bicycle *polleros* could simply wait. Foot migrants would often provoke a chase through the bush, and depending on the number of Border Patrol agents involved, the field for El Indio could be left wide open.

El Indio's group was small that day and the seven bicycles had already been lifted over the primary fence and were resting on their sides. Indio also stood against the fence. He'd decided to let the independent migrants attempt their crossing. Then he'd assess the area of operation. The cell phone's walkie-talkie soon beeped and Simon's voice came across. "They're on the inside," he said, "and they're heading for the river mouth."

Twelve thousand eight hundred ground sensors lay buried across the length of the border. Several hundred were said to exist in the five-mile stretch from San Ysidro to the ocean. These sensors were triggered by seismic disturbances—earth-shaking temblors, heavy construction, horses, running and walking people—and they were placed near known entry points and migrant trails. Their sensitivity could be calibrated according to location. Each device was associated with a number. When triggered, the sensor emitted a signal that was bounced off a repeater and then sent to dispatch. The receiving agent at HQ would pinpoint the sensor location using its number. That agent could then radio officers in the field to investigate the cause of the trigger. Faith in the sensors did not run high among rank and file, as they could be tripped by anything from rodents to corrosive elements in the soil. Or the sensors might be tripped by nothing. Sixty-two percent of their signals fell into the category of "unknown causes," as opposed to the thirty-four percent known to be a false alarm.

El Indio had no way of knowing whether or not the independent crossers Simon followed with the binoculars had tripped a sensor. But at that moment, the Border Patrol agents surged into action and trundled down off the mesa tops. Indio waited. The dust trails settled. The wind kicked up again. Minutes later Simon called, "They're going for the river. *La migra* is after them. The way is open."

The *polleros* ordered the clients to mount their bikes. "Remember, single file," Indio said. "Keep your eyes on me; don't look behind, don't look to the sides." The cyclists followed the team leader down a bumpy foot trail that eventually led onto a wide and grated dirt road. Apolo brought up the back. Indio increased the tempo to a fast but sustainable pace. The pack elongated, then pulled in again—forming a train that stirred little dust. Simon's voice came over the walkie-talkie in Indio's breast pocket. "Still clear," it said.

"And the paved road?" he asked.

"Clear for now."

The bottom of the gulch road degraded into a dry wash that lapped up on a bend of Monument Road. Before the juncture rose a brace of pale and dusty cypress trees. Nearly eclipsed by the undergrowth was a small cement marker set in place by a forgotten Boy Scout troop. Its plaque designated this location as the entry point of Father Junípero Serra, founder of Alta California's mission system. Indio brought his bicycle to a slow stop and raised his fist into the halt signal. He turned in the saddle. "Stay here," he said. Then he crept out to get a glimpse of Monument Road. It was empty. Indio waved the riders across, where they met a dirt farm lane that carried them off to the ample brush cover of the Tijuana River.

26

There are two central facts about the bicycle. First, it is the most efficient device ever created for the conversion of raw human power into locomotion. And second, there is something special about the people drawn to tinker and wrench on them. The proof is all around us—from freeways to airports to factories of mass production. The greatest by-product of the instrument that Susan B. Anthony called the "freedom machine" is the diaspora of remarkable people who had been inspired by bikes and, as a result, created a lot of remarkable things.

Many of these we just don't notice anymore. When I was about six or seven, I rode a hand-me-down bicycle with a metal seat and solid rubber tires. I loathed the tires because they spun out, absorbed little, and set me apart from the older kids on their pillowy and sleek pneumatic tires. But it turns out that solid rubber tires were an important gift, a great improvement over wood or steel wheels, given to us in the mid-1800s by Clément Ader—a Frenchman with a reedy mustache and eyebrows like a Muppet, who would go on to improve Alexander Graham Bell's telephone, install the first telecommunications system in Paris, and build three airplane prototypes that looked like nefarious and great-winged bats.

Orville and Wilbur Wright owned a bicycle shop in Dayton, Ohio. There they invented a self-oiling hub and left-handed threads to prevent pedals from coming unscrewed en route. Profits from the Wright Cycle Co. funded their work on what was known as the "flight problem," and the brothers used bikes and bike-building techniques in aspects of their gliders and wind tunnel experiments. The Wright Flyer, the first human-piloted airplane, was built in their final bike shop at 1127 West Third Street, the craft's spare lines, cables, sprockets, and chain drive leaving no doubt as to the machine that gave it lift.

Another bike shop owner and mechanic, Glenn Curtiss, is said to be the founder of the commercial aviation industry. He created the seaplane and the first American combat aircraft to enter World War I. He worked with Graham Bell on ever lighter and stronger combustion engines.

Still another bike mechanic, Henry Ford, adopted the down-the-line mass-production techniques used in cycle factories in the manufacture of another revolutionary vehicle, the Model T. Mr. Ford also borrowed from the bike components such as pneumatic tires, chain drives, ball bearings, and wire wheels. This technology, along with bike industry innovations such as steel tubing and metal stamping, enabled the United States to quickly retool for World War II.

Today's 54-million-member-strong AAA (formerly the American Automobile Association) was directly inspired by the League of American Wheelmen, a group of cyclists, clubs, manufacturers, and mechanics that actively instigated the Good Roads Movement, a grassroots campaign advocating a novel idea: to involve the federal government in the building and maintenance of uniform highway systems. Their advocacy led President Woodrow Wilson—himself a cyclist—to sign the Federal Aid Road Act of 1916, a program that lasted into the 1920s and shaped the landscape of American road travel as we know it today.

Requiring no electricity or chemical fuel, bicycles have lifted economies, facilitated industrial revolutions, and circumnavigated the globe. Their inventors and technicians gave us the motorcycle, the short skirt, the unchaperoned date, and an audacious faith in our own forward progress.

Following my visit to El Negro's ship, I was desperate to see the swamp bikes again. As a group, the bikes had become something like molecules of air or water—identical, interchangeable, and nearly invisible. I was aware of mass and movement, but I could no longer see individual bikes. My mind was just swimming with interchangeable objects I could only identify by knowing where they'd come from or where they were going.

To complicate this, the character who'd put them in the valley proved mysterious and exceedingly elusive. The various authorities who scooped bikes up offered little comment. And the vast majority of cycles fled the valley in such disparate and unforeseen ways, I felt as if the foundation of the little world I'd been circling in had steadily eroded out from underneath me. This dislocation spawned a powerful suspicion that I'd wasted profitable man-hours chasing down a funny little dream I'd had—something cute, impractical, and, in the end, unreal. So when the trail went cold like this, I found myself stretching beyond my normally reclusive nature just to be *around* bikes that *might be* the bikes I'd followed, or had crossed paths with in the street; or that might share lineages or decals or might have been manufactured in the same facility half a world away.

A friend texted a photo he'd taken of a stake-bed truck brimming with used bicycles in Los Angeles. I could see in the photo that the truck was about to enter a large metal-recycling facility. When my friend confirmed the destination, my heart made orbital loops around a hard little nucleus of anxiety. At first I thought: now this is tragedy; to melt bicycles guilty only of being abandoned. Then I wondered, could these be my swamp bikes? By 2011, America's largest export to China, by value, was scrap and waste metal. The largest market for recycled plastic and metal was also the world's largest bicycle manufacturer. Was it possible that these bikes could be crushed, shredded, melted, and then reconfigured as brake cables, handlebars, bells, and frames? How could I follow them then?

While feeling disjointed from the bike trail, one of the more logical things I did was hang around a group of punker kids who'd inherited a bicycle co-op from a lesbian organization. Their big idea was to teach basic repair skills to the public in order to get the people back into the saddles of their old beaters. It is surprising how often a flat tire can relegate a bike to oxidation and rust—which is terrible, because both are very slow-acting relatives of burning. The women who had been running it had had a good thing going with the co-op, but their base just wasn't big enough to sustain an ongoing effort of bicycle repair. So the punkers took it over. And these kids had no boundaries; they would help fix anyone's bike for free. I got the sense that it was a political gesture in the same way that they Dumpster-dived, aggressively recycled, and grew vegetables on the front lawns of their rented apartments. The bike wrenching was done at a weekly farmers' market in one of San Diego's poorest neighborhoods. This particular burg happened to be a melting pot of immigrant communities that, coincidentally, mirrored the United States' overseas interventions—there were Vietnamese, Laotians, Central Americans, Somalis, and Iraqis. These were the places my contacts at Stu Segall Productions studied in order to create facsimile training grounds.

Although tolerant of almost everybody and anything, the punkers frowned on beach cruisers as, well, simply pedestrian. Meat eating was so last century. And me, a grown man riding a 1984 ladies' Free Spirit with slim to no vintage potential—uh, well, they found me peculiar in the way that only the most generous and openhearted people can. I hung around out of some vague hope that I could learn something about the way ordinary bikes moved through the world once their commercial value had plummeted into the low two digits. At that cost, in City Heights at least, bikes beat bus fare every time. I also learned how to use a crank puller, that spit really is the best adhesive for handle grips, and that one could build a whole new society with WD-40 and duct tape. What I really discovered, however, was the exact expression on the face of a ten-year-old whose single mother worked fourteen hours, seven days a week, after you'd fixed his flat tire and he became exponentially more mobile and independent again. The look wasn't cute; it was triumphant.

On an early morning not long afterward, I was standing in my kitchen watching a new rainstorm that had set the palms outside to flapping. I switched the radio on in the event that the river valley might be mentioned. Instead, a reporter delivered a short piece about a bicycle giveaway. Christmas was just around the corner, and events like this had become popular with police and fire departments. So I listened with only a minimum of attention until I heard the radio voice mention the name of a local Salvation Army center and, importantly, that these particular refurbished bicycles were being supplied by the Richard J. Donovan Correctional Facility.

As reported by Janine Zúñiga in her 2009 *Union-Tribune* article, bikes discovered abandoned by the Border Patrol's Imperial Beach staff were taken to the station on Saturn Road, checked for drugs or reports of theft, and then stored until a batch of them could be shipped to the prison. For a quarter of a century, the inmate mechanics at Donovan had been repairing and restoring bikes and then donating them to charities and school programs. I was well aware that a portion of the swamp bikes had disappeared behind the prison gates; I just didn't think I'd ever see them again. I did, however, imagine the bicycle mechanics behind those high fences and walls, plying a craft—truing wheels, adjusting neck sets—that tied them to the greatest engineers and inventors of the twentieth century.

Soon, I found myself navigating a landscape of freeways and strip malls. The sky above was the color of cement. The pavement below had become a black lake district of interconnected potholes. The weather and traffic caused me to run late to the giveaway. The feeling of missing the bicycles by a slim margin was becoming familiar.

The pitiful gray tones of the atmosphere seemed a permanent condition until I found the Salvation Army's Kroc Center. I parked and, under a gale, scurried toward its arched entry. There I saw a splintering, kaleidoscopic explosion of color. A lanky Salvation Army major wore a pert uniform of navy felt with crimson trim. Sheriff's deputies wore their dark greens and khaki with sparkling badges of brass. One hundred and twenty-five children, six to eleven years old, writhed in their new helmets like a fleet of helium balloons—buoyant, kinetic, and waiting for liftoff. A pair of Donovan's inmate bike mechanics, with shaved heads and dressed in light blue scrubs-like uniforms, had arranged the dozens of vivid bicycles by size and style and positioned them upside down in rows. When a bike was presented to one of the children, it was ceremoniously reverted. In the turning over I could see that the swamp bikes now gleamed with new chains and freshly polished hubs and chain rings. Some frames had been completely repainted too, in a rainbow of color—all the bells and whistles had been added, literally. Scents of fresh lubricant and rubber tires almost overpowered the fast-food catering. Both inmates and corrections officers laughed. Bikes rolled. The children glowed. The hushed quality of low clouds only amplified the shrill, chittering sounds of children on squeaky new tires.

And then it began to rain again; the ceremony was cut short. Children wheeled away, padding their feet to either side while guardians walked uneasily behind as if blowing wet leaves along. The inmates were escorted into the corrections vans. I didn't like to see bicycle mechanics subjugated in this manner. Many of my new colleagues and interview subjects, including El Negro and several of Stu Segall's employees, had done time. On the border, it seemed merely a station between here and there. When existence is unlawful, a sentence isn't so much the result of poor decisions and character flaws as it is a harsh reality of life—like the flu. The fact that the inmates showed interest and skill in rehabilitating dirty, abandoned bicycles when they could be lifting weights, trading cigarettes, and watching TV helped me to see beyond the jailbird denim with the bright yellow Donovan insignia. The uniforms were temporary; the love of a bike was forever.

I left with a feeling that, for the first and only instance, seemed opposite to that of searching. It wasn't bated breath so much as deflating relief. I didn't need to follow these particular bicycles anymore. They'd found their rightful place. They'd descended through the seven rings of fire—of importation, sale, impoundment, auction, contraband, confiscation, and donation—and here they were again in the hands of fresh new cyclists. It was as if the bikes had graduated from weird times on the traveling freak show, having filled the roles of the reptile man, the fire-eater, the sword-swallower, and now in retirement they'd become staid, calm, dutiful, and serviceable again—like postal workers, customs clerks, and crosswalk guards with colorful, secret pasts.

27

"When we hear a whistle," Apolo told the men who huddled among the riverside brambles, "that means the ride is close, and we're going to run like crazy to meet El Indio."

To hurry up and wait was the hardest part. El Indio had gone to meet the *levantón*, which may have seemed a convincing next step to the *pollos* but did not always seem that way to the remaining guide. Their position could be stumbled on by a rancher or recreational horse rider. The whine of the Border Patrol quad motorbikes was sometimes within earshot, and if civilians caught a glimpse of the crossers, it was easy to assume they'd tip off the agents. During the day, that sense of apprehension was amplified by the thumping of naval helicopters running maneuvers out of Ream Field. Then, before dusk, nature took over—buzzing mosquitoes that left dime-sized welts on the skin rose out of the swamp. Worst of all was the fear that no one was coming for them. Though Apolo was new, there were rumors of migrants having to jump aboard a city bus with only the few gringo dollars their guides had given them.

But the whistle came high and clear through the reeds. The *pollos* left the bikes there on the ground and ran along a path toward Hollister Street. This time, there was a minivan—light blue with its rear window peopled by those stick-figure decals indicating family members. The bumper was plastered with sports logos. Indio had opened the sliding door and he waved the migrants forward from the bush trail. The men dashed and climbed into the cabin. Indio entered from the passenger-side door. "Okay, let's go," he said.

Apolo knew the driver to be Martín, El Indio's eldest brother. That Indio was said to have worked out a deal with his siblings, and that even his sisters had made runs, was welcome news. But the brother displayed an austere bearing. There was talk of trouble at home.

They traveled a similar route to the one Indio and Martín had negotiated that first time. They passed the community gardens the earlier group had taken for a shantytown. They passed the old cowboy bunk house that now held a county parks office. Martín slowed to a halt at the last stop sign before the bridge. After they'd crossed, he accelerated onto the wider pavement. As they approached the first, outlying tract homes of Imperial Beach, one of the passengers noticed the wail of a siren. "*Trucha*," he said—watch out.

The siren belonged to a white-and-green Border Patrol truck that now appeared in the van's rearview mirror. It was coming on hot behind them.

"*La migra*," a migrant whispered.

"Everybody relax," Martín said.

The truck soon blew through the stop sign they'd passed. It crossed the bridge and then its headlights flashed.

"Pull over," Indio said. Martín edged the van to the roadside. It was lined by a thicket of wild bamboo. Apolo noticed their clients eyeing the growth, and he soon considered the option of disappearing into the bamboo as well. The instinct to flee ricocheted through the cabin. "Everybody stays in the van," Indio said.

The enforcement vehicle and its wailing siren shot past—the windows were so tinted, it was hard to tell if the driver even looked their way. The valley quiet eventually settled back in, like a moist vapor rising from the wetland.

Had they been arrested, the agents would have interviewed everyone in the van—a central purpose of which would have been to discover the identity of the *pollero*. They would have checked the ID of each illegal against criminal databases, and asked each where he was coming from and where he was going. They would have searched their cell phone address books and call histories to make connections. The agents would have graphed how each migrant knew the others. There was a chance the relationship between Indio and Martín would have been established—which would have put their entire family in jeopardy. The migrants would have been offered immunity for their testimony against Martín and El Indio. The first offense carried a ten-to-thirteen-year sentence in federal prison.

An alternative scenario—one *polleros* drummed into their clients before allowing them to set foot on the inside—required that no one ever admit meeting or talking to a smuggler. They'd simply decided to cross together. Since the bicycle organization guaranteed another opportunity to cross should a migrant find himself deported, the likelihood was high that the clients wouldn't leak.

But even in the absence of evidence, the authorities could bounce El Indio from one institution to the next until his business failed, his family members were jailed or deported, and his marriage plans whirled into indefinite and withering limbo.

Silent and sweating, the migrants wore the slack expressions of castaways. El Indio turned to them. "*Amigos*, today is our lucky day," he said. "Those *pollos* who took to the river on foot must have been fast. Now *la migra* is rushing around the swamp trying to catch them."

Apolo could tell by his cool demeanor that Martín was a good driver. But it was Indio's words—his ability to shine through that

Oaxacan stoicism with an open and honest reassurance—that made the coyote's professionalism apparent to the new *guía*.

"So we're going to continue." Indio nodded at Martín. "Okay."

The van lurched into gear and they merged onto the road. The migrants remained shaken.

"That was a close one, *amigos*," Indio continued. "It happens. But we need to lighten up. Did you ever hear about the *malandro* who crossed through *la garita* on his bicycle?"

If this was essential information, Apolo hadn't heard it before.

"Well, this *hombre* wheeled into line with all the cars, and just like them, he was stopped at the front. The customs guy pointed to two sacks the man carried on his back. 'What's in the bags?' the man says.

"'Sand,' says the Mexican.

"'I need to have a look.'

"So, the *malandro* poured out the bags there on the concrete, and sure enough, only sand. 'Hmpf,' says the agent.

"Our guy, he refilled the bags with his hands, loaded them up on his shoulders again, and pedaled across the border. Next day, same thing. The agent demanded to inspect the two bags again. The *malandro* showed him nothing but sand. This went on every day, until one time the Mexican with the sandbags failed to appear. Some months later, the agent sees the bike rider at a taco shop somewhere around here. This *cholo*, he was now wearing brand-new tennis shoes, baggy jeans, and gold chains. The agent couldn't help himself. He taps the Mexican and says, '*Hola, amigo*, it's been a while. You really had me thinking there on the border with your bags of sand—I knew you were smuggling something. Listen, I won't bust you, just tell me what it was.'

"'*Amigo*,' said the *malandro*, 'I was smuggling bicycles.'"

A couple of the migrants chuckled, the others only smirked. Apolo was still on the job, self-conscious but observant. And through the back window, a second Border Patrol truck appeared. It was distant and slow, but steady. One of the clients began to look over his shoulder. Indio, turning in his seat, must have seen it too.

"What?" he said, suddenly animated. "You don't think that joke is funny? That's because you migrants see yourselves as the *malandro*. Am I right? But believe me, in this joke you are not the *malandro*. You, sirs, are the sandbags. *Gracias* to all of you for pedaling my stolen bikes across to the United States."

The holdouts chuckled, and Indio guffawed until the cabin eroded into laughter. At that moment the second Border Patrol truck pulled up alongside the van. The driver's window was down and an officer peered into their vehicle. Indio looked ahead and grinned. The agent was presented with a slightly used minivan displaying current tags, family stickers on the back, good tires, a driver wearing American-style clothes, and happy, laughing passengers on a sunny suburban day. The Border Patrol accelerated around them and moved on into the baked pavements of the Southland.

Before the convenience of air-conditioning, it was common practice in Mexico and parts of the West to battle summer temperatures by opening the entire house to the dark breezes of the predawn. Stars still blinked in the well of the sky and windows and doors were thrown open like the gates of a dam. Houses filled with the rushing balm of night-blooming cactus, sage, and moist earth. Before sunrise, however, matriarchs sealed the chilled atmosphere in by shuttering their windows with a series of heavy, layered drapes that insulated the home from both light and heat. Summer's daylight hours became the darkest and most still of the year as families attempted to trap morning inside like block ice in a cooler. Men returning for lunch could not see their meals. Those with a need for airy openness stayed away. And though El Indio's mother had known only windowless shacks in Oaxaca, in the United States she'd taken to shuttering the apartment as if it were a Sonoran hacienda—even while her neighbors' air conditioners thrummed.

Apolo noticed the architecture wasn't too different from that of the motel where they'd deposited the clients. The steps were made of concrete, the railings of steel; aluminum framed windows that looked shuttered by seasonal residents. Indio glanced at Martín, who only nodded up the stairs. On the landing, Martín put his key in the lock. As the door opened, a block of light expanded across the carpet. Indio followed but Apolo stepped aside in the entry. "*Madre*," Martín called. "It's not even warm today. Open some windows."

Indio turned back to fetch Apolo. "Please," he said, gesturing at his colleague.

Their sister, Josie, sat in a corner watching television; the blue of the screen seemed to hold her in its glow. She glanced at them. The room smelled of *albóndigas*. A large pot, visible from the doorway, simmered on the stovetop.

"Josie?" Their mother's voice came from a side room. "Oh," she said, stepping in and making out the forms of her sons, "the hoodlums."

The sister stood and began to draw the drapes. Sunshine lit their mother, whose brown eyes narrowed but did not blink—the eyebrows peaked into sharp angles. Her gaze leveling on El Indio, she stood like a creature without the need for breath.

"*Hola, mamá*," he said. "This is a friend—Apolo." Indio gestured toward the young man behind him. She offered no acknowledgement.

"The work that you do is dishonest," she said.

"Let him alone," Josie replied.

"It is my obligation to tell him," she said with a wave, "and to protect the family. He does illegal things and now, it seems, all of my children are helping him."

"I cross regular hardworking people," he said.

"Always wanting to do whatever you please. That's Pablito." She clasped her hands at her waist and looked at Martín and Apolo. She huffed. "I made soup. Sit down."

Josie and the men gathered around the circular dining table. There were six chairs; the immediate family consisted of seven. Some of the walls held framed family photos, but none from the village.

Their mother served the bowls of soup. She placed a spoon next to each and remained standing. "The neighbors ask questions," she said. "They see Martín come and go at strange hours—on the phone like a drug dealer. I think he is at work and his boss calls. I am afraid the man might say something. This morning I see Martín leaving without tools. I tell him if he doesn't do honest work, he can't live in my home."

"Leave it alone, Mama," Josie said.

The guests concentrated on the meal.

"And if he can't slip away, he sends your sister to do the dirty work."

Martín looked up. His chin and neck were deeply tanned but his forehead paled where the hard hat had covered it on the job. "Our baby brother needs help, it's our duty to help him." He flicked a hand at his T-shirt and jeans, always speckled with cement. He pointed at his bucket of trowels near the door. "You don't have to tell me which kind of work is dirty."

"What you're doing is wrong," she said.

The fact that the matriarch had herself engaged the services of a *pollero*, as had every person close to her, was a thread no one cared to pull. Among the men, Martín had acknowledged that during his crossing, "there was no one laughing." The coyotes kept them hungry, tired, and scared. Safe passage was the best they could have hoped for. The people Martín dropped at the hotel on Indio's behalf seemed legitimately happy. And Martín said he could see Indio confident and excited in the things he was doing and saying.

Apolo sensed that their sister, Josie, got a kick out of the work. But also that a dispute in the family, even between the siblings, "was a true chaos"—a situation that would not stand in the village.

Indio set his spoon next to his empty bowl. "Mother, what if I bought a real house for you—something nice here in San Diego. Would you be accepting and open then?"

"A house!" she said. "Oh, Pablito, isn't it nice to daydream? The only thing I have is my family, and you are putting us all in danger."

"If I buy you a house, will you help me out?" El Indio asked soberly.

For the first time, Josie and Martín looked at him as if he'd gone too far.

"Ha!" she said. "Let us see you buy a house and then, just maybe, we can talk."

When the youngest brother said good-bye, it was clear that the conversation in the apartment was going to continue without him. Finding capable pickup drivers had been a needling, and potentially disastrous, problem. On the stairs, Indio admitted to Apolo, "This is going to be more difficult than I thought."

Walking to the van, Martín said that he would try to convince their mother. El Indio took this as more than an offer and asked Martín if he really believed in him.

"The truth is," Martín said, "I don't know."

Apolo hesitated to weigh in. He saw the seeds of disaster in Indio's boastful promise of a house. He tried, in respectful tones, to explain that buying a house was much more complex and expensive than Indio might think. There was the matter of finding the right one at the right price, and then there was the paperwork, the banks, credit history, notaries, etc. "I know all about it, *hombre*, my uncle is a realtor over here in San Diego," Apolo said. "For you, I don't think it's possible."

"Your uncle?"

The man worked for an outfit called Century 21, Apolo said. Indio asked for an introduction.

"*Compa*, houses here cost hundreds of thousands of dollars, even more," Apolo said. "How are you going to pay?"

"In cash," Indio said.

Martín groaned.

It was apparent, Apolo said later, "whether they knew it or not, the family was becoming a part of El Indio's gang."

28

At eighteen, El Negro migrated from the steamy Pacific state of Michoacán to the sunny citrus belt of Southern California. For nearly three decades he resided in the suburbanized farm town of San Bernardino, California, where he worked as a bus driver and machine operator. He married, gained a green card, and raised a family of five. The trajectory of his life seemed set. He would grow old with his family rising up around him.

But early one evening in 2004, El Negro went drinking with friends after work and on his short drive home he was pulled over at a four-way stop by local police and arrested on suspicion of driving under the influence—it was his third such arrest. Without means to put up a defense, the conviction was a foregone conclusion. In addition to sentencing him to jail time, the judge stripped El Negro of his legal residency and ordered his deportation following completion of his term. Expelled onto the streets of Tijuana with nothing but his memories and his wits to sustain him, El Negro remembered, "I was scared, man. Even in prison I heard shit about Tijuana."

He'd been convicted, but the real-life consequences far surpassed the mandatory sentence. El Negro lost his income, career, home, wife, children, legal status, and identity. The weight of the guilt and remorse he suffered in exile was crippling.

Eventually Negro made his way along the boundary to Playas de Tijuana. At this tiny corner of northwestern Mexico that widened and shrank with the tide, the dreams of the disconnected were sustained in small ways. At that time, families separated by the border wall could converse through the pylons at the beach, for instance, or at Friendship Park. The myriad smugglers, their astounding techniques, and the stories of successful crossers brightened the deportee's meager existence with an alluring ray of hope.

While acquainting himself with Playas, El Negro stumbled upon a construction site near the old lighthouse. He saw that the dark red earth of Monument Mesa was being prepared for something, but that the handful of workers present seemed simply to mill about. So Negro struck up a conversation. A worker told him that a nonprofit organization was building bathrooms there and planning a park, but that the man hired to operate the backhoe had failed to show.

"So now what?" El Negro asked.

"I don't know," the man said. "We might just leave."

"I can drive a backhoe," Negro said. "If you want to work, let me help you."

The man consulted with the crew and soon enough El Negro was in the seat of the intimidating machine. He showed smarts and ability, and he was invited to stay on in several capacities. Following completion of the project, the organizers held an opening ceremony in the new park. Negro was asked to work at the bathrooms on that occasion, a kind of concierge of the establishment. And as the event came to a close, almost as an afterthought, an administrator informed Negro that the position was open, and his if he wanted it. He did, and he soon took up residence in an ample supply room in back, almost hidden by the circular design of the structure.

The municipal bathrooms proved to be a nexus point. Plumbing infrastructure was not the beach area's strong suit, so locals frequently stopped by. From them, El Negro gleaned layers of gossip that came to form an intricate picture of his surroundings. He got to know Playas in less convenient ways too. Not long after he'd taken the new job, Tijuana police picked him up for walking without identification. En route to the police station the officers answered a call concerning the robbery of an area 7-Eleven. On arrival, a gun battle erupted between the officers and two *pistoleros* fleeing on foot. Negro was handcuffed in back of the patrol car. Bullets penetrated the metal like staples through paper.

Another time, he'd cut into an empty lot on the way to the Comercial Mexicana for groceries. In the fading light he came upon some plastic trash bags surrounded by splatters of something wet and black—fresh blood, he discovered as he bent to look. Then Negro noticed the decapitated head set openly on the mound of plastic. The bags were filled with the body parts of three men. The blood at his feet had yet to coagulate. He's done the math a million times. Negro escaped a run-in with the murderers by a matter of minutes.

One day a man in a white pickup stopped in the loading zone at the bathrooms. He was a bigger guy, and as soon as he stepped out of the truck Negro could see that the man still had the way of the ranch about him. His cool gaze traveled the landscape as if assessing the quality of the range. The bed of his pickup was filled with men, day laborers, it looked like. The man approached Negro at the bathroom entrance and introduced himself.

"*Buenos días, señor.* My name is Roberto. You don't know me. I work in the area. And I've noticed that you have a little room there in back of the bathrooms." A pause settled between them like a centavo coin spinning and shivering to a stop on the concrete. "It is helpful to be observant," Roberto said.

"That's where I am living," Negro said.

"Yes, well, I've got these *pollos* here," he waved at the pickup, "and I've had some arrangements go bad today. If the police see them in my truck or on the streets, these men won't get to where they need to go. If you hide these men in your room there, for just a short time, it would be a great favor."

"For them?"

"And for me."

"For them it's not a problem," Negro said, taking his key chain from his belt. The eleven men were granted entry to his small space in back. Negro moved his bedding and accommodated them as best he could. Then he returned to his station outside the bathroom entrance.

Sometime later, this man Roberto returned with a white van. He greeted Negro in the same calm, respectful manner. The two of them ushered the men out of the room and into the idling vehicle.

Roberto turned to Negro and said, "Thank you for the hospitality," and he withdrew a roll of cash. He peeled off a few bills and extended them.

Negro waved them away. "I appreciate the offer. It's not necessary," he said.

"Why not accept a small tip?" Roberto asked. The bills lay like limp fish in his hand.

"I have compassion for my people." Negro shrugged. "I've been a migrant like them. And if they are sent back here, I have been that person too. I can't take money."

"Okay, *amigo*," Roberto said, tapping the brim of his Stetson. "Maybe you will let me compensate you next time."

"Good luck," Negro said.

In this way, he became known as someone who helped exiles. Others brought clothing and sometimes food to be distributed at Negro's leisure. A charitable person once delivered a box of professional attire—dress shoes, clip-on ties. On a slow day at the bathrooms, Negro noticed a group of grubby migrants and waved them over.

"Men," he said, "you can't go to an interview looking like that. Look, I've got this box of clothes over here; pick out something for yourselves. Take whatever you have a need for."

The men rifled through the box and donned items that appealed to them—pants, suits, and sports jackets. They had just gathered to look each other over, inventing new occupations for themselves, when a police car pulled up and an officer lowered the window. "*Oye*, bathroom guy," the officer called to Negro, "where are all of the *pollos* at?"

Negro raised a hand to his brow. He looked down at the beach. He surveyed the park and the sidewalks. "I guess this isn't the place today, officers," he hollered back. The patrol car sped off. Negro then appraised the men in their new costumes again. They looked, he thought, like a conference of lawyers.

By the beginning of 2005, housing prices in California, Arizona, and Nevada had jumped 25 percent over the previous year. Across the Southwest construction boomed to meet demand—and a web of industries, from complex financial instruments to raw materials, surged with it. According to the Bureau of Labor Statistics, the unemployment rate had ebbed to 5.2 that January and was still steadily sinking. These conditions created a vast market for cheap undocumented labor—which was mostly filled by Mexicans. The action in smuggling that labor over the boundary was as hot as any other fed by the bonanza, and in Tijuana, it was hottest at Playas.

Around that time a middling *pollero* we'll call El Ratón—the Mouse, for his oversized ears and shifty gaze—insinuated himself among a significant band of smugglers based near the bullring. Each of his colleagues was known for certain techniques, successes, or feats in the field. There was an attractive young woman who called herself Viva Mexico, for example, who was famous for having cut a garage-door-sized partition in the fence with an arc welder. Her crew then rigged the piece with hinges and meticulously fit it back into place—so as to access the portal again and again. Another operator employed a grappling hook fashioned from rebar with a knotted rope ladder attached to it. The hook would be thrown up onto the fence line and the *pollo* would climb the rope, straddle the fence, toss the rope over to the US side, and climb right down. This wasn't a simple thing to do. Incidents of broken ankles and legs had skyrocketed at the border fence.

El Ratón, however, was not a specialist. He bought, sold, and crossed *pollos* in the most readily available ways. More than cunning, he was known for an accessory. El Ratón carried a handgun in the band of his trousers and he was rumored to have killed a man in a dispute. When asked why he carried a weapon, El Ratón commonly replied, "It's a dangerous border, a dangerous business." Few of the other *polleros* armed themselves—getting caught with a gun in the United States would immediately finger them as smugglers and invite a slew of additional charges. Further, the *polleros* understood El Ratón's comment as self-reflective—that he intended a dangerous business. This was a fragile and perilous boast. Handguns were highly illegal in Mexico. If police caught El Ratón with the weapon, and he hadn't already fostered a financial relationship with them, the Mouse would be looking down the barrel of a thirty-year sentence. If he ran into men who truly used their weapons as business tools, his chances would be worse.

One day Negro was tending the bathrooms at the lighthouse when El Ratón approached, his beady eyes darting about. He wore a collared shirt and baggy jeans cinched around skinny hips. A light jacket purposely left open revealed the revolver.

"*Mira*, Negro," he said, looking right and then left. "I heard that *pinche pollero* Roberto was here talking to you." He flicked his chin upward. "Where is he now?"

"I don't have that information," Negro said with a shrug. He continued to break off squares of toilet paper, folding them into personal allotments for his customers.

"You are *amigos*, no? You tell each other things."

"I work at the bathrooms. He is a client. He used the bathrooms and he left. The people give me five pesos, not their day plans."

"We both know that is bullshit," El Ratón said. "So let's agree that when you see Roberto again, you come and find me, *comprende*? I am the only *amigo* you have now. That Roberto, he is a dead coyote. Nobody takes *pollos* off of me."

Ratón made a show of peering downward. He hunched his shoulders and hollowed out his middle, a gesture that popped the pistol grip from his waist. In this posture, he looked at Negro, his small eyes unusually still. He sucked at his front teeth, tea-colored chalks rimmed in silver.

He said, "Don't end up on the wrong side of this."

El Negro did spy Roberto again, of course, and as the white pickup casually rounded the curve about the lighthouse, Negro flagged it down. The truck came to a slow halt. Negro then noticed an associate of Roberto's sitting shotgun. This was El Oso—the Bear. The nickname was not an ironic description of his size.

Wearing the Stetson and dark sunglasses, Roberto leaned on the steering wheel and spoke past this man. "*Compa*," he said, "*que onda?*"

"*Qué onda*," Negro replied. "Can I have a word with you?"

"Go ahead," Roberto said. "You know El Oso."

"*Hola*, Oso," he said. "No, Roberto, over here by the bathroom, *por favor*."

Roberto pursed his lips, put the vehicle in park, and stepped out. His associate remained on the vinyl bench seat.

Roberto stood a head taller, which forced El Negro to look up when they faced each other. "El Ratón was here flashing his pistol thirty minutes ago," Negro explained. "He said you are a dead coyote. Nobody takes his *pollos*."

"*Sí?* El Ratón? Here, eh? What else did our colleague have to say?"

"That when I see you, I should tell him."

Roberto whistled. "Yet another complication to the day, *compa*." He held his chin in thought. "But we can accommodate our friend. What do you say? I don't think he's playing."

"No, I don't think he is playing," Negro advised.

Roberto walked back to the truck. At the passenger-side window he took off his hat and sunglasses and handed them through to El Oso. Then he gave this man directions. El Oso placed Roberto's hat on his own head and slid over the bench seat to the steering wheel. He situated the sunglasses upon his brow, put the pickup in gear, and drove away.

Bare of his Stetson and shades, Roberto peered about Monument Mesa. He draped an arm around Negro and said, "Make me a guest in your home for a little while. I would appreciate it."

Within a half hour or so, Negro recognized Roberto's *pollo* van circling the block. Then, in short succession, five of *el coyote*'s workers approached the bathrooms on foot, identified themselves, and asked also to be guests in Negro's home.

"*Pasele*." Negro waved them through. They opened the steel door at the rear of the structure and entered the supply room in the deft silent file of smugglers.

El Oso eventually returned along the lighthouse road in the white pickup. He parked at the curb in front of the bathrooms. He took his time getting out, and placed the Stetson on his head. He waited in the plaza. He looked at the sky, checked his watch, and then approached and handed El Negro his five pesos. Negro traded them for a fold of tissue and Oso entered.

It wasn't long before El Ratón came loping around the green coconut stand on the opposite corner—but still it was surprising, the way a hunting thing, however quiet, could come side-winding along at the critical moment. His jacket was closed this time. He nodded at the truck.

"You didn't come get me," he said to Negro.

"I can't leave my job," he said.

"Inside?" he asked.

"*Sí.*" Negro nodded with gravity.

"With his pants down already?" Ratón winked at the bathroom attendant and stepped inside. On finding the stalls empty, Ratón called out, "Eh, Negro, where's your *amigo*?" El Negro shut the front steel door of the men's bathroom and locked it—a round click of cylinders sinking into place. "Eh?" Ratón said.

The barge-like groan of the supply room door sounded, and then Roberto's voice. "No need to yell, Ratón," he said. "I'm right here."

Negro placed the CERRADO sign at the entrance. And standing outside, he could hear a scuffing and shuffling of feet, a flurry of muffled sounds like flags flapping in a stiff wind, and then a pronounced moan. "No," El Ratón said, "think about it."

"In all of my years as a *pollero*, I have never owned a gun," Roberto's voice then said—reflective, warm almost. "And now, when I have been openly threatened, just the weapon I need finds its way to my hand." The measured clip of pacing was detectable. "You paid a lot for this, I'm sure, carried it around—right there in your belt—a mother kangaroo warming its little baby in her pouch."

"No, Roberto," Ratón repeated. "Think for a minute."

"Last week you crossed four *pollos* that first came to me. I did not go hunting you with a pistol. You did me a favor—a load was lifted from my back, and people who wanted to cross were able to do so. Those people will call their village: 'I went to Tijuana,' they'll say, 'and two coyotes worked together, and here we are.'"

"*Puto,*" Ratón spat.

"Then I crossed some of your *pollos*, a favor. And you present this."

The attendant heard sobbing. Roberto said, "Okay, let's go." And then, "*La puerta, por favor.*"

Negro unlocked the bathroom door. The men walked out holding Ratón by the arms. He didn't appear beaten, but simply smaller.

Roberto stepped out last, wearing his Stetson again. He stuffed some bills into Negro's tip cup. He said, "Thank you, *amigo*." And then he and El Oso walked off to the pickup alone as his men whisked El Ratón in the other direction.

El Negro never heard the report of a pistol. He never saw El Ratón again. He never asked after him.

29

Marta asked Solo to help her make a migrant pickup at a location near the San Ysidro port of entry. This was the busiest land port in the world. Cars and trucks often waited for two to three hours in order to enter the United States. Knickknack shops dense with goods lined the idling thoroughfare. Pixilated billboards flashed. Engines revved and horns honked. The spaces between vehicles were populated. Street performers juggled colorful illuminated balls. Ragged street vendors paced, hawking peanuts, gum, chips, tacos, fruit, churros, paintings of Christ's last supper, ceramic pitchers, blankets, soccer jerseys, and ice cream. Many of these workers had been deported and now lived in the river. They received a small commission for their sales. Self-appointed line bosses decided where freelancers could operate, reserving the cash-fat beginning for themselves. This meant that the vendors grew increasingly desperate approaching the border markers. This was where the beggars and nuns and sellers of plaster Bart Simpson statuettes worked.

Roberto did a lot of business in the area. For his high-end clients—whom he passed right through customs with counterfeit documents—he kept an apartment above one of the central pharmacies. The building was big and pink and garish. Inside the apartment, however, the atmosphere was surprisingly tranquil. Sunlight filtered in through curtains. The noise of the borderline was dampened to a low bubbling buzz.

Marta surveyed the room and asked the ten or so *pollos* who were there to ready themselves. In her new look—work slacks and sensible flats—Marta was businesslike and efficient. The *pollos* tended to mind her commands as they would their eventual *mayordomos*. Maybe it was her posture, but Solo noted her field-manager-like effect on the *pollos*.

He stepped through the kitchen and between rooms to help with whatever bags they might have. At one point, Marta slumped into a living room loveseat, a shift in her bearing that caught his attention. This wasn't a job for sitting—a poor representation for the migrants, something she normally would have stressed. They'd been going hard lately. Solo wasn't the type to judge. But she must have opened the curtains and window, too—not a load-house practice. A view of the traffic and the customs booths loomed beyond. It looked like one of those paintings made exclusively of dots, but shiny and brighter. On second glance, the cityscape took on a boiling aspect. It was a cauldron of refracting light and movement. The vehicle exhaust could be nauseating, too. Marta looked suddenly blanched, a pallor that worried Solo. He could handle the *pollos* alone, but how could he care for the boss as well? They needed to get a move on. He directed his attention to the migrants.

Moments later, Marta called out to Solo. She'd withdrawn her cell phone and was dialing. The clients perceived that something was amiss and suspended their packing—they seemed to track him, but watch her.

"*Mi amor*," Marta said into the device, "can you come to where I am right now?" Obviously, it was El Indio at the other end. She gestured for Solo to wait."Roberto's apartment at *la garita*. I'm feeling really bad," she said. "Just . . . different. Awful, I don't know. Please come here right now."

Her figure slumped then. Solo dashed, but she quickly slid off the chair and onto the floor.

El Indio arrived fresh out of the canyons. The police officer who had driven them, his siren splitting traffic, trailed the young *pollero* into the apartment. They found Marta on the floor, a pillow positioned beneath her head. Solo crouched at her side.

"She fainted," he said. "She came back, then in and out."

Indio bent to her, as well. Marta's complexion seemed almost translucent—a milk bottle emptied of milk. One of her eyelids was not quite shut. He placed the back of his hand to her lips. Her breath was slight but steady. He touched her forehead. It was not hot. Migrants occupied the doorways of adjacent rooms—the energy of their preparation withering in the presence of the policeman, and the possibility of a derailed crossing.

Two uniformed paramedics arrived and pulled Indio and Solo from Marta's side. One kneeled to check her vitals; he opened her mouth and peered in. With a thumb and forefinger, he parted her eyelids. The other uniformed man peppered Solo with a series of questions about Marta's condition before the loss of consciousness. A gurney was brought in. The paramedics lifted Marta onto the stretcher and carried her out. Those remaining—Indio's police guard, the migrants, and Solo—looked to Indio for direction.

"Take the people to Los Laureles," he said. "Javy is there. Tell him and the others that everything is fine. Be alert and do your jobs."

As Solo moved them into action, Indio dialed his cell phone.

"Roberto, I need a favor. Can you meet your sister and me at the hospital?"

The doctor was young-looking and seemed to choose his words with care. "From what we can observe, Marta's circulatory system—her blood vessels—relaxed and widened, as part of her condition," he said. "This increased blood flow to the womb but slowed its return to the brain. The lower-than-usual blood pressure reduced oxygen to the brain and she fainted."

"'Womb'? 'Condition'? What do you mean?" asked Indio.

He and Roberto stood with the doctor in the tiled hallway of Hospital General de Tijuana. Marta had regained consciousness and had since been subjected to a number of tests. Feeling well enough, and propped up by pillows, she wanted to assert her independence and go home, maybe even catch up on the work they'd lost. The incident for her, it was clear, had been an embarrassing one.

Alone with the men in the hall, the doctor responded, "I say 'womb,' *Señor*, because the patient is pregnant—likely a factor in her loss of consciousness."

Indio regarded Roberto, he outstretched his arms for an embrace.

"*Compadre!*" Indio said. "You know you are going to be the baby's *compadre*, right?" Indio's face beamed.

"Congratulations, *amigo*," Roberto said. "Of course I will be godfather to the little one."

Indio couldn't seem to contain himself. He raced off to share the news with Marta. Roberto began to turn as well, but the doctor caught his arm.

"Apologies. You are the brother, correct?"

"Yes."

"I wasn't finished with the assessment. We believe we've identified something of concern in Marta's right hemisphere. Unfortunately, we can't make a diagnosis at this time."

"Something of concern?" Roberto asked.

"A spot," the doctor said.

"What do you mean, 'a spot'?"

"A tumor." The doctor made a grave, affirmative nod.

"In her brain?"

"Marta's emotional state, given the pregnancy, is our highest priority. It is extremely important not to add stress. If it is a neoplasm, it may be benign. The condition is treatable. In my opinion, it's best that she not be alarmed. After we receive additional test results, there is a chance that I will recommend a specialist. This might take time. In the absence of further fainting or nausea, she will be free to go tomorrow."

"Thank you, doctor," he said. The men shook hands.

Roberto walked to the open doorway of Marta's room—four green walls and a high window that allowed a raking light into the small space. The metal bedframe was bookended by cabinets that held monitoring equipment. Indio kneeled at the bedside, his hands clasped over Marta's, which she rested on the blankets over her belly. Marta's long dark hair lay slack on the pillow, framing a face just a shade off her normal energetic self. On catching her brother in the doorway, Marta raised her eyebrows and mouthed the words, "I'm pregnant."

A dull, throbbing headache roused Marta most nights.

"What can I do for you?" Indio would ask.

"Nothing, I think."

In the rare moments that she did complain, Marta described a pressure on the right side of her head that felt like a pulsing balloon. Rubbing her temples with her fingertips alleviated the pressure at times. Painkillers did not prove useful, which was okay, because she did not want to take medication for the sake of the baby. In the daytime, she admitted, there was occasional nausea and vomiting—a natural symptom of pregnancy.

What followed was a state of blankness that wasn't sleeping or unconsciousness but a feeling of having gone away and returned without knowing where from. A length of time couldn't be assigned to the absence—if one could think of it as such. Better to think of the moments as spells, "pregnancy brain," and wave them off as a kind of aftereffect of the fainting.

When Indio raised concerns Marta hushed him and admonished him to get some sleep. She was still able to perform some of her duties with the *enganchadores* via cell phone, but Indio needed his feet on the ground and his wits about him. For her, the coming baby only heightened a palpable sense of risk in their work.

There hadn't been an occasion, given her fainting spell, to discuss the problem of finding reliable pickup drivers. Indio listed those from his contacts in the Zona Norte who failed to show, or those who made excuses at the last minute. And he explained how he increasingly tapped his brother Martín, who brought in the other siblings.

"Good," she said. "If you have to count on someone, count on family."

"It puts everybody in danger," he said. "And plus, the price is, maybe, too high."

"They want more than the others?" she asked.

"I promised to buy my mother a house in exchange for her cooperation."

"Oh," Marta said.

The ensuing silence, Indio believed, was occupied with her estimations of the cost, as well as the resources that would not be going to their own start in life. She knew the books better than he. But maybe it was the idea of things going unsaid that concerned her, because what she said next was: "I think a house for your family is a good idea. Your mother would always have a place, and when you and I are ready to cross over, so will we."

"Listen, Indio," Roberto said over the cell phone, "your business is never going to have this moment again." The old coyote had seen enough ups and downs to know, he said. This was El Indio's high water and he'd better haul some goddamned buckets. "Me, I can afford to take the time."

The specialist recommended for Marta's care practiced at a research clinic in sprawling Mexico City—1,700 miles south of Tijuana. Roberto did not inform Marta or Indio about the true nature of the recommendation. Neither did he want to give Marta the opportunity to decline the trip as trivial, so he purchased the airline tickets immediately.

Indio's resistance was unexpected. Impending fatherhood seemed to have sparked a protective streak in him.

"I don't feel right about you going; the obligation is mine," he said.

Roberto could hear the voices of the *pollos* and workers on the other side of the line. "*Amigo*, my little sister's welfare was my obligation long before it was yours," he said. "Let's make a deal. Including travel, the doctor said to plan on three days. I'm certain the fainting and headaches are just a part of the process for her, and the tests just a precaution. We'll shoot back right away. On the chance that she requires more time with them, you and I can swap, and you can fly to Mexico City to be with her. *Está bien?*"

Indio was hesitant. "Okay," he said, "that's fair."

"All right, go make some money."

To Marta, Roberto pitched the trip as simply going the extra mile for the health of the baby, something people did in *el Norte* all the time. To his surprise, Marta proved receptive to the idea. She wanted the best possible advice, and a thorough exam might relieve her needling fears. Roberto asked her to pack for the week, just in case.

Many of Roberto's international clients arrived in Mexico City. An underground network of fixers, drivers, and safe houses ushered them north. In this instance, Roberto simply reversed his well-oiled machine.

When they arrived at the hospital, Marta was assigned a locker for her things and given a flimsy hospital gown that tied in the back and a cheap pair of earplugs. The MRI machine was described to her as a giant magnet. She was allowed to wear underthings but not her bra, which contained a metal underwire. Checking again for her usual thin chain, Marta touched her neckline. She then handed the locker key to the technician. He helped her to lie down on the sliding table where her shoulders fit into a plastic brace. She'd been told a couple of things: not to move and that it would be loud. But no one mentioned the impossibility of modesty in the presence of the male technician and her brother. He'd been allowed to accompany her into the room for the test, provided he remove his significant belt buckle, and he stood to the side—a rigid figure dressed like a cowboy.

Marta inserted the earplugs, and the technician rolled her table into the dark, narrow bore. The technician's voice then boomed over an intercom. Then there was clicking, and then a volley of sound like laser fire or a printing press at capacity.

This was not the only test. One required her to wear an apparatus on her head and look at flashing lights. For another, a dye was injected into her bloodstream. The nurse who performed the sonogram was not associated with the oncologist or any of the technicians and let slip the sex of the child. "I'm having a boy," Marta told Roberto with a light in her eyes, and for the duration of the return trip this was all she talked about. Would he play baseball or soccer? From her he'd inherit a love of school. And, she suspected, he'd learn to speak English too. Given his father's long-standing dream, this child might be an American boy.

Indio greeted Marta and Roberto at Tijuana International Airport holding a bouquet of her favorite flowers. He hugged and kissed Marta, who seemed to hum with the vibrancy of her news: a boy, a boy, a man. He kissed her on the cheeks and twirled her around. When they finally parted, Indio thrust a hearty hand at Roberto and said, "Good to see you, *compadre*."

Roberto took the hand but, attending to the luggage with unusual concentration, he failed to meet El Indio's eye.

30

A man missing his right leg below the knee labored by on crutches. Dried blood covered his uniform. It was hot, and he was sweating. Thunderclouds formed above the interior mountains. A guy standing on a roof looked down on the scene and called to the amputee, "What's up, smiley?" Another soldier followed. He was dressed in desert camouflage. An eyeball hung by bloody sinews from his right eye socket. The white of the eyeball bounced lightly upon his cheekbone as he traipsed along.

A stagehand passed in the opposite direction. "Hey, you get dizzy yet?" he asked. "I wore that thing once. I started to spin after a while."

The soldier with the dislodged eyeball shrugged and grinned. "Not yet."

A call to prayer rose from tinny, blown-out speakers. Women wearing black head-to-toe abayas jogged by as if late for Friday services. What I took to be makeup artists, because of their contemporary hairstyles and clothing, ran by holding jugs of what looked to be fake blood.

This parade took place in the relatively sedate moments between explosive training scenarios at one of Strategic Operations' simulation venues. The actors, whether playing civilians, attackers, the wounded, or the dead, hustled to take up new positions before the next group of navy corpsmen entered the scene. This was to be the troops' final training before deployment, and the atmosphere was riven with a theatrical sense of ceremony and graduation.

"I've got all kinds of shit going on," said a large man who waved me over. "So if I'm not around—and anybody asks—you just tell them that you're with Johnny Hoffman."

Strawberry blond and grizzled, Hoffman seemed all-American in that genre of the high school football hero turned bad. He was well built, had a ruddy complexion, and wore the uniform of a California vet—a tank top, surf shorts, military-issue boots, and grim tattoos. One read BEYOND GONE. Hoffman strode through the fake village like Robert Duvall opining on the smell of victory as Lieutenant Colonel Bill Kilgore in *Apocalypse Now*. Between calling shots, he narrated a personal vision shaped by war. It included stints in Grenada, Panama, Haiti, the Balkans, and Afghanistan. "I've been going to war one way or another for thirty years," he said.

Hoffman then introduced me to an assistant, a young bearded guy—also a vet—whose countenance suggested not quite military or civilian, but freelancer. Hoffman led us through the set to a steel ladder behind one of the structures. He pointed up. We climbed to the top of some shipping containers and met an unbroken view of the amorphous Middle Eastern square. Detritus from previous explosions littered the ground below. The smell of explosives, like cap gun smoke, hung in the air. The next role-play was about to start.

"You'll see a rocket come over that wire," Hoffman advised.

If Kim Zirpolo and her boss Bill Anderson were the designers of these pageants, Hoffman was the choreographer. I gathered that he'd held the position from Strategic Operations' humble beginnings. He mentioned experimenting with the initial decoration himself. Bicycles, he noted from his time in the field, were a natural fit. None of the original crew had known the business would grow the way it had, or that their need for people and props would expand in such a manner. They had been, in fact, a startup at the forefront of a new industry called "atmospherics." The speed of their growth hadn't sunk in until the work at Fort Irwin—an early apex for the company—when Hoffman found himself directing thousands of role-players.

On top of the shipping containers, when I should have been mentally prepping, I found myself scanning the set for bicycles. I caught sight of a bedraggled BMX with a rusty chain that looked familiar. A last-minute worker ran by clutching a bloody leg. It was stiff and bent at the knee.

Hoffman nodded. "In Africa, the skinnies would eat that."

The "skinnies," I took it, were natives. Hoffman turned to sort out some last-second technical issue. The bearded assistant mentioned, casually, that the old soldier held some kind of record for knife kills in the field. I didn't know how to process this detail.

A formation of navy corpsmen then entered the village. A woman in an abaya bolted from a hiding place. The soldiers followed her with their rifles. They discovered more locals in an alcove and detained them. Then the rocket, just as Hoffman had said, rose over the wire and exploded much too close and much too loud.

"Damn," I said, raising a hand to one ear and a notebook to the other. Fragments scattered. More smoke.

"Ha ha. I told you," Hoffman said.

Below us, the blast sent the troops into fevered action. In a state of dislocation brought on by the ringing in my ears and the sudden clapping of gunfire, I glanced across the village at a thirty-foot tower where, under an awning, with the brilliant white thunderheads behind, stood Stu Segall. In the newspaper, he'd been described as "cherubic." But with his potbelly, polo shirt, and reddish beard, he looked like one of those dried apple characters on a stick, shriveled and wrinkled without having lost the color.

At Segall's side stood a gathering of dignitaries. The older men looked down upon the movements of the trainees. They were Roman heads of state observing gladiator practice. One of the men with Segall I recognized as Congressman Brian Bilbray, a border hawk, member of the "drone caucus," and former chairman of the House Immigration Reform Caucus, who'd lobbied extensively for the new forty-nine billion-dollar border wall.

In recent years, the real meat eaters of the military contracting jungle had taken note of what Segall's Strategic Operations had been doing. And employing Segall's own techniques, these well-connected corporations easily snatched large atmospherics contracts out of the studio's hands. At the time of this visit, a wave of fiscal belt tightening was about to sweep through the nation's capital as well. Services like those provided by Stu Segall Productions were seen as low-hanging fruit for cuts. Everyone on set could see that the salad days were coming to an end. The Strategic Operations team had already been whittled to a fraction of the size it was at its height. Further cuts were coming. Segall's hosting of politicians at this late stage looked like a last-ditch effort to gobble up the scraps. "We are going to suffer," Hoffman said. "Contractors are the first to go."

The role-play concluded without any point I could have summed up. As far as I knew, it was all sound and fury, signifying nothing. I asked Hoffman what was really going on here.

"I don't care how many times you practice," he said, "your first firefight is pretty fucking terrifying. You can't ever simulate that, but this gives you something to fall back on."

Hoffman looked at the young soldiers. They seemed to be working through a series of mental stages—from fantasy to the shores of reality—smoke wafting all around. Wistfully, he said, "A year from now, all these guys will be downrange. Some will be dead."

We watched Segall and the rest of the delegation walk through the war-torn movie set. I'd been severed from employment enough times to know—from their postures and cadence, this looked like an easy letdown. The age of sequestration was at hand; contracts were drying up. Hoffman didn't have to mention what I suspected to be the case: the cutbacks meant that the "swing gang" I'd heard so much about, after having been deployed with the bicycles to military installations all over the country for the better part of five years, were now coming home—not because the conflicts were over, but because they were being laid off.

31

Roberto invited Indio out for a couple of beers. There was something he hoped they could discuss. Riding on the bench seat of the old white truck, Roberto found himself heading out toward the dusty eastern edge of Tijuana, and to a neighborhood called el Gato Bronco, the Tough Cat. The bar he had in mind shared the name, and there was always some confusion as to which came first, the settlement or the watering hole. A sleek new highway was being built in the trough of the desert valley that held the few homes there, forecasting the next run of Tijuana's liquid-like sprawl. They traveled fresh federal pavement for a distance. Then, without signage, the road just ended in dirt and they continued on a temporary road before uniting with the old one again. The bar was nothing special, but Roberto had had good times there. It was somewhere he'd take foreign clients who weren't able to cross at that time, for whatever reasons, and had been cooped up in his house too long. As the drive extended, however, Roberto questioned the choice. It was more remote than he recalled, but maybe that was best.

Stepping into el Gato Bronco felt like entering a dark closet. The eyes needed time to adjust. There was a musty stillness. A few small tables came into focus. Artificial light emanated from weak lamps behind the bar. There were just two people in the room, a waitress poised against a barstool and a bartender who was, at that moment, stocking ice. After appraising the men, the woman stood and withdrew a couple of chairs from one of the central tables. "Please come in," she said. "It's bright out there."

The men took the seats.

"Something to drink?" she asked.

"A bucket of Tecates," Roberto said. He winked at Indio. "My brother's brand."

Indio smiled. "Eventually, even the blind dog gets a bone."

The woman merely nodded at the bartender, who rose with a wince and stepped to the cooler. He was old, past seventy, and fat—which suggested to Roberto a kind of health. He knew many old men, all of them bone-skinny, even if they'd once been plump. The waitress eased back onto her stool to wait, and this time positioned herself to observe the men.

The bartender raised his head from the bottles. "You look familiar," he said, pointing the opener at Roberto.

"I haven't been back in a long time," Roberto answered. "But I always liked the place."

"I'm glad that you paid the visit," the bartender said. The woman placed the tin bucket on the bar before him and the bartender filled it with the bottles and ice. "We won't be here for much longer," he said.

"True?" Roberto asked.

"The new highway, it will pave right over us."

"This very spot," the waitress added.

"That's too bad," Indio said.

"Yes," said the bartender. He slid the bucket of beers to the waitress and then plunged his trowel back into the ice. The woman stepped across linoleum the color of burnt sugar. As their eyes adjusted, detail emerged. Vinyl seats frayed and splitting, a cracked mirror. Roberto remembered the jukebox and the plunking sound of its plastic keys.

"Amigo, I once gave you a hundred bucks. A week later, you still had that note in your pocket," Roberto said.

Indio nodded.

Roberto regarded the young man's wide features, his eyes shaped like a pharaoh's, his quiet yet intensely alert demeanor. "How many *pollos* have you crossed this month?" he asked.

"A few hundred," Indio said, but then corrected himself. "Two hundred twenty-six."

"You're joking me."

"No," he said.

"Pace yourself. A lot of *polleros* don't cross a thousand people in their careers."

Indio shrugged.

Roberto waved his finger. "No one is giving out gold medals to smugglers."

Indio finally cracked a wide, straight smile. He said, "We're thinking of naming him Roberto."

"The little one?" Roberto's gaze narrowed. "You can't give an angel the name of a *malandro*."

When Indio laughed, Roberto thought he looked like a boy.

"You're not a *malandro*," El Indio said. "I owe you everything."

Roberto didn't know where to begin. He certainly didn't want to take Indio to the cave of thorns where his own heart suffered. Yet it was *el coyote*'s business to ferry seekers from one reality to another. And it was his duty to deliver Indio to the truth—facts that he himself did not want to hear spoken out loud.

Roberto began by talking about what had happened in Mexico City—not to Marta, exactly, but to him.

"You know my friend Julian," he offered. "Julian has been in this business since 1960, a first-generation coyote. Seen it all. He has a complete infrastructure down there—for the international clients. He gets them visas meant for visiting artists and performers, almost as good as a diplomatic visa. Julian's driver, Alejandro, is the same one who meets my clients at the airport there. So I made the call and Alejandro picked us up. Absolutely no stress in that regard; he took us right there to the clinic, and afterward, to Julian's house. Nice place."

The men sipped their beers. The lengthy description, the far-flung el Gato Bronco bar, the speed with which Roberto was drinking, and the speaker's unhealthy pallor may have caused Indio's brow to rise.

"The specialist was older—a good man I think—and smart," Roberto said. He relayed the fact that Marta's symptoms—the headaches, nausea, vomiting—were often the same for difficult pregnancies as for this other thing that the doctor had been thinking. So the doctor's people worked really hard to get the right results. "She had, I don't know, many different tests. And all the way through she was as strong and courageous as you would expect Marta to be. The sonogram made her really happy."

While his sister was with the sonographer, the old doctor had called Roberto aside to present a preliminary diagnosis. The results of some tests took time, the oncologist admitted, but he'd seen enough. "The tumor is malignant," he said. And unfortunately, it was not a solid mass but a web enmeshed with critical areas of brain function. Hormones associated with the pregnancy might have fueled the aggressive cell division, but they couldn't know for sure. "In either event," the doctor said. "I am afraid that there is no cure."

In the dark bar, the two men locked eyes.

"I pleaded with him, *amigo*, I did. I said, 'What can we do? I would trade my life for Marta's. Money is not a problem.' The doctor said only, 'Make her happy for the time God grants her. It won't be long.'"

The ridges of Indio's forehead bunched up. His welling brown eyes shimmered, a look of disbelief at first. He didn't breathe. "And the baby?" he asked.

Roberto shook his head.

Indio stood. "Let's go. I need to see her."

"No, *compa*." Roberto raised his hands, fingers spread wide—a gesture of surrender. "As her brother, I cannot allow her to see you like this. Marta will know then. She will know and her last days will fill with mourning for the boy. I can't have that."

Indio lunged across the table, snatching up Roberto's shirt. "Give me the keys."

"No, brother."

Indio shook Roberto, his energy feverish, fitful, incoherent.

Thin tears brimmed at the corners of Roberto's wide, still eyes and spilled over. Indio released his grip, and slumped back into his chair. His head dropped. He began to sob.

Roberto raised a finger to the waitress. "A bottle," he said, "the big one." The bartender tipped it down like a book off a shelf. He blew the dust from the label and handed it to the waitress. She set the golden bottle on the table, placing two shot glasses beside it. A question rose to her lips. Roberto waved it off. He looked at El Indio. "We are not leaving until it's finished."

Indio grabbed the bottle's neck and broke the seal. He sent the shot glasses to the floor with a forearm and turned the tequila up, drinking the burning liquid down.

"Another bucket of beer," Roberto called. He stood and pulled the bottle from Indio. He poured it into his own throat. The new bucket arrived. The bottle passed like a pistol between men contesting a round of Russian roulette. Slivers of daylight weakened around the windows and doorway. After-work patrons entered, drank, and left without notice. The bottle drained down to a stubborn little hue of vapor and the pain was still there and there wasn't enough alcohol in the doomed little bar to kill it. The men climbed to their feet. Indio withdrew a roll of dollars as thick as an ax handle. He peeled a limp sheaf of hundreds off onto the table. The bartender and the waitress wished them luck from the other side of their blurry oblivion. The men found the door, and then that the world beyond had become cold and dark.

Indio slid behind the wheel. Roberto crawled in on the passenger side. Indio pulled the keys from his hand. The engine ignited, the lights flared, and they roared into the desert valley. The tawny roadside flicked past, twigs and brambles flaring in the headlights. Fewer than five miles on, a rampart of tumbleweeds reflected the light and signaled a curve in the road that Indio failed to account for. At the sight of the berm he yanked at the wheel. The bed of the truck traveled around and the bumper forged their way, spinning and bucking into the brush. A trench pitched the Ford onto its two driver-side wheels. It slid like this, on the verge of tipping, of rolling, but then slowed just short of a deep arroyo. When the truck came crashing onto all four tires again, the engine died.

Indio opened his door and fell out. He crawled on his knees, retching, vomiting, and then sobbing. He pounded the desert floor with his fists. He screamed at the stars.

Roberto exited the cab, stumbled down the arroyo bank, fell onto his side, and remained there. The dirt was cool and granular. He could smell the wild sage, the earth churned from the crash, and spilled antifreeze and exhaust. He eventually came around and made his way out. He found his *compadre*, picked him up, and pushed him back into the cab. Roberto got the engine started and eased the truck back onto the road, which carried them along a tributary and then the river and eventually back into the heart of Tijuana and the red neon lights of the Zona Norte, where the brothers really lost control.

32

In 2010, after Solo came up in casual conversation in the Zona Norte, El Negro uncovered a cadre of lower-level workers in the bicycle coyote operation. There was El Ruso, El Cholo, El Sombra, and Juan and Javy and Angel. Through them, Negro learned of the operation's general, Marta, and her connection to Roberto. It was the first time El Negro had linked the high-level *pollero* to the bicycles. As the brother of the woman in charge, Negro reasoned, Roberto must know something the others did not. But El Negro realized that in order to get the story straight, he'd have to play a card he'd never considered. To obtain an interview with *el coyote* concerning this illicit business that somehow touched the baby sister, Negro might have to allude to a certain situation that concerned an armed and aggressive *malandro* and Negro's assistance in that serious event.

Surprisingly, when Negro reached out to his acquaintance in the white pickup, no reference to the past proved necessary. Roberto revealed himself to be gracious and amenable, almost as if he'd been waiting some time for this very request from his old *compa* at the bathrooms. El Negro was invited into *el coyote*'s home, where he spent long afternoons with the family, in the kitchen and outside by the garden. He saw the hallway of rooms, and the hustle and bustle of internationals being escorted in and out.

Though I had faith in El Negro's growing body of research, even as the details turned fantastic and bizarre, I was never dead certain as to his own personal motivations. Negro was sticking his neck out. He banged on the doors of shacks where he was unwanted. He was threatened, and pleaded with, to ask no more questions. And while the work was going well, I suppose, I buried the question as to why he persevered. I vaguely aligned his dedication in uncovering El Indio's story with his desire to help migrants and deportees. El Negro had little power and no money, but he could do this—he could tell their stories. What I didn't understand was why any of the smugglers would openly describe their activities to Negro. The bathroom worker wielded an undeniable charisma, but I didn't believe that was enough. There was a reason they trusted him; I just couldn't be sure what that reason was.

The question of motivation swung both ways. After our first visit, Negro chastised Dan Watman for presuming to bring around a strange gringo asking dangerous questions. Over time, his doubts seemed to mellow: he said he saw a passion in my eyes. But once he'd conducted his first interviews with Roberto, El Negro's willingness to suspend his disbelief about my background and motivations evaporated like water flicked across a sizzling-hot taco-cart grill.

The trust and protection of Roberto was not worth spilling on a wild goose chase.

So Negro made a point of catching Watman near the native garden on the following Sunday. He asked him pointedly if I could be working with Homeland Security, or the CIA, or the FBI, or any number of interested parties. "How do you know him?" El Negro asked.

"He just called me one day," Watman admitted. "I guess I *don't* really know him."

"Could Kimball be an agent?"

"I don't know," he answered. "Maybe."

And Watman, unable to stay silent when it would keep people from connecting over contentious boundaries, called me and spilled his guts as to Negro's reservations. This far into our research, they were hard doubts to hear.

I'd once given El Negro a copy of a story collection I'd written. I mentioned this fact to Watman then, suggesting that it might be evidence—the physical volume might prove that I was a writer. While talking to Watman on the phone, I picked up another copy in my office and turned its smooth surface over in my hands. The back cover carried a small author photo, a younger version of me. Considering the situation from Negro's point of view, I was compelled to ask myself: Could a government agency one-off such a volume in short order to bolster a cover story? Of course it could. Neither the book nor my credentials were proof of anything—that I was not an undercover agent, a garbage collector, or a candlestick maker.

In truth, I had realized that there are many ways to prove what one is, but very few to prove what one isn't. Further, I knew that to be suspected as an informant was the most dangerous position I could find myself in. A real informant, at least, would likely have the support of his or her real agency. All I had was a story. My disappearance could cost as little as fifty dollars. I would not see the threat coming until it stood in front of me. I'd not know the cost until it was paid. That drive into Tijuana to meet El Negro and convince him of my authorship, regain his trust, and learn the tale fresh from the lips of *malandro* royalty was the scariest drive I've ever made.

After Ben McCue's wife showed a lack of interest in the Free Spirit, the ladies' ten-speed he'd purchased from Terry Tynan on our first meeting, I borrowed it—replaced its slashed tire, fixed the brakes, and added a new seat—and I coveted the little burgundy machine. I would sometimes ride it around Playas de Tijuana, the boardwalk's planks making a ticky-tack sound under the wheels, while I looked for El Negro. He didn't have a cell phone or a tendency to stay in any one place for long, so the search for him took on the guessing, traveling aspect of a scavenger hunt. This time, however, I rode the Free Spirit because I didn't want to be recognized, which I suspected I might be in my usual pickup. I couldn't know what or whom I was afraid of, and I suffered a case of paranoia that I found very difficult to peel away from the truth.

Finally, I discovered El Negro sitting outside the bathrooms on the south end of Playas de Tijuana—next to the only lifeguard tower on the beach and kitty-corner to an open dirt lot where the city's surfers congregated and appraised ocean conditions. These bathrooms were white and airy and to sit on benches in the plaza outside of them conjured sensations of the Mediterranean.

On greeting me Negro did not appear suspicious or inimical or hard. He said, "Kimball, I've been waiting for you. Did Daniel tell you about the interview?"

"Yes," I said, and I wondered if maybe Watman had misunderstood Negro's questions about my occupation.

"Hold on," he said, "let me get my folder." El Negro stood, but then a bathroom customer arrived. He made the transaction with this customer and then some acquaintances waved from across the street and Negro went to meet them. I continued to sit and enjoy the warm sunlight and crisp sea breeze. I watched the surfers in the dirt lot, so much like surfers anywhere on the coast.

I wasn't paying much attention to anything until a man stood before me. His hair was dark, greased, and combed back. His face was acne-scarred and seemingly hemmed in by the tattoos crawling out of his hairline and up his neck. Several teardrops were inked and dripping from the corner of his right eye, which, along with its mate, was just a fully dilated black pupil. He stood about six foot, but hunched.

A prison gym physique bulged from his neatly pressed white T-shirt. He wore tan chino slacks with a crease down each leg and a mesh belt that hung alongside. I thought he was yet another gangland soldier scooped up from Los Angeles and dumped here. I might have shrugged him off as a mental case, or a drunk, if not for his intense focus on me.

"That's a nice pen," he said in Spanish, nodding down at my hand. I looked too. It was just a clear plastic ballpoint with blue ink. "I like that pen better than my pen," he said. A silence passed between us. He withdrew a skinny Bic from his pocket. "Why don't you trade pens with me?"

Gambling that this trade would end the encounter, I handed over the clear pen. He took it and put his own back in his pants pocket. Then he clasped the clear pen in his fist as if it were a knife or a shiv.

"*Dios o Diablo?*" he asked. What was he really asking? I was confused. "*Dios o Diablo?*" he repeated. A riddle? Or was he demanding that I choose a side? God or the devil. God or the devil. I saw the pen in his hand like a dagger. "*Dios o Diablo?*" I knew that God was the answer, in this Catholic country especially. But this man looked like he worked for the devil. Directly. The repetition of the question acted on me with the fury of a carnival tornado. I sat in a shiver of sensory confusion, unable to reply. If not a test, it was the torture of the victim before the first puncture. I believed I had been set up. "*Dios o Diablo?*" This is it, I thought I am going to be the writer stabbed with his own pen for asking too many questions.

"*Dios*," I said.

The gangster's senseless repetition eased into a quiet stare. He raised the pen to eye level and appeared to appraise its point. Then he clipped the pen to his T-shirt collar. "*Dios*," he said, and he walked away.

Negro returned from his chat with friends. He held his black plastic folder and sat down next to me, oblivious or resolved. He'd received the all clear, maybe. There wouldn't be a murder.

"Who was that man?" I asked.

"What man?"

"That man." I pointed to the white T-shirt receding down the lane.

"I don't know that man. *Mira*," Negro continued, opening the folder.

"Has he seen me?" I blurted.

"Who?"

"Either of them. Roberto or . . . Indio."

"I don't know, maybe."

"What do they look like?"

"Regular."

"Regular?"

"Yeah, regular. I don't know what it is you're asking about. But maybe you have seen Roberto."

"Where?"

"On those wanted posters over there at the border where you walk into Mexico." Negro looked at me. He saw the anger. "Do you want to hear this story or not?" he asked.

I took a breath. Through my teeth, I said, "That is the *only* reason I'm here."

He thumbed through the now familiar pages filled with tiny, misspelled words so thick with slang and borderland speak that most educated Spanish readers could not begin to wade into it. And then Negro looked up at me and his eyes were brimming with tears.

"Why are you crying?" I asked.

"Because this," he said, wiping at his eyes with the backs of his hands, "this is a very sad story."

33

Juan and Javy found Indio and Roberto slumped in a corner booth of the Chicago Club. It was 8:00 AM on a Monday. Daylight spilled from beneath the heavy front door. The room smelled of the previous night and, under this, the nights of the past. The *polleros* were not asleep, exactly, but they were not quite conscious either. Between them were bottles and glasses. These shared the table with peanuts and several little plastic plates that belonged to the taco vendor. Indio, his neck crooked, was almost prone. A parted eyelid revealed an eerie white crescent. Vomit stains mottled his shirt. Roberto's hat was gone, his hair awry; spittle marked the corners of his mouth. From the empty drinks, it looked like women had been with them. The bartender, waitstaff, and doormen had been either too respectful or too fearful to ask the men to move on.

Javy placed a hand on Indio's shoulder and shook it. "*Jefe*," he said, "we need you in the canyon." Juan stood close behind Javy. The workers were concerned. Indio always drank in moderation; they'd never seen him in a stupor. With additional prodding, the boss shifted his weight but failed to respond in any coherent manner. "Come on," Javy said, again rocking his old friend from the bus station. "It's time to go to work."

Roberto sat up gasping. He exhaled and blinked several times. Then he turned on the workers with yellow, bloodshot eyes. An eyebrow raised; his complexion was ghostly. "What the fuck do you want?"

Neither worker had ever exchanged words directly with Roberto; had never really met the man's gaze. "We need *el jefe*," Javy said, pointing with a limp finger.

"We're busy here," Roberto said.

Juan stepped forward. "*Disculpe, señor,* Solo sent us. The *pollos* . . . we have so many, and the cops want the money. The recruiters too. Bikes are missing. We need Indio."

"The pace is . . ." Javy began.

"*Silencio*." Roberto waved his palm.

His attention settled on an abandoned shot of tequila. He picked it up and threw it back. Then the old coyote withdrew from the booth and stood. Bracing himself on the table, he edged around to Indio's side. He planted his left palm on the bench back. With the right, he reached in, grabbed his *compadre* by the shirt, and pulled him up. Indio said something inaudible. Roberto adjusted Indio's head cautiously, as if righting a portrait, and turned to Javy and Juan. He pulled a fold of pesos from a pocket and regarded the colored paper like a thin taco. He shrugged.

"Take this. Go buy me a new shirt and a pair of jeans, like these, and some socks," Roberto said. He looked at Indio. "And new clothes for him as well. You know the shit he likes. Where's my hat?"

Roberto escorted the slumped figure of El Indio to the hotel next door, a place where street prostitutes took their clients. It rented by the half hour. The man at the desk informed Roberto that sheets for the bed were extra, a twelve-dollar rental fee.

"We won't be sleeping," Roberto explained.

The man insisted on the sheet fee. Hands to his breast pockets, Roberto realized he'd given his stake to Juan and Javy. He stepped to the bench where he'd placed Indio and patted him down, the action of fluffing a pillow. He found the roll of American dollars, then leaned in on the clerk.

"Two *cholos* will come here," Roberto said. "Don't be frightened. They'll have my clothing." He paid the man double. "Send them directly to the room."

Roberto put Indio into the shower fully dressed. He reached in and turned the handle. Only the cold water worked. In a minute or two Indio came around but leaned silently in the downpour. Juan and Javy arrived with parcels—a large cowboy shirt and jeans for Roberto, a white T-shirt and khakis for El Indio. Juan revealed the brand-new pair of black Nikes with the white swoosh, but Indio made no response.

The four *malandros* walked out of the hotel and caught a cab to a quiet bar on Calle Sexta. Weak pink light radiated from behind rows of bottles. The ceiling was low. Painted in white on a wood beam above the bar were the faded words AHORA O NUNCA—now or never—and TODO O NADA—all or nothing. The *polleros* administered a steady series of *Bucanas*, tequila, and *micheladas* to the boss. Indio accepted the drinks but stared vacantly at a black-and-white framed photo in the corner of the bar. It was of Pancho Villa's bullet-peppered corpse, taken after seven assassins ambushed the Mexican Revolutionary general on the road from Hidalgo del Parral in 1923. The men noticed the object of Indio's attention and began discussing Villa's death.

"It happened in a Dodge," Juan said. "I could never drive a Dodge."

"It happened because he wanted to be president," said Javy. "Do you know that a thief stole Villa's skull right out of the casket?"

"It happened because of fate," Roberto said. "There is nothing else."

"Where the fuck were you guys? My head is about to explode," Solo said.

Indio, Javy, Juan, and Roberto found him in the pit of Los Laureles Canyon before the man-sized drainage pipes that lead into the Tijuana River Valley. He had about two dozen *pollos* there, the first of two trips that day, and only the mechanics El Ruso and El Cholo to assist him. He hadn't heard from the chief *levantón*. The *gancho* was just sitting up on Spooner's Mesa twiddling his thumbs, waiting for the go-ahead. Solo figured that he'd act as both the *comunicador* and the *guía*, hoping beyond hope that there would be a ride there to meet them.

Men and women sat astride their *bicicletas*, readying themselves. They fidgeted and checked the brakes. One man was dressed for an interview—slacks and shined shoes—rocking a mountain bike back and forth. A middle-aged woman sat perched on a child's bike. A young man carried a bulging black trash bag slung over his shoulder. With his cap pulled low and a steady, marauding gaze, he hunched over the bars of the BMX—a tortoise on wheels.

"I'll confirm the pickup," Indio said. He raised his phone to his ear.

"We'll guide them," said Juan, indicating himself and Javy.

"What's left to do, *mi* Solo?" Roberto asked.

Solo nodded at an older couple idling nearby. "They don't know how to ride."

It must have been clear to Marta that a change had come over Indio. He was affectionate but distant—more introspective even than usual. They were no longer in the field together. Aspects of their day-to-day lives that had always seemed so natural now seemed like space in a growing chasm. The Sunday night that Indio didn't come home wasn't completely out of the ordinary. He occasionally crossed to the inside and was unable or too busy to call. Either way, it wasn't in his nature to offer explanations. Marta didn't ask. With so many of her duties curbed by the fainting and the pregnancy, it was important that she remain confident and strong—if for no other reason than the family's peace of mind. Yet it wasn't a secret that her man bit his lip when he worried, and this tell wasn't something she'd have missed.

The most obvious cause of the change in Indio's demeanor was the stress of the work. Marta continued to direct the recruiters via cell phone. She was aware that the number of customers had picked up dramatically. Bikes, bike parts, men to make the repairs—these were all in short supply. The motor vehicles also required service. Managing people anywhere had its complications; the border only multiplied them: *pollos* lost, or caught and deported, or caught and never heard from again. Families called. The more migrants, the more complications. Her main communication point, Solo, was frenzied by the increased responsibility and the volume, but even in this, he seemed a version of his normal self. Solo was the more outspoken of the two—a link to Indio's childhood, and since she loved Indio, she would have likely carried some affection for Solo as well. Marta communicated with him daily. They were teammates in the field. Had Indio confided any part of his current concern to Solo, she couldn't guess its nature, and it was not Marta's position to ask.

When not managing her duties by phone, Marta prepared for the baby. The house was abuzz and a room had been set aside for a nursery. One day, as she embroidered a light blue one-piece, Roberto and Indio entered through the kitchen. Her brother remarked on the smell of the fresh baking bread in their father's clay oven. That Roberto had so heartily stepped in to help her fiancé in the work—the two men were together in that way that Roberto and Marta once had been—was not lost on the family. A silent, devoted camaraderie was evident even when they entered the house and parted without words. Indio appraised Marta's handiwork. He appeared overwhelmed and proud.

For days, Roberto and his large *socio* El Oso formed a tight huddle around the young coyote. And they bookended him on the Ford's bench seat as the men made rounds and attended to his bicycle business—which, these days, encompassed the entire city. There was Indio's old room in the Zona Norte and the safe house in El Soler and Roberto's apartment at *la línea*. The workers thought Indio's company odd, especially since he'd bought his own new four-by-four pickup. But these associates were highly esteemed, and there was so much work to do that few had time to question the motives of the boss.

The trio had just dropped some *pollos* at the safe house. And somewhere in town, at that moment, El Indio's brother Martín was riding around with a large packet of American dollars—money to be distributed to the police, the customs agent, and the workers, and to be otherwise laundered and banked. Martín was also the courier of some papers regarding a significant purchase Indio was making on the other side. He'd crossed on foot and was now traversing the city in the back of a white cab. That the eldest brother and strongest earner had risked everything to act as Indio's driver, and that he now crossed into Tijuana on errands, was a serious concern for their mother. But the siblings were now in so deep, her admonishments passed like assessments of the weather. She worried that, eventually, the family would be permanently divided by the border. Between Indio's and Roberto's operations, however, Martín never had trouble finding a way to cross back over; he had choices. It was like asking a man in a family of cooks if he'd been eating.

The brothers miscommunicated the meeting point. Then Indio lost his connection to Martín's American cell phone and was unable to reconnect. Roberto pulled his Ford along the river before they decided to head back to his house, just a couple of miles away and one of the few places Martín knew in Tijuana.

Roberto repeated a similar refrain each time they neared the house. "Okay," he said, "put your clown faces on." They'd made a pact, he, Oso, and Indio: their emotions were their own; let the family enjoy life as they understood it. Who could say what fortune held? Roberto then received a call on his personal cell phone. He withdrew the device and looked at it. The number on the screen was the house line.

"*Bueno*," he answered. "*Sí*, we're only a couple of blocks away." He listened for a moment and then said, "*Ya veo.*"

"Martín is there already?" Indio asked.

"No, brother," he said. "That was my mother." Roberto turned to Indio and Oso, silver wedges brimming below his brown eyes. "Marta is gone."

On entering the house, the men were met by the *llantos*—the sobbing and the weeping. Chedas appeared and drew her husband aside. El Indio went directly to the room he shared with his fiancée, the mother of his unborn son. The door was open, and Indio left it that way. He lay on the bed, next to the still figure below the sheets. He held her form. He wept. Other moans, from the other rooms, drowned his sobs. There was a time when Indio lifted the sheet to view a face that looked only asleep. There was hope and rage and sorrow and hope and rage. He put his cheek to Marta's cheek, bone against skin and bone, and he held her. In the following moments, all sound subsided. The life of the house itself seemed to expire.

El Oso appeared, filling the doorway. "*Compa*," he said.

Indio understood the gesture. He sat upright.

"Oso," he said without looking, "please bring me that bottle I have there in the kitchen." Oso knew the bottle. It was a premium tequila called Cazadores that El Indio had bought in the presence of the men, intended for the celebration of the birth of his son.

Two workers with Servicio Médico Forense arrived for the body.

Oso and Chedas pulled Indio from Marta's bed and escorted him to the living room, where her mother and father sat at the edge of the couch as if awaiting further news. The mother wore a house robe, her posture correct; he was dressed for the ranch. Roberto stood to the side, his hands clasped over his belt buckle. Lupita looked at

Indio as if not seeing the man at all but an empty space between the moment and what had to be done. She said to Roberto, "Son, make certain that the little angel boy is buried separately, right away. He was never born, he never left the side of God. Look at me: The angel must have his own casket."

The twelve mariachis walked single file up the shaded gravel road of Panteón Jardín. Their wide sombreros careened to either side, creating a writhing effect as their bodies remained in step. Their *trajes* consisted of white shirts, bow ties, and short, heavily embroidered jackets. Their pants were tight, and gold medallions rippled down the legs. There were violins, trumpets, guitars, a folk harp, an accordion, and a *vihuela*, or lute. The man who wielded the *guitarrón*, a voluptuous bass guitar, nearly disappeared behind the instrument. Twenty paces from the grave, the trumpeters sounded the first notes of "Despedida con Mariachi" ("A Mariachi Farewell"). The violinists joined in, and the accordion followed.

As at Puerta Blanca, from the grounds of Panteón Jardin one overlooks the border wall, the Tijuana River Valley, and the United States. The garden cemetery, however, is at a higher elevation and lush, defined by large acacia trees and a gently sloping lawn. Light fell on it differently—bright but filtered through the greenery. Rather than mossy crypts and sepulchers, the well-spaced, orderly tombstones of Panteón Jardín were clean and maintained. The care of loved ones was evident in the flowers and gifts placed before many of the graves. Local custom dictated that the deceased were to be interred at the cemetery closest to the family home, so as to be near. El Indio and Roberto talked it over and chose Panteón Jardín because it was closest to the canyons where Marta did the work that she loved. Roberto persuaded the director, who made a choice location available.

El Indio was dressed conservatively in black, as were most of the bereaved. His stubby nose and dark lips were slightly swollen. He stood with the immediate family and El Oso before the open grave. Next to the hole in the earth was a small patch of flat tan dirt where the little boy had been buried the day before. Indio purchased mahogany caskets for both Marta and their son, but he never saw the little one as he'd agreed with Lupita's request to bury him as soon as possible. In the outer ring of guests stood many of their neighbors and a great number of Roberto's associates; some of them El Indio knew but some he did not. Among these were members of Tijuana's eleven *polleros viejos*, the council of elders. Marta had known them and their families in one way or another, so they'd come both in mourning for her and out of respect for Roberto. Within the group of neighbors was a girl named Marlene. She was about twelve years old and had silky black hair. The girl had wildly admired Marta, and often brought her small tokens of friendship. Marta had agreed to serve as Marlene's godmother at her first communion, and so Marlene was already calling her *madrina*. The girl's eyes were rimmed in red and her face was puffy but by the time the mariachis arrived at the gravesite, she'd stopped crying. Marta's parents sat in wood chairs before the large, deep-brown casket. They looked smaller somehow, and more frail—but dignified. Indio's own parents were not present. By the second song—"Amor Eterno"—most eyes had dried. Somewhere in the back of the crowd a mourner began to sing along. Others joined in.

The next day Indio found Solo at work. The crew was preparing for one of three crossings they'd orchestrate that day. Solo hadn't been invited to the funeral; neither had any of the workers. In fact, they'd passed a couple of dozen clients below the funeral as it unfolded at Panteón Jardín. Solo didn't understand his exclusion but he didn't resent it either. Indio wouldn't stop. In the canyon, he opened the passenger-side door of his new truck and grabbed some shopping bags. "These are for you and everyone," Indio said with a wave.

Solo looked in. The bags contained black T-shirts and black pants.

"I understand," Solo said, accepting the parcels. "How did it go?"

"I think it was beautiful, as much as it could be," Indio said.

"Listen, Pablo," Solo said. "I don't think you should be here. Why don't you take time for yourself?"

"Are you telling me that the people don't need to cross anymore?"

"No," Solo said.

"Are they crossing themselves?"

"No. I'm saying that this is critical work. If your mind isn't right, you shouldn't be here."

"*Amigo*, no matter where she is, I am a reflection of her. She worked up to her last day. I'm not going to stop."

34

The building was low and flat—an insignificant aside to a wide palm-lined street that ran from the Coast Highway down to the railroad tracks. The empty spread of asphalt summoned a forlorn sense of Los Angeles noir. One could smell but not see the ocean. Abandoned-looking cars occupied curb space. Errant grocery carts were parked on grassy, overgrown meridians. Nothing inside the building broke the spell. It was cool and dark and filled with the presence of large men. The sensation was of entering an arboreal longhouse with vague questions about lost people and things. I didn't have much of anything to trade for the information other than my enthusiasm—or rather, a middling obsession. The truth was, if not for Kim Zirpolo, I would not have been greeted at the door. She arranged the meeting, calling the men "my boys" or "my guys."

"Imagine my guys," she said. "They're huge, intimidating, and most likely wearing their gang colors. They've got a truck full of bicycles and guns, and they're driving through Texas. There's no paperwork. What would happen, God forbid, if they got pulled over by some ranger? How would they explain, if they didn't get shot first?"

The moniker "swing gang" emerged from the era when multiple movie sets occupied one studio stage; via the swinging of hinged walls into and out of place, the sets could be efficiently changed. The nickname was originally used for the workers who moved those walls, but the position grew into any kind of breaking down, transportation of props, or set dressing. And it might have been inaccurate to describe the men who worked for Stu Segall as a swing gang, because they did anything and everything to pull the job off. They were the strategy behind Strategic Operations.

Most of them hailed from Oceanside, California's significant Samoan community—known as a tough crowd in one of the coast's last rough-and-tumble beach towns. I was hesitant to approach them about an interview at that time because the most esteemed citizen Oceanside had produced, NFL linebacker Junior Seau, had recently shot himself in his beachfront home. The Samoan community was tight and extremely family oriented. Seau's death came as a sudden blow. He was their icon, their star. Further, the guys I'd come to meet had just been severed from employment with Stu Segall Productions. They'd seen it coming since talk of cutbacks in government spending began. But I didn't imagine they'd be in the mood to share tales of high times on the trail of coyote bikes.

The black vinyl chairs sat low and wide, as did the coffee table between us. I had to gaze up to meet the eyes of my hosts. Aaron Garrison, who sat across the table, looked something like the actor known as the Rock—handsome, intelligent, amiable, oversized. Eric Amavisca was tall and slender with bright blue eyes. Ron Nua stood a bit shorter, with thick rounded shoulders. He spoke with a raspy swagger. His sentences were peppered with "bitch" and "shit." And within minutes of entering, I discovered that I really liked these guys. They laughed easily. Each of them could tell a story. They were fans of off-color details, and they never framed their answers to place themselves, or anyone, in a softer light.

The work had started with Garrison. In the late 1990s, one of his football coaches at Grossmont College happened to be a ranking member of the local filmmakers' union. He helped Garrison get work on a series of Mexican soap operas called *telenovelas* that were filmed in San Diego. In time, Garrison brought friends from the neighborhood into the business. Around 2000, work with the *novelas* waned and so they "filtered" over to the only other gig in town, Stu Segall Productions. This trio represented the core of the swing gang. They confirmed that Kiser had turned Zirpolo on to Terry Tynan's swamp bikes. And one day when the workload at the studio was light, Zirpolo sent Garrison, Amavisca, and Nua down to the Kimzey Ranch with directions to load three hundred bikes onto a stake bed.

"That shit was a bike cemetery," Nua said. The hemmed-in feeling of the border, broken-down ranches, dirt roads, and the demand for cash all evoked the foreboding of a strange deal. They described Tynan as an oddball. "He was *into* the bikes, the most I've ever seen in my life."

But Tynan greeted the men much as he had me, with an unmasked appreciation of his own good fortune. He indicated the trails where he did his collecting. He walked through his piles, organized by style and quality, and separated the studio sales from the pack. In the beginning, it was the junk bikes for Segall. "Some had no seats. They were just bombers—two tires, a chain, and half a handlebar," Nua said. Then Terry popped the doors of the wood garden shack, and "it was like bike heaven in there."

There were vintage Italian racers and pristine Mongoose and Diamondback BMX bikes from the eighties.

"I was always looking for a bike," Garrison said. They all were, in fact—everyone who ever marveled at the swamp bikes. Nua had his eye on a Redline, a model he remembered from his childhood. Amavisca developed a possessive fondness for a murdered-out beach cruiser that he'd later hide around the studio lot lest someone else admire it too. The men marveled at Tynan's operation. "He was making money," Garrison said, "and not just off us."

Nua called it clockwork. "We'd want to make an order, and he'd be like, 'Give me another week,' and then there'd be another five hundred up in this bitch."

The swing gang never questioned the origin of the bikes. They never considered the fact that each bike represented at least one new migrant. They admired certain machines but mostly, "We just put 'em on lots."

This was not as easy as it might seem. Like the troops for whom they did their work, the men experienced a kind of deployment. They'd receive a packing list, broad instructions, and keys to a truck or a one-way plane ticket. They could remain on the road for six-to-nine-month stretches, unaware of the next destination, or the final one. Their per diem food allowance could be set as low as the cost of meals at the base cafeteria. In Louisiana, it was $11.25. Their salary was comparable to an army private's, but half of a base janitor's.

There wasn't a whole lot of support from Strategic Operations headquarters, either. For whatever reason, be it the fly-through nature of the movie business or the culture at Stu Segall Productions, permissions, forward notices, and paperwork on the dangerous loads were considered only in the rearview. Nua was once sent to Canada with a truck that contained bicycles, props, and sealed boxes. After a three-day drive that crossed state and international boundaries, Nua opened boxes to discover that they contained authentic AK-47 assault rifles. Nua was on parole at the time. A pull-over, or a single curious inspector, and there was a strong chance he would have been returned to prison. "Even the fake shit looks real as fuck," Nua said.

"You really have to grab it and have a look at it," confirmed Garrison.

Another contingent of the swing gang drove a load of pyrotechnic explosives to a base in Virginia. The studio had not communicated with the officer receiving the shipment. So the men spent their day standing outside the base gates with rifles trained on them as soldiers searched the truck and verified identities.

"You're definitely scared," said Amavisca, describing the experience of approaching any kind of state or Border Patrol checkpoint. The swing gang knew that in most instances, officials refrained from unpacking a fifty-three-foot truck. Still, Garrison said, "It's our job to drive. So we drive—and we have no idea."

Garrison once worked at an East Coast facility for a week before his background check came through. It indicated a previous arrest for arms possession. The facility was an arms depot. He was kicked off but merely directed to another base. In Virginia, he'd just finished situating props when a small squad of soldiers entered the set. One of the troops looked around the street scene Garrison had just finished building. The man dropped his rifle in the dirt, threw up his hands, and ran away. "I thought, *wow, that's crazy*," Garrison said. "I thought he was going to get in trouble because—well—that's some bitch shit, just running away."

Garrison later learned that the fleeing soldier had just returned from Iraq, where he'd taken a bullet in a firefight—a shoot-out on a street that looked, apparently, just like the replica.

Desert winds, humidity, driving rain, hail, and snow—over distance and time, for the swing gang, the Baby Baghdads installed at disparate locations became, if not reality, a way of living real life. "When they throw the role players in there, it's like, you are there," Nua said.

At a village built in the Nevada desert, role players lived on set for twenty-one-day stretches. They commuted and ran errands on the swamp bikes. They shopped in fake markets that became real markets. They repaired their real bikes at the fake gas station. Because training exercises were ongoing, the swing gang was required to wear Iraqi "garb" while at work. The pyro explosions rattled even their private thoughts. Special Forces training at the facility didn't live in the village but occupied the surrounding mountains. They raided the hamlet at night and at random intervals—shakedowns that put the swing gang on edge.

"Where exactly did you take the bikes?" I asked.

"Everywhere. Every set had bikes there."

Garrison, Nua, and Amavisca began dropping place names like Ping-Pong balls in a lottery drawing: Hawaii, Canada, Louisiana, Texas, Florida, South Carolina, North Carolina, Virginia, New Jersey, New York, Michigan, Nevada, California, and Arizona. "Bill Anderson is in Japan right now, at Okinawa—he's got bikes," Garrison said.

The place names became a blur of camps, forts, and airfields, but then as they dwindled, the men began to mention the places with no names. Nua described a "compound" near Fort Bragg, North Carolina, that was limited to Special Forces training. The outer perimeter of the installation was odd, like a rectangular box with the far two corners sheared by walls set at angles. The main building was three stories high and had a walled balcony.

"The inner layout was a maze that they told us to build," Nua said. "Some hallways led to nothing."

He was describing what he said he later came to believe was a replica of Osama bin Laden's estate in Abbottabad, Pakistan. "I shit you not, this compound we put up with these big-ass walls: when I seen [bin Laden] got caught, I was on it. I was like, 'Whoa, that's like the shit we built out in North Carolina.' I mean, to the exact T."

I asked if he brought bikes to the location. "Yeah," Nua said.

"We took bikes everywhere," Garrison said.

I asked again because, well, Nua was suggesting the possibility that SEAL Team Six members, the killers of Osama bin Laden and, for a time, the most celebrated defenders in America, might have trained in the presence of—and, if other scenarios are any example, likely pedaled—the same bikes that El Indio's migrants used to infiltrate the United States.

Kim Zirpolo doubted that Strategic Operations contributed to the re-creation of the Abbottabad compound. And there might have been more than one. When I talked to the swing gang on August 22, 2012, however, no details of the top-secret training facility had been released. Only a select few in the world knew for certain that it existed, and where. Then, former SEAL Team Six member Matt Bissonnette's book *No Easy Day*, which described the training and hunt for bin Laden, was published on September 4. A paragraph placed the "mock-up" where they had trained in North Carolina. Two months after I met with the swing gang, a whistle-blower website called Cryptome.org referenced *No Easy Day* and posted old TerraServer satellite images housed on the Bing search engine. These revealed a compound of near exact proportions to that of bin Laden's Abbottabad compound. It had the high walls and shipping containers. It was located near Fort Bragg in North Carolina.

Bissonnette described the compound as constructed of plywood and shipping containers. He complimented the construction workers who built it. "The level of detail on the mock-up was impressive . . . changes were made. The construction crew didn't ask why and they never said no."

By way of advice, Garrison warned me off the search for the bicycles. He described a fairly open base in Louisiana. "The townspeople would come in and steal a bike. Once we were done training in [any] village, people would steal bikes. And I've never been to a spot where the POC [point of contact] wasn't saying, 'I want a bike. I need a bike.'"

Eventually, I'd reach Bill Anderson on the phone, and he'd describe a similar scene. "The bicycles tend to walk away. Marines would pull up and throw them into the back of their pickups. They're just kids. They will do stupid stuff. You see 'em riding around on the bikes, doing wheelies. Kim would yell at them and say, 'Get off those bikes.' But pretty soon everyone in the lot would end up with a bike to ride."

At the end of our meeting in Oceanside, Garrison said, "The only place you're going to find those bikes is on San Clemente Island." He was describing a crescent-shaped desert island forty miles offshore, the southernmost rock in the Channel Island chain. Part of the island was used as a bombing range for cruisers. Regardless, the whole thing was off-limits to civilians. The swing gang had once been sent there with props and bikes.

"They told us we were going to be gone for four days"—but the gang was stuck on the island for two months, wearing the same four sets of clothes. They knew how hard it was to get off that island.

35

The status they'd attained felt something like that of a plucky local soccer club on an unexpected rise from the bottom of the draw. If not stars, they were lauded as wily, cunning, and brave. The money that came with that success was something none of the *polleros* had ever experienced. There were rumors of El Indio having thrown lavish parties for authorities, the chief of police among them—one in which he had entertained the attendees with an unannounced performance by the famous cumbia group La Sonora Dinamita.

Solo, however, had fallen deeply in love with a local girl, and so certain was he of their future together, he quit the people-smuggling business in its headiest days. El Negro found Indio's former lieutenant in the Postal neighborhood with a new baby in his arms. Solo was surprised to see the bathroom worker, but he was friendly. He said he worked in his mother-in-law's packing plant now, and because he'd been focusing on his family, he was living up to his solitary nickname more than ever. Solo hadn't talked to his childhood friend and former boss in some time. He described his final days with the operation, when El Indio, in the smoldering energy of his loss, pushed the gang to cross more people than ever. The week following Marta's funeral, Solo said, they crossed 495 migrants. At some point, Solo felt he couldn't expose his young wife to the risks they were taking on the border and he quit. Because of this, he said, he didn't know what had happened in the end. Solo could only judge the outcome according to alternating rumors he'd heard: that El Indio was in prison, or that El Indio lived in security with his parents and siblings on the other side.

El Cholo, the deportee who'd stumbled into El Indio's camp nearing the point of starvation—"dog hungry" is how he described it—and worked his way from bike mechanic to the bagman who personally doled out bribes to customs agents and police commanders, also retired in 2007. He now owned a house with a bit of land near the border. He pointed out the new cars in the driveway and the fact that he was able to pay for his mother's hernia surgery as indications of his windfall. Like Solo, El Cholo had no knowledge of the gang's final days. In his heart, he believed that El Indio had been caught, and that was why the operation ceased so suddenly and the workers scattered so completely.

Juan, El Indio's early friend from the bus station, was more difficult to find because he'd fled Tijuana for a safe house in Tecate. As the drug wars escalated in 2008, Juan got caught up in some bad dealings—unrelated to migrants, though he wouldn't be specific—and there were people who wanted to "take [him] down." Early in his flight, El Indio had sent Juan $30,000 to help his *compa* make a new start. But because, as Juan said, "I can't go back to Tijuana if I want to stay alive," he had lost all communication with the gang. El Negro found Juan through a mutual acquaintance, a taxi driver, and this only after El Negro displayed the scrawled pages of his interviews there in the back of the cab.

Javy was also residing in Tecate, and though prior arrangements had been made, he was not at all happy to be visited by El Negro. He didn't like the idea that a gringo writer knew anything of the bicycle business. And he didn't want the story told. With his gains from the smuggling operation Juan had purchased a couple of party vans, and he ran charters. He didn't want to put his business, or himself, in jeopardy. El Negro suspected that his own personal appearance was what had sparked Javy's reassessment of the situation. Negro pegged Javy as arrogant and vain. Negro was dressed in his normal, well-worn clothes. And it dawned on him that Javy had expected to greet a journalist wearing a crisp suit, maybe followed by a cameraman, and now Javy was biased against Negro and declined to talk.

Seated in the shade on a park bench, Javy and Negro argued. With his reading glasses resting on the bridge of his nose, El Negro reminded the young man that Javy himself had promised their mutual friend Solo that he'd be open and honest. Only on the strength of that promise had Negro made the expensive trip from Tijuana. Javy seethed. Negro then threatened to relay the details of their encounter to a dear friend of his, a man named Roberto. At this—because, Javy said, he thought so "highly" of El Negro's friend—the interview proceeded, halting with intermittent argument until Javy bellowed, "I can't understand journalists. They always get involved in stuff that they shouldn't. That's why they get killed."

The interview degraded into a trade of insults and character judgments that precluded further inquiry into the ultimate fate of El Indio, or anything else.

El Sombra figured El Indio was dead. El Ruso said he was imprisoned, not in the United States but in Mexico, which, in his opinion, was much worse. So Negro tracked down the police officer who'd provided protection and escorts for the operation from the lookout at Summit Canyon. "El Indio disappeared like magic," the officer said. "Everything ended without us knowing anything about his whereabouts, where he was headed, or if something had happened to him. Maybe he is in Paris—a man with money is appreciated everywhere."

I was pretty certain of El Negro's declaration on the day we met, the day I first heard the name El Indio: "You are never going to find that person."

Given the discrepancies in the accounts of their final days, it is interesting to note that the *polleros* seemed to settle with finality, as a group, on a single number: seven thousand. Independently, each of them said that they crossed seven thousand cyclists beyond the most enforced and technologically advanced five miles of a two-thousand-mile border—that they then dumped the bikes and delivered the people to their destinations.

Accurate migration numbers are so difficult to come by that Customs and Border Protection is unable to supply Congress with the real numbers that might put their successes or failures into context. A simple reason for this is that successful crossings go uncounted and, most often, undetected. Many in Congress have demanded a border security plan that would stop 90 percent of all illegal entries. The obvious question is: 90 percent of what? It's just not possible to estimate a percentage of an unknowable number. The bicycles, however, left an interesting tally. A bike cannot pedal itself. Presumably, each abandoned bicycle represented one or more migrants. After talking to the residents of the Tijuana River Valley, I could account for roughly half the volume of bikes that El Indio's *polleros* claim to have shepherded across.

Yet, I arrived at the border much too late in the game. Abandoned bikes had been wheeling back into America's streets, uncounted, in every imaginable fashion for two years. It is more than likely that copycats picked up the trade, too. There is also anecdotal evidence that bikes were collected from the valley floor and sent back to Tijuana and returned with a new migrant on top.

If the bicycle *polleros*' claim is true, however, at $4,500 per migrant—in Tijuana, an average sum for the time—El Indio's gang pulled in over thirty-one million tax-free dollars in under three years. Everybody along the chain was paid: the customs agent (who bought a Lincoln Navigator), the police (who were soon swept up in Tijuana's most violent period ever), the American police departments that sold the bikes, the truck drivers, bike mechanics, recruiters, *checadores, comunicadores, ganchos, guías*, and *levantons*. In every operation, *el coyote* received the largest chunk. Which would suggest that a child whose parents left him with an elderly grandfather in an impoverished village, who attended school part-time to the seventh grade, came to the border, lost everything dear to him, and became a millionaire.

Then, he vanished.

Around about April, I finally accepted something I'd long suspected in Dan Watman. It occurred in the obvious, sudden way one discovers that the Easter Bunny isn't real. It was that Watman possessed almost no ability to lie. Moreover, he was terrible at withholding information of any kind. At first I thought he'd made a philosophical stand related to his activism. Watman's group was called Border Encuentro—border meeting—and its primary purpose was to get people talking across the boundary. To show any tendency to fabricate, I assumed, ran counter to his faith in complete and open dialogue. The problem with this was that Watman worked on a dangerous border, and communicated with everyone from petty criminals and smugglers to enforcement agencies like Customs and Border Protection and the Border Patrol. All of these people lied to Watman. Be it inability or moral stance, his transparency placed him on a lonely one-way street.

There was, however, one curious instance in which Watman withheld information—for a little while at least. He lived in Tijuana and crossed the border daily to teach Spanish at a law college in San Diego and to work with other activists. But because he had a punk streak in him, and just didn't care for the whole idea of a militarized wall separating our sister cities, one day, he presented himself to customs agents at the end of the long line to cross the border and refused to produce documentation, his identity, or any citizenship status. To questions, he replied, simply, "I don't want to say."

The customs agent said, "Don't give me any drama." This caused a stalemate. He was sent to "secondary." His obvious American accent and Caucasian looks would have created a dilemma for the agents. They couldn't just kick him back to Mexico because he could be a terrorist. They couldn't let him pass without documentation. So the agents took Watman to a back room and interrogated him. His demeanor exacerbated the situation; he was committed but never heated. He answered their questions with a simple, "I don't want to say."

After a number of hours, the lead agent admitted that, well, despite this being the most voluminous land crossing in the world, Watman had presented them an entirely novel problem. "I have never seen this before," said the agent. Honored, Watman sought to take credit and soon offered up his name and citizenship. So, with better things to do, Customs and Border Protection allowed Watman into the United States despite his deliberate lack of documentation. In his retelling of the story, the strongest element I took from it was Watman's great relief in unburdening himself of the information he'd held for eight hours, and his pride in never having actually lied to the agents.

El Negro's stance on fabrication and withholding, however, was quite a bit more nuanced and artful. From the start, he withheld information from me like a master. I was the dunce before a shell game. But there was more. For example, on a few occasions he'd relayed the story of his first crossing to the United States. It was standard: in the 1980s he walked across at Otay with a close friend from his home village who had made the trip before. One day, however, El

Negro told me about a rare return to Michoacán he'd made ten years later. As soon as he struck the dusty streets of the village, he ran into his original crossing partner, which was a godsend. Despite their tight bond, life in the United States had separated them over the decade. So El Negro suggested they grab a couple of beers in the village cantina before he sought out his mother's house. The friend was agreeable, and rather than two, the pair downed several beers, talking all the while about their lives and adventures in *el Norte*. Finally, El Negro said he really must complete the trip to his mother's house, and the men parted with hearty hugs and a vague plan to meet again in the future. When El Negro reached home, he found his sisters and his mother beside themselves. "Where have you been?" they asked. "We heard you were in town, but you never arrived. We thought something terrible had happened to you."

"Oh no, nothing terrible at all," said El Negro. "I ran into Eduardo, and we haven't seen each other in years. And he's such an old friend, we drank a few together. I'm sorry I'm late. But what a time we had catching up."

El Negro's family looked at each other; they looked at him. The mother said, "*Mijo*, Eduardo has been dead for two years now. He's buried over there in the cemetery."

El Negro told me this story as if it were something that had happened during his shift at the bathrooms. He could both share in my disbelief—because it *was* fantastic—and confirm the tale as a truth. It was as real as a thing—as thin and gauzy as the sheets of toilet paper he handed to his customers, and as essential to everyday life as well.

It wasn't the first incident that gave me pause. El Negro was no longer just a source, he was a research assistant. He tended to drop weight rather noticeably from time to time—because he was so poor, he couldn't always buy food. I began to hand him cash here and there, enough to eat, anyway. I needed to keep El Negro alive. But this changed the status of our relationship. As long as I was paying him, the incentive was only to become more elaborate, more wicked, and to stretch the search to the grave. I considered the characters he interviewed—each ingeniously eccentric, they popped up and disappeared like a game of Whac-A-Mole. I'd seen some of the peripheral characters with my own eyes and confirmed the existence of others; but still, the one figure who mattered most—El Indio—remained a mystery. And because of this, I swam in a still pool of doubt. I began to suspect many conflicting things: that El Negro himself was the bicycle coyote, or a version of him. Or that El Negro had made the whole thing up, or a large portion of it anyway. Along the border, a story that is not worth embellishing just isn't worth telling. Was it possible that El Indio represented something like the ghost of El Negro's friend in Michoacán—both nonexistent and essential to the experience of migration as well?

The bowl-cut *pollero* I encountered in front of the bathrooms on my first visit to Playas had confirmed the moniker El Indio as belonging to the famous bicycle coyote. And then, without knowing me, or my purpose for being there, he and the bathroom worker had discussed this person with a sort of regard that reminded me of the way local ballers might mention a big leaguer who'd dropped by the neighborhood court one day.

Mateo, the man who lived adjacent to the bicycle gang's favored little canyon, independently confirmed that trucks carried bikes into the declivity in the same place and manner that El Negro described, aligning the period of time the gang lasted and the numbers of crossers as well. He identified the policeman El Gordito, who would later appear in El Negro's interviews, but Mateo would not even mutter the nickname of the figure who ran the operation almost on his doorstep.

With a scholarly approach, Oscar Romo studied the cycle excursions mounted from Los Laureles Canyon, the structure of the *polleros*' organization, and the volume of their clientele, but he was not privy to the main actors' identities—only what he saw as the fun and resourcefulness of the idea.

That each of the ranches along Monument Road, as well as the state and county parks, received a share of the abandoned bikes suggested the breadth and diversity of the coyote's tactics. But really, the cycles themselves told so much more. They were so varied—from style to price point to national origin, with their police auction stickers, city registration labels, and shop emblems—that few who came into contact with them believed that the bikes had sprung forth, with any consistency, from Tijuana's streets—these were American bikes.

Although Customs and Border Protection has been derided as one of the most opaque and obfuscating American bureaucracies (one investigator told me she took a "tongue lashing" for even speaking to me), border communities eventually become the agents' homes. I talked to friends of friends. I met with willing yet anonymous agents to discuss both smuggling and enforcement tactics and to put the screws to the plausibility of this bicycle *pollero's* claims. One of these continued to send cell photos of migrant bikes discovered long after El Indio was said to have retired. Environmental activists in the valley, likewise, sent photos of bikes obviously abandoned by migrants as late as 2014.

I'd heard the term *garantizado* some time before I came across the case of the Villarreal brothers. "Guaranteed," in this sense, meant that illegal migrants traveled under the ironclad protection of immigration officials. This mind-twisting reality only became clear once the Villarreals—Fidel and Raul, former Border Patrol agents who fled in the face of an internal investigation—were repatriated from Mexico and placed before a federal court. They had been esteemed professionals—one had been a spokesman for the agency—and they had been crossing migrants in Border Patrol vehicles while on the job. The price per migrant was $12,000.

I attended the federal trial to confirm the tactics of both Border Patrol and smuggling operations. The case was seen as a black eye to Customs and Border Protection, even at a time when hundreds of agents had been indicted and convicted of corruption since a 2004 surge in new hires. And the case was a rare airing of the agency's dirty laundry. I'll never forget a *levantón* prosecutors brought to the stand. He was a young, squirrelly Mexican American who I swear could have been in my high school algebra class. He was currently serving time on a drug conviction and was led into the court in cuffs. Until that point, the defense had been focusing on every detail of the agency's kilo trucks, which the Villarreals sometimes drove—basically, a full-sized truck with a metal camper that served as a jail cell mounted in the bed. But on the stand, this *levantón* began to describe a planned meeting at Smuggler's Gulch—a pickup of nineteen migrants—and he said that he'd met one of the Villarreals, who was driving a Border Patrol jeep.

Spotting an obvious hole in the getaway driver's story, a defense attorney immediately interrupted the testimony. All along they had been talking about kilo trucks with the ability to transport large groups. Nobody had yet mentioned a jeep. And *how* was it possible that nineteen people could be transported in a jeep?

The courtroom hushed. It looked like the *levantón*'s credibility was about to crumble. This was when he leaned into the microphone and, with the confidence of an ironworker talking iron, said, "Sir, I happen to know from experience that you can fit nineteen people into a jeep."

He knew, and he knew it with such a steely certainty that, suddenly, we all knew that you could fit nineteen human beings into a bucket-seat jeep. And the entire courtroom erupted in laughter.

Much later, I found myself waiting in the greenroom of our local public radio station. I was there to discuss an article I'd written. A serious-looking man with a shaved head and a navy-blue jacket entered the room. He wore a small Border Patrol pin on his lapel. This was Shawn Moran, a spokesman for the Border Patrol agents' union, and he was there to discuss the wave of Central American children who were crossing the border in the summer of 2014. We struck up a conversation about the cunning and curious techniques of smugglers, a favorite topic of mine and of many agents. Then Moran happened to mention that, until recently, he'd been stationed in Imperial Beach, a stint that had lasted well over a decade.

Oh, I said, so he must know all about the abandoned bikes.

Know about them? He'd pursued their riders on several occasions. And Moran vividly recalled a chase that had occurred one Christmas Eve a few years back.

"How many bikes would you say were abandoned?" I asked.

"Hundreds."

"I know a rancher who said he collected a thousand in six months," I said.

"I believe that," he said.

Then Moran was whisked away to opine on an even more daunting crossing—occurring at that moment—undertaken by tens of thousands of children with no wheels at all.

From my own investigations, I could confirm the *what*, *where*, *when*, and *how*. But only El Negro's interviews elucidated the *who* and *why*.

I had many doubts. But then I would sift through the cache of interviews again. I thought: if this grade-school-educated Playas de Tijuana bathroom worker who lived in a fake ship could create these characters and this story from thin air—all the while nailing the cadence, vocabularies, dispositions, personal histories, and knowledge sets of a cast of desperados who had convened at the border from all over Mexico and the United States, situating their testimonies in a time frame and geography corresponding to the observations of my outside witnesses—then the world had let an awesome talent slip past on a river of poverty, because El Negro was, if not an honest investigator, a master storyteller.

I confessed my concern to Dan Watman. Because we'd become friends, I assumed that Watman and I could argue the finer points of reality versus illusion in confidence. In effect, I suspended my earlier assessment of Watman as someone who was unable to lie or withhold information. I asked him if *he* thought El Negro could be inventing part, or all, of Indio's story. Watman said only, "Hmm, I don't know." And sure enough, on next meeting El Negro in the binational garden, Watman spilled his guts about my doubt, my disbelief.

El Negro and I had been working together for nearly three years. His early and increasing skill at investigation and interviewing nurtured in him a pride that lifted his posture, even. It offered an identity other than deportee, pauper, *indigente* sheared from his family and life's path. In many ways, that journalistic skill set was his most tangible possession, and in my presence he had openly questioned why he hadn't discovered this gift until so late in life. He'd told me he'd pondered that slight of fate, until one day he realized that, "No, this thing didn't come too late, but just in time."

Understandably, Dan's revelation of my doubt caused a falling-out between my research assistant and me. And because he didn't own a telephone, lived in another country, and tended to disappear, the break was all the more severe.

"You won't believe how we crossed," said a young woman sitting in a shack where she and a friend had recently found themselves guests. El Negro supposed she was about twenty-four years old. She'd offered the statement as a challenge. And having issued it, she bunched up her soft lips, threw her shoulders back, looked at her girlfriend, and awaited a response.

In combing the streets of Tijuana, working his contacts, and ferreting out the story, El Negro truly had found his passion. His first interviews were good, he felt, but when he read them beginning to end on cold nights aboard the ship, he really saw the growth in each subsequent piece. And in that summer's vacuous heat, when El Negro and I believed we'd discovered everything we could concerning the tale of a ghost coyote called the Indian, El Negro decided to write his own book—an account of Tijuana's deported.

To do this, he employed the same techniques he'd developed in our search for El Indio. Deportation stories were a dime a dozen. He wanted the good ones. As we talked through the border fence one day, me on one side and El Negro on the other, he said, "A story is like a machine: you need all the parts for it to work right." And in speaking to a woman in the Zona Norte, he learned of two girls residing in *el Cañón de los Laureles*—they'd both crossed and were deported together. El Negro had documented the stories of several men, and he thought the perspective of two women might deepen his piece. He mostly hoped their story had all the parts.

Leti wanted the chronicle to start at the beginning, and she wanted El Negro to hazard a guess, a flip of a coin at the start of a match. "You won't believe how we crossed," she said.

Okay, El Negro thought, assessing her demeanor and social status. "In the trunk of a car," he said.

"No."

"You swam around the sea fence."

"No."

"As a passenger in *panga* fishing boat, then."

"No."

"You climbed a rope ladder over the fence . . . Someone cut a hole in the fence with an arc welder . . . You passed through a water culvert or a sewer pipe."

"No, no, no."

"You went through a drug tunnel."

"Keep going."

"A customs agent was bribed and waved you through."

"This way of crossing was different. It was fun," the other one, Julia, said.

"You crossed in the mountains and the coyote met you with packhorses," El Negro said.

"No."

"You rented one of those little personal submarines and it carried you to Coronado."

"You'll never guess," she said.

"Okay, tell me, then. How did you cross into *el otro lado*?"

"On bicycles!" said Leti.

El Negro didn't say a word, because he didn't want anything he might say to influence the direction of the story that followed. He'd been at this awhile, and he knew that the details come of their own accord. So, there was a distinct and awkward pause, one that could easily be taken for doubt. In the little shack, Leti, Julia, and El Negro looked at each other. "Yes, it's true," Julia said.

El Negro listened to their story then, not letting on, and the two young women explained that they'd come to Tijuana with little money but struck an arrangement with the bicycle coyote. He would cross them despite their inability to pay. He would help them find work, and they would repay him somehow. The coyote dispatched the women in two separate groups, first Julia, whose group was picked up by a man driving a van. Leti and her smaller group were met by a woman in a car. In both instances, the drive was relatively short. Julia said they came to a house in a wealthy enclave of San Diego; the neighborhood was hilly and filled with views of the ocean. The van slowed at a driveway and an automatic garage door lifted before them. The driver pulled the van into the roomy space, and he told the passengers to remain in their seats until the door was completely shut. Afterward, they were led through a side door that opened into a kitchen. The house was "very spacious and beautiful," with many bedrooms and bathrooms. The matron—an indigenous-looking woman—appeared and set down some rules. Before their departure, no one was permitted to leave the house for any reason. Both the front and back yards were off-limits. The drapes and curtains, which hung thick against the western sun, were not to be touched.

La señora then pulled Julia aside and informed the young woman that she wouldn't be leaving with the rest of the group. Because of her debt, Julia would live and work there at the house, helping one of the matron's daughters with housekeeping. On her arrival, Leti was placed in the service of the kitchen. Both women helped on the three big shopping days per week. The volume of food purchased and prepared astonished them. In time, they came to know the family—and that both the male and female *levantones* were siblings of El Indio. The matron, who owned the house, was his mother. And El Indio himself appeared once a week, usually on a Saturday. Congenial with the neighbors, he helped with sprinklers and tree planting; there was talk of the family launching a landscaping business. And Indio often hosted large *carne asada* cookouts on the back porch. The guides and drivers sat outside with El Indio. Leti served migrants in the dining room first. They could watch TV there, but were not invited outside. Likewise with the neighbors who sometimes drifted over. Guests were kept on the porch and directed toward the restroom in a back house, should they need it. No matter their number on these occasions, Julia recalled, "the *pollos* wouldn't make a sound."

Leti and Julia, however, did meet some neighbors—one of them sold the young women an old Toyota Celica for a very good price. On this basis, they became friendly and were invited to events outside of the home. At one of these, a tanned and talkative couple rather knowingly probed Leti and Julia as to their "work situation." The women shared, maybe, more than they should have. But the American couple didn't appear to judge them. The woman offered to get them jobs with a friend in Los Angeles. She insisted, in fact. "Easy work with good wages," said Leti, "giving massages."

In the kitchen not long after, the girls from Sinaloa broached the possibility with their matron. They explained that all of the training for these positions was done on the job. Leaning over a pot, Indio's mother looked surprised. If it meant doing better for themselves and prospering, *la señora* said, she was happy for the girls. Leti and Julia waited for El Indio's next visit to ask for his blessing and to thank him. He'd still not charged them for the crossing, and he even paid them a bit besides. Here they were leaving after a short time, but El Indio said, "If this is your decision, go ahead. You've helped me a lot. If someday you need me, look for me and I'll do whatever I can." He withdrew some bills and handed each of them $500. "Please take it," he said.

The girls packed their few belongings into the Celica and drove to the home of the elegant couple. "They were expecting us," Leti said. "We left for Los Angeles that day. And I swear, if we knew what lay in store for us there, we never would have gone."

El Negro didn't have to ask about the road their travels had taken. Leti's verve had become anger. It was clear that she and Julia had been escorted to Los Angeles and turned into prostitutes. The massage parlor must have been raided down the line, El Negro thought, and now, here they were.

"The truth is, things have been bad for us," Leti said, "and worse, we aren't able to find El Indio anywhere."

Later, El Negro sat at a simple wood table in a dark kitchen. The scents of percolating coffee and baking bread added a familial intimacy that he missed in his solitary life aboard ship. The squat clay bread oven emitted a comfortable heat and an amber light. It flickered on the gilded portrait of Marta—sitting upright and proud in her traditional attire—which was mounted next to the table. Marta's mother, Lupita, worked at the kitchen sink.

Negro had come to Roberto's home mostly because the story of Leti and Julia lacked important parts—a happy ending for one and, two, the central character. That El Indio was not dead or imprisoned was a revelation only slightly less jarring than the fact that Roberto had failed to confide it in him. He realized the friendship went only so far. One man helped thwart an attempt on his life, the other had been like a brother. Understandably, Roberto always refused to discuss the day of Marta's death or her funeral, and having reached that limit, their conversations ended in a reconstitution of their masculine stoicism—a drying of eyes and straightening of shoulders, and going no further. El Oso had been more open about that day, but still there were limits: the experience had been too painful. El Negro also assumed a dreadful end for Roberto's *compadre*, yet another wound. To probe further into the gracious family's tragedy posed a challenge that, as an investigator, El Negro was not willing to hazard. He thought it was the same as the kicking of the down-and-out. But the morning of Negro's arrival at the home, Roberto received his friend from Playas with *abrazos*, excusing himself only so that he might finish some business before they talked.

In Roberto's absence, El Negro spied the opportunity to visit with Lupita. She placed coffee before him but returned to the sink. To her back, then, El Negro suggested that maybe she'd accept just a short interview. "And if there is something you don't want to discuss . . ."

"What I feel most," she said, rinsing a plate, "is sorrow in my soul that such a man's heart was undone. But the most important thing is the great love that God gave the both of them." The speed of her reply led Negro to understand that she'd long had words for him. Lupita turned to face her guest. "I know so because, for a time, my daughter was the happiest woman in the world. And Indio tells me that Marta still comes to touch him in his sleep. But enough. I tell him, 'Son, those are just thoughts. Don't long for her so much. Find a woman and get married.' He tells me not yet, that he's waiting for God to heal his heart fully."

"Apologies," said El Negro. "You still speak with Indio? Do you have plans to get together?"

"Not a week goes by that we don't communicate. He says he likes to be with me because I look like my daughter. Last week he was here, we went to eat at Popotla."

"He visits?"

"You know that," she said.

Of course, El Negro observed many strangers there. Clients and guests, Mexican and foreign, such as the Indonesian family with the lovely daughter, and many more besides, were compartmentalized in his memory like rooms in that house. Plus, Negro never truly knew the spectrum of Roberto's associates. It wasn't a home where one inquired into the business of fellow visitors. Severe men came and went. There was an instance, however, when upon entry El Negro met the gaze of a young man wearing an expensive-looking green sweater. In a corner, the youth had stood in consultation with the man Negro knew as El Oso—and there had been something in his regard that El Negro felt in the marrow, a deep appraisal. Again, Negro thought it had to do with his own poor state of dress. Unfortunately, it was the best he had. But then Roberto appeared and whisked Negro into the backyard where guests had gathered, food was being served, and music piped through. He didn't see the young man again that day, and wasn't sure if he'd seen him before. The memory of that brief encounter didn't surface until Lupita suggested that Negro had been in El Indio's presence, from time to time, all along.

"At the restaurant in Popotla, in fact, you came up in conversation," Lupita said to Negro. "In some ways I agree with El Indio—he didn't do anything that merits a story. He told Roberto, 'Look, God was on my side for this, but now I think the devil wants to stick his tail in.' But Roberto thinks so highly of you, Negro. You don't know how much he's gone through with El Indio because of these interviews you've done. You're the fly that's in the milk all of the time. I don't say this to upset you. There is almost nothing that Roberto would refuse you, but I don't think he has skipped out on the bill here. He has given you plenty, risking so much."

El Negro assured her that names would be changed. "No one will know who it is except the one who knows his own life," he said. Lupita inhaled and sighed heavily at the counter. They were quiet. El Negro then thanked Lupita for her honesty. "You have always been very nice to me. I am grateful," he said.

"You're always welcome here, Negro." She tossed the rag into the sink. "Really, I don't understand any of it."

36

In November, I stood on the loose talus slope of Spooner's Mesa with Chris Peregrin, Border Field State Park's Acting Reserve Manager. His colleague Greg Abbott, wanting to keep his hands in the dirt, waved off such promotions just as he had as a lifeguard. And at that moment, he was busy planting cholla cactus somewhere in the land below us. The hilltop we occupied overlooked that saucer-like bull-ring of Playas de Tijuana, the rambling border fence, the brown and russet colors of the Tijuana River Valley, and an empty white beach that ran into the cityscape of San Diego.

I rode this ground on the Free Spirit sometimes, imagining the rush had the authorities been looking to snatch me up. But since they weren't, I could take time to stand on the mesa and let the landscape seep in. Ninety degrees left offered an intimate view of Los Laureles Canyon—the dusty hillsides of its crevasse terraced with plywood and tin-roofed shacks, their foundations made of the spent car tires that had drawn me here in the first place. An equal turn to the right, and I caught the gleaming downtown towers of San Diego, the harbor, the navy fleet and leisure yachts, the palisades of Point Loma.

"We're in luck," Peregrin said, pointing down toward the wetlands that snaked through rust-colored grasses and green thickets between us and the city. "The tide is really full today. You can see the whole system."

The highest tide of the year, actually—and thus the lowest low—came in November. And as Peregrin pointed out, the crystalline blue of the ocean had slinked past the sandy gates of the Tijuana River mouth and crept miles into the American valley—lighting every torpid bend, oxbow, and dead end. Stretching from Otay Mountain to the Pacific, this was the last unbroken watershed in Southern California. And the vibrant blue illuminated all of its inner workings to the naked eye. Without the tide, the sandbanks and vegetation-choked arteries of the wetland would have gone virtually invisible, would have blended into a gradient of browns. The tide acted like dye in the plumbing.

This was the very role of the bicycles that wheeled over this same topography. Just as seawater defined the tidal lands, the bicycles revealed America's economic and social systems by floating through its bloodstream and coloring—with sparkling chrome, metallic paints, a whir of spokes and a flicker of handlebar ribbons—the murkiest corners and farthest reaches.

In the end, I understood few aspects of this story with complete fidelity. Chief among the things that I knew to be true was the fact that a lot of bicycles had come to rest, abandoned and ownerless, in a strange and forgotten valley at the southwesternmost corner of the continental United States. For many months, and at various points since, I believed this was all I'd ever know.

Yet bicycles hold very special attributes that grant them access. They are both the object and the means by which to move that object. Like a dollar bill, once a bicycle leaves the hand of its owner it becomes general, joins the ambiguous idea of the thing—the sea of dollars, the sea of bikes.

In the dust trails of their travel, I thought I glimpsed answers to the way things worked. I believed their unique qualities were what led the swamp bicycles to illustrate, for me, certain central equations. Take value, for example, how an object or service is worth nothing until somebody wants it. How once we prohibit something of value, we instantly create a smuggler. The more resources we put into enforcing the prohibition, the higher the value of the thing being smuggled. The higher the value of that desired item, the more incentive there is for the smuggler, whom we created, to smuggle it. How the business and jobs of enforcement rely, in the end, on the business of smuggling. An endless cycle that also helps to explain how these criminal and enforcement worlds overlap like rings on a pond. And how once you begin to pedal among either smuggling or enforcement circles, the circles only become smaller and more elite as you naturally travel up, until one day you're pedaling around in a specialized training scenario meant to replicate a compound in Pakistan where commando forces practice for an operation whose success the president of the United States will hang his hat on—will win an election on—and will change the way we view our place in the world.

By now, the shiny new border construction responsible for filling in Smuggler's Gulch with 1.7 million yards of dirt had been completed to the sea. One could argue that this edifice put an end to the bicycle coyote's technique. Yet I continued to receive photos and reports of new bikes found in the valley. A plan to replace the entire string of aging seismic censors failed to receive funding.

In an interview that El Negro conducted with Roberto's mentor Julian, a *pollero viejo* who had observed changes in the business since 1960, Negro asked, "With all of the walls being built, do you think someday you won't be able to cross people into the United States?"

"Of course I don't believe that," Julian said. "One door closes and another one opens."

Roberto was more specific on this point. He said, "The deal with walls is just, you could say, smoke and mirrors. They're built in order to say that the United States is fighting the flow of immigrants. In reality, it's nothing. What's happening is that more people are working in government, and they all have opportunities to make illicit money through their work."

Smugglers understood that by erecting an ever more massive border complex, by doubling and tripling agents and resources, the government was also building the pipelines through which people and contraband might pass. This wasn't only a matter of gaming physical obstacles and boundaries. Social scientists, internal affairs investigators, and attorneys general have often estimated a 10 percent rate of corruption among various law-enforcement entities. This number is sometimes dismissed as insignificant. Yet Homeland Security, of which Customs and Border Protection is a part, is the country's largest enforcement agency. And that scale matters. In fact, when CBP fired James Tomsheck, its head of internal affairs, as the agency suffered a wave of corruption cases and a leaked audit that suggested it did little to investigate allegations made against its officers, Tomsheck went on record as saying he was scapegoated by a corrupt system. He estimated 5 or 10 percent of CBP's agents were already corrupt, and "the system was clearly engineered to interfere with our efforts to hold the Border Patrol accountable."

This point about percentages is one that smugglers claim to manipulate at ground level. The number of Border Patrol agents was doubled under the George W. Bush administration, when the agency eventually grew to employ twenty thousand officers. This gave smugglers a possible two thousand agents to work with. The heavily debated border-reform bill, the Secure Our Borders Act, called for another doubling of agents. Rather than concern coyotes, this effort suggested there could be as many as four thousand amenable officers on their side.

"The United States government does visible, grandiose things in order to be seen," Julian said, "like the enormous walls they build. But they themselves know it does no good. They do it just so the people will see they are doing something to combat the flow."

There was another high point nearby that I'd long admired for its vantage. Peregrin and I could see its pinnacle from Spooner's Mesa. Even before I glimpsed the coyote bikes, I'd pedal or hike up to certain lookouts on Point Loma—the swayback peninsula that rises to 422 feet to face the broad Pacific—always on the first evening of a Santa Ana wind. These breezes that start off cool in the box canyons of Utah cross the desert and bloom into hot, offshore gusts that completely transform the face of the south coast. Tan, chalky cliffs, slate-blue ocean, and dusty green hillocks warm into the true colors following a morning rain—but with something else, an atmospheric patina reminiscent of an old photo. That past-meets-present clarity is what takes me up to the lookout. Because on the horizon at sundown, San Clemente Island looms out of the west nearly fifty miles away. Normally the island is completely invisible to the naked eye, but at times like this, landscape detail emerges from a great distance.

I often thought about the last bikes trapped out there on a craggy, mysterious island that appeared only during rare atmospheric conditions. Part of the appeal had to do with the restricted access, as civilians weren't allowed near it. After the swing gang mentioned that, given the speed with which bikes disappeared from military bases, San Clemente Island was probably the only location where the swamp bikes could be said with certainty to exist, I had the occasion to interview a lobster fisherman who happened to work the backside of the island every fall. As he regaled me with the terrifying details of a boat sinking he'd survived out there, I found a question rising to my lips. I was about to ask the man for a ride on his new boat, out to the island, where I imagined myself scaling its desert cliffs and scouring the topside for junk bikes probably rusting away in the dirt somewhere. That's when I stopped. I finally realized how far I'd overshot my mark. Bicycle brakes never really were that good.

Months later, Watman sent word that El Negro wanted to see me. And I took this as an opportunity to make amends. En route, I tried to script an explanation for my doubts. I didn't want to lie, yet I couldn't frame up an honest answer without poking at the old wound. But when I found Negro socializing near the bathrooms below the lighthouse in Playas, no trace of a grudge could be detected.

He said, "Did Daniel tell you?"

"Tell me what?" I asked.

"I found him."

"Who?"

"El Indio," he said. "Come on, there is a message for you."

We hurried along the promenade, past the coconut seller, bars, and taco stands where freelancing mariachis idled, thumbing the strings of their guitars.

"What does he look like?" I asked.

"A young guy. Regular, not real good-looking."

"You mean he's indigenous, and you're not going to tell me anything more."

"*Sí*," he said.

Negro opened the black doors of the ship, and I could see that it was not rotting but was finally taking shape as the themed restaurant it was always meant to be. We took up chairs on the plank flooring. I admired a fake new chandelier made of rebar. Negro fetched his notebook. He sat and explained how he continued to visit the home of Roberto and his family until Negro's presence had passed annoyance and merged with the everyday, like an ugly sofa. And then, one day, Indio was there. The bicycle coyote was not thrilled to be confronted, but he wasn't combative with his pursuer either. El Negro showed Indio his interviews, and they discussed the characters who filled them. Indio didn't think it was a very good story at first. But the investigator and his subject met like this several times, until, finally, El Indio was persuaded there might be something to his adventures after all. On that occasion, they sat at Roberto's small kitchen table and, because they'd become friendly, they drank Tecates together. The men looked over El Negro's notes again, and afterward, Indio dictated this letter:

First, I'd like to say thank you, because I never thought that an American would have focused on me, or something as insignificant as crossing our people to the other side. In that respect, I hadn't given the experience a lot of thought, much less to honor it by writing it down. But now I can see that, yes, it is a good story. Believe me, I would have really liked to put down the real names of the people important to this story. Because each of them deserves the mention. As I'm sure you can understand, the possibility remains that we could all end up in prison in one country or the other.

El Negro and I have had disagreements. He is a very insistent person. I sense the majority of the time he comes out with what he's looking for. And I think this is an exception, a unique time, you could say, because he is impossible. He's always gotten some kind of response. He has insisted that I do an interview with you, and I've turned him down and I'll continue to turn him down because, well, some things hurt me too much to talk about. As I imagine you already know, Marta was the grand love of my life. A great collaborator, one of whose many gifts was this business that prospered beyond our dreams. Take care of those close to you, there is nothing more fragile than a family.

I hope you don't get offended by what I've said. I would have liked very much to have met up with you some time. I only know you by the picture. El Negro gave me a book of yours that you had given to him. He gave it to me as proof. I feel that I know you now, by the company you keep, and by the photo. It is not easy for me to trust a citizen of the country into which I passed so many of us illegally. Pardon my sincerity. Really, you don't need me at all. What you needed, you already have.

When you're finished reading this, please drink a chelita *[cold one] to my health. And I will do the same and toast your work.*

Gracias amigo,
El Indio

I continue to visit El Negro aboard his ship. The themed restaurant opened for one week and closed. For El Negro's sake, I hope it's for good. We talk about tunnels and submarines and other mysterious things. We talk about writing and the machinery of stories. He tells me that El Indio did something no millionaire American would do—he took up a career in manual labor. Indio bought a truck, a lawn mower, some rakes, shovels, and Weedwackers—and he started a landscaping business. He goes to work every day. Negro says El Indio is softening to the idea of the three of us getting together, drinking some cold ones, and talking about bikes. At these times, I wonder if El Negro himself composed that letter from El Indio. If he did, it wasn't his best work, really. So I continue to believe that it came from the bicycle coyote's lips, and I believe all of the other bits El Negro tells me, even about ghosts who sometimes sit down to drink with you and tell you what they've been up to *en el otro lado.*

I continue to pedal the Free Spirit around the neighborhood and the city. There isn't a day that goes by that I don't spot a landscaping truck, its bench seat burdened with workers. I always look—especially when I'm on the saddle of the Free Spirit. I look through the windshields and into the cabs of those trucks for a worker with an eye for a bike; the narrowed gaze of appraisal, the glint of familiarity. I'm sure I've made a number of landscapers pretty uncomfortable. The moment will pass. I'll ride on—and then I'll imagine all of the swamp bikes still out there, ferrying new people to new places, their spokes a blur spinning out new stories into the world, the details of which I'll just never know.

A Note on Sources and Acknowledgments

While researching the development of the bicycle, my reading stumbled upon historical accounts that, for me, have become like favored items I keep in a kind of mental *Wunderkammer*—a cabinet of curiosities. Often, in the process of writing this book, I'd return to these images, dust them off and spin them around. One is set at the Paris *Exposition Universelle* in the summer of 1867. Inside beautiful fair buildings, artists, explorers, and scientists had assembled a collection meant to represent the forefront of human knowledge. So much effort had gone into selecting these astonishing displays that, it seems, the entire endeavor overshot a development that had occurred practically in the shadows of its scaffolding: the humble bicycle.

French inventors had just recently given the bicycle pedals, an event that held implications for all forward movement. Yet the bicycle was not admitted among the achievements of the exposition. The slight did not matter: regular Parisians rode their new bikes to the fairgrounds anyway, and, at the exposition steps in the *Champ de Mars*, they pedaled their wheels in lazy, entertaining, joyous circles.

Twenty-six years later, the main attraction at Chicago's World's Columbian Exposition was none other than George Ferris' monstrous wheel, a contraption that looped thirty-six passenger cars 264 feet into the sky. It was an iconic engineering achievement intended to rival the Eiffel Tower, as well as, essentially, just a giant bicycle wheel: axel, spokes, rims and all.

Another scene I return to occurred indoors on wooden, elliptical rinks. As the bicycle craze of the late 1800s hit America, manufactures realized that a major impediment to sales was the fact that potential customers didn't know how to ride. The go-around was to establish cycling schools. When I discovered, through El Negro's interviews, that the bicycle coyote organized such lessons for migrants who had not yet learned to balance on two wheels, the distance between the very first beginners and those on the border with El Indio's gang collapsed for me—I saw only gyrations through time.

I suppose what my visual curios have in common is a type of circular synchronicity, pictures and stories that always come back around to their beginnings. Outwardly, the developments of the US–Mexico border and the bicycle don't have much in common. But they do share this circular nature, this piquant for irony. Some of the stories that occurred on the border were just too thick with it to include. For example, a common legend has it that construction on the earliest government fence was contracted out to American ranchers. Upon completion, the very next act of those locals was to cut holes in the fence to give themselves access to Tijuana's delights. Or, in more recent times, the government contracted with a firm to extend a physical boundary into San Diego's interior. This fence company was later charged with having used illegal labor in the building of the fortification designed to keep such labor out.

The search for El Indio took on a similar character, always cycling back to the few bits we could be certain about, variously plying the story with deeper mysteries. For El Negro, the characters involved in the bicycle operation appeared and disappeared again, as is the nature in a city where modern communication can be an expensive luxury.

The odd numbered chapters that explore the rise of El Indio are very much the result of having learned the coyote's story over time, from the memories of disparate individuals. El Negro conducted dozens of interviews with the gang, beat cops, and other officials, often returning for critical details. Illustrations of the same events, depending on the teller, differed in shape and scope. El Negro and I probed the veracity of these tales by visiting the scenes of the events—Panteón Jardín, where Marta is buried, or El Gato Bronco, or Los Laureles. Separately, I traveled to Oaxaca, Mexico, to small villages like the one where El Indio was born, to learn something not only of the place, but of the era in which Pablito and Solo resided there.

To understand the experience of migration I spoke to people who lived in the Tijuana River, deportees I met in Playas, people who had returned from the US to Oaxaca, people who had once crossed illegally but had obtained citizenship, and also to Dreamers, the children of crossers. The federal case against the brothers Raul and Fidel Villareal, the Border Patrol agents who were convicted of crossing migrants in Border Patrol vehicles, was especially enlightening. Enforcement agents I'd met, speaking on condition of anonymity, were extremely generous with their time and experiences. Victor Clark Alfaro, a human rights activist and lecturer at San Diego State University, invites human smugglers and street prostitutes to his office in Tijuana, where the subjects explain their work for his SDSU students via a video feed. I was able to attend one of these events at his office, and found Clark's use of primary sources in this field unparalleled. What I learned in person was aided by the books and articles of Peter Andreas, Lawrence A. Herzog, and Joseph Nevins.

So many people contributed to *The Coyote's Bicycle* in small ways, I could never thank them all. Early readers Chris Patterson, Brian Taylor, Cameron Taylor, Angie Fitzpatrick-Taylor, Zach Plopper, and Tim Barger helped to foster the work along. Grant Ellis labored over rugged terrain to capture the cover image. Shawn Bathe acted as both my Baja co-pilot and artistic collaborator. Almost all of the principals and interview subjects in this story were unstinting with their information. I'd like to thank: Dick Tynan, Terry Tynan, Carol Kimzey, Sharon Kimzey-Moore, Jesse Gomez, David Gomez, Greg Abbott, Chris Peregrin, Mike McCoy, Serge Dedina, Oscar Romo, Janine Zúñiga, Eric Kiser, Kim Zirpolo, Tarek Albaba, Johnny Hoffman, Brian Anderson, Ron Nua, Eric Amavisca, Aaron Garrison, Maria Teresa Fernandez, Ana Teresa Fernandez, Eric Blehm, William Finnegan, J. Jesus Cueva Pelayo, Vianett Medina, Amy Isackson, Gabe Duran, Steve Hawk, Ian Taylor, Ken Gomez and the volunteers of Bikes del Pueblo, the Binational Conference on Border Issues, Squaw Valley Community of Writers, Tony Perez, Nanci McCloskey, and the staff of Tin House Books.

And in hopes that what El Negro promised his sources—"No one will know who it is except the one who knows his own life"—is indeed the case, I'd like to thank El Indio, Solo, Roberto, et al.

Notes and Sources

CHAPTER 2

page 17: most crossed international border zone . . . "Number of Border Crossings Stabilizes," Sandra Dibble, *San Diego Union-Tribune*, July 11, 2010

page 17: brought several forty-foot Dumpsters' . . . Interviews with Dick Tynan, Greg Abbott, and Chris Peregrin

page 18: the flood cycle at seventeen years . . . "Historias de las Inundaciones in Tijuana," *El Mexicano*, January 23, 2011

page 18: was caught by currents . . . Ibid.

page 18: The bridge to San Diego collapsed three times . . . Ibid.

page 18: Tijuana's original horse track . . . *Tijuana: Identitades y Nostalgias*, Francisco Manuel Acuña Borbolla, 2002; *Seabiscuit: An American Legend*, Laura Hillenbrand, 2001

page 18: a flash flood caused a landslide . . . "Historias de las Inundaciones in Tijuana," *El Mexicano*, January 23, 2011

page 18: a commune of farmers . . . "The Little Landers Colony of San Ysidro," *The Journal of San Diego History*, Winter 1975

page 18: A dairyman . . . *San Diego Union-Tribune*, February 2, 1993

page 18: A raft of wooden *. . . Imperial Star News, March 2, 1980*

page 20: "When I bought" . . . Interview with Ben McCue

page 21: There was actually a guru . . . "The Flow of Used and Waste Tires in the California-Mexico Border Region," 2009, Institute for Regional Studies of the Californias, San Diego State University

page 22: "This valley is forgotten" . . . Interview with Dick Tynan and Terry Tynan

page 23: Until Santa Anita opened . . . *Seabiscuit: An American Legend*, Laura Hillenbrand, 2001

page 23: Movie star cowboy Roy Rogers . . . "Roy Rogers' Horse Trigger (1932?-1965): A Biography," RoyRogersWorld.com; Interview with Dick Tynan

page 23: Actor Jay Silverheels, who played Tonto . . . *San Ysidro and the Tijuana River Valley*, Barbara Zaragoza, 2014

page 23: automobile magnate Charles S. Howard . . . "Charles S. Howard, Owner Of Seabiscuit, Noor Dies," *San Diego Union*, June 7, 1950; "Howard Ranch," *San Diego Union*, January 1, 1969

page 27: Horses had even drowned . . . "Horse Owners Surprised by Flood Waters," *San Diego Union-Tribune*, December 18, 2008

page 27: not one little piece . . . In June of 2013, a fire that began on the All Bikes lot quickly grew into a blaze that consumed an estimated nine thousand bikes and motorcycles.

CHAPTER 4

page 39: women of the 1890s . . . *Bicycle: The History*, David V. Herlihy, 2004

page 40: the most militarized portion . . . "Background to the Office of the Inspector General Investigation," Office of the Inspector General, U.S, Justice Department, 1998

page 41: had sold for decades . . . Sears contracted with numerous manufactures to produce a range of styles under the Free Spirit brand. Some were made in the US by Huffy and Murray, but many more were made overseas, in Europe and Asia. I gleaned this information from knowledgeable enthusiasts on several cycling forums including BikeForums and oldroads.com. Under the tag, alanbikehouston, one Free Spirit buff had this to say on BikeForums, "During the 1960's and 1970's, probably half the bikes in any given small town in America were labeled 'Free Spirit.' Most were sturdy bikes for their specific price range. An oddity of 'Free Spirit' bikes in the 1968 to 1980 period was that Sears would buy bikes of similar appearance from suppliers in Austria, Belgium, France, Germany, and Japan. So, although the bikes looked like the same model, they might use different size rims and tires."

page 42: It was set at yellow . . . Chronology of Changes to Homeland Security Advisory System, http://www.dhs.gov/homeland-security-advisory-system

The color-coded advisory system lasted for nine years, ending in 2011. According to the DHS, it was going to be a "comprehensive and effective communications structure." CNN commentator Bruce Schneirer wrote, "It was introduced after 9/11, and was supposed to tell you how likely a terrorist attack might be. Except that it never did."

page 42: The ranks of the border patrol agents . . . "Border Patrol has lots of agents . . . in wrong places," *Associated Press*, June 29, 2014

page 42: least open or transparent . . . "Reporting Around DHS Opacity," *On the Media*, October 25, 2013; "Shedding Light on DHS," *On the Media*, February 28, 2014

page 42: In his 2009 memoir . . . *The Test of Our Times: America Under Siege . . . and How We Can Be Safe Again*, Tom Ridge, Larry Bloom, 2009; "Ridge Says He Was Pressured to Raise Terror Alert," Associated Press, August 20, 2009

page 43: Back in 1980 . . . Interviews with Mike McCoy and Serge Dedina

page 43: But in 2002 . . . "An INS Project Threatens Southern California Lands," Deborah Knight, *Grist*, January 31, 2003

page 43: The California Coastal Commision . . . "Border Field State Park and Its Monument," Nancy Carol Carter, *Eden: Journal of the California Gardens & Landscape History Society*, Fall 2011

page 44: 1.7 million cubic yards . . . "U.S. Smooths Away an Illegal Border Crossing Wrinkle," Richard Marosi, *Los Angeles Times*, January 4, 2009

page 44: It was on the tops . . . *La Gran Linea: Mapping the United States-Mexico Boundary, 1849–1857*, Paula Rebert, 2001; "La Mojonera and the Marking of California's U.S.–Mexico Boundary Line, 1849–1851," Charles W. Hughes, *Journal of San Diego History*

page 45: Having missed the founding phase . . . Monument at Initial Point, *Personal Narrative of Exploration and Incidents in Texas, New Mexico, California, Sonora, and Chihuahua*, John Russell Bartlett, 1854; "La Mojonera and the Marking of California's U.S.–Mexico Boundary Line, 1849–1851," Charles W. Hughes, *Journal of San Diego History*

page 46: But the men attached to the Boundary . . . Interview with Gabe Duran, International Boundary and Water Commision; *The Great Reconnaissance*, Edward S. Wallace, 1955

page 47: Arguello Adobe . . . *San Diego's Lost Landscape: La Punta*, John Blocker

page 49: The problem started in the 1880s . . . "U.S. Smooths Away an Illegal Border Crossing Wrinkle," Richard Marosi, *Los Angeles Times*, January 4, 2009

page 49: Nearby is Russian Hill . . . Interview with Oscar Romo

page 51: Kumeyaay people's clam harvest . . . Tijuana River National Estuarine Research Reserve, High School Curriculum

CHAPTER 6

page 63: I came across a photo . . . "A Vehicle for Quick Crossing," Janine Zúñiga, *San Diego Union-Tribune*, January 30, 2009

page 64: She cowrote a lengthy series . . . "How boy from San Diego became accused cartel hitman," Morgan Lee, Janine Zúñiga, *San Diego Union-Tribune*, July 13, 2011

page 65: interned during World War II . . . "Japanese in Tijuana River Valley," Steve Schoenherr, *South Bay Historical Society*, 2015; Interview with Dick Tynan

page 68: After years of watching . . . Interview with Maria Teresa Fernandez

page 69: One artist had . . . The sky-blue section of the border fence at Playas de Tijuana was the work of Maria Teresa Fernandez's daughter Ana Teresa Fernandez, an acclaimed artist who lives in San Francisco and travels widely. At the time of publication, Ana Teresa was painting a section of the fence in Nogales, Sonora, the same sky blue.

page 69: She'd found a hole . . . This anecdote came about in conversation with Dan Watman, who has worked closely with Maria Teresa Fernandez. Both are members of Friends of Friendship Park.

page 72: I found Greg Abbott on a clear . . . Interview with Greg Abbott

page 74: Abbott spotted . . . The original report of this rescue was provided to me by the California State Park lifeguards at Silver Strand State Beach.

page 74: the first sea fence . . . "Background to the Office of the Inspector General Investigation," Office of the Inspector General, U.S. Justice Department, 1998

page 76: Drowning victims . . . Interview with Chuck Chase, former lifeguard supervisor

page 79: this was the example . . . *Operation Gatekeeper: The Rise of the "Illegal Alien" and the Making of the U.S.–Mexico Boundary*, Joseph Nevins, 2002

CHAPTER 8

page 93: images of the globe at night . . . In 2012, NASA released a composite animation of the globe at night that had been compiled from data gathered by the Suomi NPP satellite.

page 93: Cali and Medellin cartels . . . *El Narco: Inside Mexico's Criminal Insurgency*, Ioan Grillo, 2011

page 94: as many as forty thousand lives . . . At the time of my reporting, this estimation of deaths caused by the drug wars that took place between 2006 and 2012 was widely reported. It has since been adjusted upward to sixty thousand by Human Rights Watch. Other estimates go much higher.

page 94: The war revealed . . . "Letter from Tijuana: In the Name of the Law," William Finnegan, *The New Yorker*, October, 13, 2010

page 94: Calderòn was accusing . . . "Mexican Cartels Move Beyond Drugs, Seek Domination," Associated Press, August 4, 2010

page 95: One of the first events . . . "Three North County Kite Surfers Robbed at Gunpoint in Baja," Amy Isackson, KPBS News, September 10, 2007

page 96: Each border reporter . . . Interview with Amy Isackson

page 96: Bodies were hung . . . "Tijuana Drug War Violence: 2 Bodies Hung From Bridge, Man Beheaded," Mariana Martinez, Associated Press, November 19, 2010

page 97: 843 murders citywide . . . "2008 winds down with 843 killings in Tijuana," *Associated Press*, December 31, 2008

page 97: a visit by President Calderòn ... "Tijuana Sees Beheadings, Bodies Hung From Bridges Days After Mexican President Touts City," Mariana Martinez, Associated Press, October 13, 2010

page 97: "Obviously, they [narco gangs] don't want ... Ibid.

page 98: secondary border crossing ... *Juan Soldado: Rapist, Murderer, Martyr, Saint*, Paul J. Vanderwood, 2004

page 98: fifty million crossings ... San Ysidro Chamber of Commerce and Business Association, http://sanysidrochamber.org/about_us.php

page 98: strongest emitters ... "Greenhouse Gas Emissions Due to Vehicle Delays at the San Diego-Tijuana Border Crossings," Suzanne Louise Barzee, San Diego State University, 2010

page 99: unsanctioned tour of Puerta Blanca ... This tour was led by Turista Libre, whose generous spirit and "atypical day treks" helped bridge the divide that widened between California and Baja during the drug wars of 2006–2012.

page 99: The drug warfare had pushed a large percentage ... "US a Haven for Tijuana Elite," Richard Marosi, *Los Angeles Times*, June 7, 2008; "Tijuana kidnappings causing mass exodus to San Diego," Amy Isackson, KPBS, July 17, 2006; "Exodus of the Rich," *San Diego Reader*, Ernie Grimm, September 28, 2006

page 100: El Pozolero—the Stew Maker ... "Families want answers from man who says he dissolved 300 people," Richard Marosi, *Los Angeles Times*, February 9, 2009

CHAPTER 10

page 124: Tijuana's original migrant slum, Cartolandia (Cardboard Land) ... Beginning in the 1930s, Mexican emigrants to the relatively new city of Tijuana took up residence along the banks of the Tijuana River. The community grew over the following decades, and was known as a home to artisans who sold their wares on Avenida Revolución. Although organized, the neighborhood was also known for severe poverty. In step with local Catholic charities, relatives on both sides of my family traveled to *Cartolandia* with donations of food and clothing. During a rainstorm in January of 1980, Tijuana officials opened gates in the Rodriguez Dam, less than ten miles upriver. The resulting torrent completely destroyed the community, washing much of it into the United States. The land once occupied by *Cartolandia* in now some of the most upscale in the city.

page 127: the silt from another such site . . . Interview with Oscar Romo

page 128: This was an ancient landscape . . . Ibid.

page 129: rain had been falling for four days . . . "Mother Crushed by Loss of Children," Sandra Dibble, *San Diego Union-Tribune*, February 11, 2010

page 130: some of the more distinctive items . . . The act of setting plastic baby doll heads in strange locations is common throughout Baja California. One instance made the cover of the *San Diego Reader* (volume 43, number 47). When I ask residents of areas where these instillations occur why the act is so prevalent, most describe a sense of humor that veers toward the macabre.

page 130: Desert Angels volunteer Ricardo Esquivias Villegas and his dog Loba . . . "Child's Body Discovered in Tijuana River Valley," Leslie Berestein, *San Diego Union-Tribune*, January 28, 2010

page 131: led him to dream up a tour of sorts . . . "San Diego Drain Is Mexican Port of Entry for a Day," Associated Press, June 4, 2011

page 132: If former Tijuana mayor Jorge Hank Rhon hadn't been arrested . . . "Ex-Mayor of Tijuana Jorge Hank Rhon Arrested," Richard Marosi, *Los Angeles Times*, June 5, 2011. The military raid uncovered eighty-eight weapons, two of which were later linked to murders. Hank's arrest and the ensuing charges and trial impacted national politics in Mexico.

CHAPTER 12

page 143: one story about a massacre . . . "For Tijuana Children, Drug War Gore Is Part of Their School Day," Richard Marosi, *Los Angeles Times*, October 25, 2008

page 143: a group threw a birthday party for a giant pothole . . . "Tijuanans Throw Birthday Party for Pothole," Adrian Florido, *Fronteras*, February 26, 2013

page 145: in 2006, when the Department of Homeland Security . . . Interview with Dan Watman

page 145: Watman was most famously detained . . . Interview with Dan Watman; "Saving Friendship Park," Jill Holslin, *Wounded Border/ Frontera Herida*, 2011

page 146: "suffused with a feverish neon glow" . . . *Corpus of Joe Bailey*, Oakley Hall, 1953

page 147: "a throbbing dynamo of commerce and pleasure" . . . *Desert Solitaire*, Edward Abbey, 1968

page 148: manipulated a loophole in Customs and Border Protection rules . . . "The Only Way to Walk Across the Border in 5 Minutes," T. B. Beaudeau, *San Diego Reader*, November 23, 2011

CHAPTER 14

page 171: They say addicted gamblers get a bigger jolt . . . "The Almost-Winning Addiction," *The Economist*, May 6, 2010

page 172: even to pass a seed across . . . Interview with Dan Watman

CHAPTER 16

page 186: experience, one repeated every two and a half minutes . . . National Bike Registry

page 186: in England's Selby train station . . . "Bicycles Theft Hunt," *UK News*, October 6, 2012

page 186: responding to suspicious online ads . . . "S.F. Bicycle Thefts Plummet after Arrest," Vivian Ho, *San Francisco Chronicle*, July 18, 2012

page 187: North Vancouver man established Bike Rescue . . . "Vancouver City Police Put Brakes on 'Bike Rescue,'" CTV British Columbia, January 4, 2008; "RCMP Shut Down Controversial Bike Rescue Business," Tyler Maine, CTV News, November 28, 2009; "Bike Rescue Founder Pleads Guilty to Fencing Stolen Goods," Claire Piech, *Pique* newsmagazine, January 15, 2010; "Bike 'Rescuer' Arrested Again," James Weldon, *North Shore News*, October 21, 2012

page 187: Chrisman rode her Giant touring bike . . . "Davis Community Replaces Stolen Bike," Jennifer K. Morita, *Davis Patch*, September 8, 2012

page 188: automobile assumed total dominance of American streets . . . *Bicycle: The History*, David V. Herlihy, 2004

page 192: Border Patrol calls a group . . . Interview with Border Patrol agent, name withheld

page 193: trucks over abandoned bicycles . . . Interview with Terry Tynan

page 193: storage capacity at the station . . . "A Vehicle for Quick Crossing," Janine Zúñiga, *San Diego Union-Tribune*, January 30, 2009

page 194: the hustle of missing bikes proved formidable . . . "Who Pinched My Ride?" Patrick Symmes, *Outside* magazine, January 11, 2012

page 195: wanted his specific black-and-gray Fuji . . . "Chasing My Stolen Bicycle," Justin Jouvenal, *San Francisco Bay Guardian Online*, February 13, 2007

page 196: survey of everyday cyclists . . . "These 8 Depressing Bike Theft Statistics Show Just How Bad the Problem Is," Eric Jaffe, *CityLab*, April 6, 2014

page 196: FBI fact sheet listed . . . "Crime in the United States 2011," FBI, www.fbi.gov

page 196: Financial upside for bike thieves . . . "What Happens to Stolen Bicycles?" Rohin Dhar, *Priceonomics*, August 28, 2012

page 197: Sheriff's Department routed a trio . . . "Sheriff's Department's Major Crimes - Metro Detail Dismantles Bicycle Burglary Ring," Los Angeles County Sheriff's Department, May 9, 2012

CHAPTER 18

page 209: rusted metal sheets of the wall built during . . . *Operation Gatekeeper: The Rise of the "Illegal Alien" and the Making of the U.S.–Mexico Boundary*, Joseph Nevins, 2002

***page 211: The agency prefers the word* fence** . . . Interview with Friends of Friendship Park members

page 211: Richard Nixon launched Operation Intercept . . . *Operation Gatekeeper: The Rise of the "Illegal Alien" and the Making of the U.S.–Mexico Boundary*, Joseph Nevins, 2002

page 211: Since Jimmy Carter . . . Ibid.

page 211: Ronald Reagan extended . . . Ibid.

page 211: Bush Senior intercepted . . . Ibid.

page 212: Bush Junior's gift wasn't so generous . . . President George W. Bush signed the Secure Fence Act of 2006 on October 26, 2006, which ordered seven hundred miles of additional barriers along the border.

page 212: high-tech surveillance towers . . . "Watching the Border: the Virtual Fence," Steve Kroft, Keith Sharman, *60 Minutes*, 2010; "Homeland Security Cancels 'Virtual Fence' After $1 Billion Is Spent," Julia Preston, *New York Times*, January 14, 2011

page 212: Obama's legacy might be in the sky . . . The first cross-border drone use took place way back in 1916, when the US Army's 1st Aero Squadron sought out Mexican revolutionary general Pancho Villa. By signing the Secure Fence Act of 2006, George W. Bush authorized the use of drones and other technologies in border enforcement. I attribute the Customs and Border Protection drone program to President Obama here, because the country's four National Air Security Operation Centers, which operate CBP drones, weren't in operation until 2011, well into the Obama administration. The overwhelming number of flight hours and program development also occurred under the Obama administration's watch. "Customs and Border Protection Drones," Center for the Study of the Drone, Arthur Holland Michel, January 7, 2015; "Unmanned Aerial Systems: Department of Homeland Security's Review of U.S. Customs and Border Protection's Use and Compliance With Privacy and Civil Liberty Laws and Standards," Homeland Security and Justice, September 30, 2014

page 215: US soil extends three feet south of the wall . . . Interview with James Brown, Friends of Friendship Park

page 216: She once slipped and fell . . . Interviews with Ana Teresa Fernandez and Dan Watman

page 217: "I just ran along the wall" . . . Customs and Border Protection considers this a "self-deportation," and sightings of such acts can be added to their tally of total deportations.

CHAPTER 20

page 227: agents sometimes dusted the bikes for fingerprints . . . Interview with Border Patrol agent, name withheld

page 234: Thirty thousand additional troops were being prepared for deployment . . . "How Obama Came to Plan for 'Surge' in Afghanistan," Peter Baker, *New York Times*, December 5, 2009

CHAPTER 22

page 243: on account of a story traded . . . Interview with Brian Taylor

page 247: an impressive margin . . . The prices of the bikes at various stages come from my interviews with Terry Tynan and Kim Zirpolo, and my observation that Tynan charged $20 for bikes on the Kimzey property.

page 247: infamous $640 government-contracted . . . The Grace Commission, or the President's Private Sector Survey on Cost Control, was ordered by Ronald Reagan in 1982 and presented its findings to Congress in 1984. The report mentioned a number of everyday items for which the federal government paid contractors exorbitant prices. The toilet assembly for P-3C Orion aircraft became infamous partly because of a joke made by Senator William Cohen during a hearing before the Senate Armed Services Committee. The $640 toilet seat, he said, "gives new meaning to the word throne"; "Adjusting the Bottom Line," *Time*, February 18, 1985

page 247: well known for refusing interviews . . . Caitlin Rother, "Modest Mogul," *San Diego Union-Tribune*, October 8, 2006

page 247: It had been described as "spicy" . . ." Ibid.

page 247: Just about every production . . . In consultation with film industry professionals with experience in Los Angeles and San Diego markets, as well as employees and contractors at Segall Productions

page 248: felt primarily by the workers . . . Interviews with Ron Nua, Eric Amavisca, Aaron Garrison, Kim Zirpolo, and Tarek Albaba

page 248: Born just after Christmas . . . Caitlin Rother, "Modest Mogul," *San Diego Union-Tribune*, October 8, 2006

page 249: Segall got his start "as a porn actor working for Ted Paramore" . . . *History of X: 100 Years of Sex on Film*, Luke Ford, 1999

page 249: Segall told Senn . . . *The Most Dangerous Cinema: People Hunting People on Film*, Bryan Senn, 2014

page 249: that featured explicit sex . . . "History of Sex in Cinema," Tim Dirks, *Filmsite*

page 249: when Deep Throat premiered . . . *Hollywood V. Hardcore: How the Struggle Over Censorship Saved the Modern Film Industry*, Jon Lewis, 2000

page 249: Godfrey Daniels . . . http://www.imdb.com

page 250: Spirit of Seventy Sex . . . According to IMDb, Stu Segall worked under multiple alias, in this case Ms. Ricki Krelmn.

page 250: Department of Justice released . . . "Organized Crime Involvement in Pornography," United States Department of Justice, June 8, 1977

page 250: Organized crime had moved into the pornography business . . . *History of X: 100 Years of Sex on Film*, Luke Ford, 1999

page 250: Zaffarano was a big guy . . . *Donnie Brasco: My Undercover Life in the Mafia*, Joseph D. Pistone, 1989

page 251: But this would not be the fate . . . "55 Indicted by U.S. as Pornographers and in Film Piracy," *New York Times*, February 14, 1980; *Donnie Brasco: My Undercover Life in the Mafia*, Joseph D. Pistone, 1989; *History of X: 100 Years of Sex on Film*, Luke Ford, 1999

page 251: Agents also raided an office located at 1600 Broadway . . . "55 Indicted by U.S. as Pornographers and in Film Piracy," *New York Times*, February 14, 1980

Also see: Attorney General's Commission on Pornography: Final Report (Meese Report), Part 4

page 251: Agents found his crumbled figure . . . *Donnie Brasco: My Undercover Life in the Mafia*, Joseph D. Pistone, 1989; *History of X: 100 Years of Sex on Film*, Luke Ford, 1999

page 252: Segall's home in Los Angeles . . . Attorney General's Commission on Pornography: Final Report (Meese Report), Part 4, Chapter 4

page 252: In 1991, Godfrey Daniels had . . . http://www.strategic-operations.com/team/stu-segall/

page 252: One day—the story goes—DEA agents . . . Interview Kim Zirpolo

page 253: Even in make-believe, problems arose . . . "Wounds in Simulated Capture End Lance Corporal's Career," Debbi Farr Baker, *San Diego Union-Tribune*, October 15, 2007; "Former Marine Who Sued for Millions Gets $91,000," Debbi Farr Baker, *San Diego Union-Tribune*, December 11, 2007; "Training lawsuit returns to court," Gidget Fuentes, *Marine Corps Times*, November 30, 2007

page 253: according to an employee . . . Interview with Kim Zirpolo

page 254: "misguided and wasteful spending" . . . "Safety at Any Price: Assessing the Impact of Homeland Security Spending in U.S. Cities," Senator Tom Coburn, December 2012

page 254: HALO Corporation and the organizer of the summit . . . "Marines, police prep for mock zombie invasion," Julie Watson, Associated Press, October 27, 2012

page 254: "It's embarrassing, really" . . . Interviews with Kim Zirpolo and Bill Anderson

CHAPTER 24

page 268: keep squatters from commandeering the ruin . . . Interview with El Negro

page 271: entirety of the new $70-million-per-mile US Border . . . "Study: Price for border fence up to $49 billion," *San Francisco Chronicle*, January 8, 2007. The $70-million-per-mile estimate is a simple dividing of the Congressional Research Service's estimate of $49 billion by the proposed length of the fence, 700 miles. But this cost still does not include the price of acquiring land or labor if contractors are used, and is thus a low-ball estimate.

CHAPTER 26

page 283: the most efficient device . . . *Bicycling Science*, David Gordon Wilson, 2004

page 283: that Susan B. Anthony called . . . *Sports in American Life: A History*, Richard O. Davies, 2012

page 283: solid rubber tires were an important gift . . . Ibid.

page 284: Orville and Wilbur Wright . . . *It's All About the Bike: The Pursuit of Happiness on Two Wheels*, Robert Penn, 2010; *Bicycle: The History*, David V. Herlihy, 2004

page 284: another bike shop owner and mechanic . . . Ibid.

page 284: Today's 54-million-member-strong . . . Ibid.

page 286: America's largest export to China . . . "Scrap Really Is Our Top Export to China," Scott Jacobs, University of Michigan, January 3, 2013; http://www.gltaac.org/scrap-really-is-our-top-export-to-china

page 286: inherited a bicycle co-op . . . Interview with Ken Gomez, Bikes del Pueblo

CHAPTER 28

page 301: At eighteen, El Negro migrated . . . Interview with El Negro

page 302: stumbled upon a construction site . . . "New Park Turns Attention From a Forbidding Border Fence to a Welcoming Ocean," Ann Jarmusch, *San Diego Union-Tribune*, August 21, 2005

page 305: jumped 25 percent over the previous year . . . "In Come the Waves," *The Economist*, June 16, 2005

page 305: in Tijuana, it was hottest at Playas . . . "Background to the Office of the Inspector General Investigation," Office of the Inspector General, U.S. Justice Department, 1998

page 306: Incidents of broken ankles and legs . . . Interview with Border Patrol agent, name withheld

page 306: down the barrel of a thirty-year sentence . . . Consulate General of the United States, http://tijuana.usconsulate.gov/tijuana/warning.html

CHAPTER 30

page 321: he'd been described as "cherubic" . . ." Caitlin Rother, "Modest Mogul," *San Diego Union-Tribune*, October 8, 2006

page 322: Congressman Brian Bilbray . . . "The Drone Makers and Their Friends in Washington," Jill Replogle, *Fronteras Desk*, July 5, 2012; "Government Issues Waiver for Fencing Along Border," Randal C. Archibold, *New York Times*, April 2, 2008; "Mr. President, Build This Wall," Rob Davis, *Voice of San Diego*, January 8, 2007; "Time for Border Security?" Robert Costa, *National Review*, April 28, 2010

page 322: real meat eaters of the military . . . Interview with Kim Zirpolo

CHAPTER 32

page 331: when Negro reached out to this acquaintance . . . Interview with El Negro

page 332: Negro made a point of catching Watman . . . Interview with Dan Watman

CHAPTER 34

page 348: Most of them hailed from Oceanside, California's . . . Interview with Ron Nua, Eric Amavisca, and Aaron Garrison

page 350: Their per diem . . . Ibid.

page 353: described the training and hunt for bin Laden . . . "No Easy Day: The Firsthand Account of the Mission that Killed Osama bin Laden," Mark Owen aka Matt Bissonnette, Kevin Maurer, 2012

page 353: TerraServer satellite images . . . Cryptome.org, https://cryptome.org/2012-info/obl-raid-mockup/obl-raid-mockup.htm

CHAPTER 35

page 358: Accurate migration numbers . . . Bureau of Justice Statistics, http://www.bjs.gov/content/pub/pdf/fleo08.pdf

page 358: security plan that would stop 90 percent . . . This demand is nearly as old as the debate on illegal immigration itself, and thus has its own highs and lows, but roared back to the forefront in 2013. "Congress Aims to Stop 90 Percent of Illegal Border Crossing," Barbara Corbellini Duarte, *SHFwire*, May 16, 2013

page 358: At $4,500 per migrant . . . El Negro's interviews

page 359: One curious instance . . . Interview with Dan Watman

page 363: The price per migrant was $12,000 . . . Federal trial of former Border Patrol agents Fidel and Raul Villareal in San Diego, August 2012

page 364: Even at a time when hundreds of agents . . . "Border Agency Report Reveals Internal Struggles With Corruption," Andrew Becker, Center for Investigative Reporting, January 29, 2013; "Border Security: Additional Actions Needed to Strengthen CBP Efforts to Mitigate Risk of Employee Corruption and Misconduct," United States Government Accountability Office, December 2012, https://www.documentcloud.org/documents/551713-gao-13-59.html; "Crossing the Line: Corruption at the Border," Center for Investigative Reporting, http://bordercorruption.apps.cironline.org

CHAPTER 36

page 376: highest tide of the year . . . Interview with Chris Peregrin

page 377: illustrate, for me, certain central equations . . . *Border Games: Policing the U.S.–Mexico Divide*, 2nd Edition, Peter Andreas, 2009. Andreas is one of our foremost border experts, and *Border Games* helped me understand what I was discovering on the ground.

page 377: Smuggler's Gulch with 1.7 million yards of dirt . . . "U.S. Smooths Away an Illegal Border Crossing Wrinkle," Richard Marosi, *Los Angeles Times,* January 4, 2009

page 377: plan to replace the entire string . . . "Border Agents Relying On Outdated Surveillance Equipment," Brian Bennett, *Los Angeles Times*, October 19, 2012; "Homeland Security Delays Plan to Place Sensors on U.S.–Mexico Border," Robert Beckhusen, *Wired*, February 11, 2013

page 378: Social scientists, internal affairs investigators, and attorneys general . . . "Corruption in Law Enforcement: A Paradigm of Occupational Stress and Deviancy," Francis L. McCafferty, MD, Margaret A. McCafferty, RN, *Journal of the American Academy of Psychiatry and the Law*, Vol. 26, No. 1, 1998

page 378: when CBP fired James Tomsheck . . . "Former Border Protection Insider Alleges Corruption, Distortion in Agency," Carrie Johnson, *Morning Edition*, NPR News, August 28, 2014

page 378: The number of Border Patrol agents was doubled under the Bush Administration . . . "Border Patrol has lots of agents . . . in wrong places," *Associated Press*, June 29, 2014

page 378: The heavily debated border-reform bill . . . H.R.399 Secure Our Borders First Act, https://www.congress.gov/bill/114th-congress/house-bill/399